IT AIN'T OVER 'TIL THE
Fat Lady
SINGS®

REGISTERED TRADEMARK OF HOWARD G. PERETZ

IT AIN'T OVER 'TIL THE FAT LADY SINGS®

The 100 Greatest Sports Finishes Of All Time

Howard G. Peretz

Event Text by Phil Berger

BARNES & NOBLE BOOKS
NEW YORK

This edition published by Barnes & Noble, Inc.
by arrangement with Howard G. Peretz
1999 Barnes & Noble Books
ISBN 0-76071-7079
M10987654321

Copyright © 1999 Howard G. Peretz

It Ain't Over 'Til The Fat Lady Sings® is a federally registered trademark of Howard G. Peretz
All drawings are under federal copyright protection under the name Howard G. Peretz

Illustrations by Paul Kirchner

Excerpt from *Nice Guys Finish Seventh* by Ralph Keyes Copyright © 1992 by Ralph Keyes
reprinted with kind permission of Ralph Keyes
Visit the Fat Lady online at http://www.fatladysings.com

A Balliett & Fitzgerald Book

To my dad, who took me to the big ballyard in
the Bronx to watch the Yankees play and always win;

To my daughter Lauren, who began as a ballet
dancer in Los Angeles only to become an attorney
and avid Knicks supporter;

To my son Michael, who rejected tennis for golf but
still passes me the basketball on Monday nights
even if I'm not the first option;

And especially to my wife Geri, who while not
always believing in the message of the Fat Lady, has
always encouraged me to play the game.

—Howard G. Peretz, April 1999

Contents

Growing up in New York City in the 1950s, I was an avid Knicks fan, so much so that I was even the president of the Carl Braun Fan Club. In those days the Boston Celtics were the hated enemy, hated because they were always better and smarter than the opposition, but mostly because of the architect of their success, the legendary Hall of Fame basketball coach and general manager, Arnold (Red) Auerbach.

Described by Boston Globe columnist Bob Ryan as "a brash, bombastic, opinionated, and highly intelligent coach," Auerbach led the Celtics to nine championships in ten years, a dynasty which established the still-emerging world of pro basketball as a major spectator sport.

Red pioneered fast-break basketball in the NBA. He perfected the use of the sixth man beginning with Frank Ramsey, started defensive stalwarts Tom (Satch) Sanders and K.C. Jones, and originated the power-forward position with "Jungle" Jim Loscutoff. In addition to drafting wisely, Red was a very shrewd trader, making deals for players such as Bailey Howell, Nate (Tiny) Archibald, Paul Silas, Dennis Johnson, Charlie Scott, M.L. Carr, Bill Walton, Gerald Henderson, and Robert Parish.

Auerbach also had a remarkable ability as a coach and as a General Manager to grow talent. Celtics stars developed by Red seemed to have a clear road straight to the Naismith Memorial Basketball Hall of Fame. Bob Cousy, Bill Sharman, Frank Ramsey, Bill Russell, K.C. Jones, "Easy" Ed Macauley, Tom Heinsohn, John Havlicek, Dave Cowens, and Larry Bird all played on the old parquet floor of the now-demolished Boston Garden, under the sharp eyes of Auerbach.

Watching the Celtics walk from NBA title to NBA title was deeply galling to New York sports fans who believed their city, and especially Madison Square Garden, to be the true karmic center of basketball. The regular parade of shamrocked champions gave us a bitter taste of what it must have been like to not be a Yankees fan, a prospect which even today I find unsettling.

For many of us, this vast dislike of all things Boston Celtic—so broad in its annoyance with brilliant play, unflappable confidence and class—sharpened and fixed on one thing: Red Auerbach's cigar. Whenever a Celtics victory was assured during those long ago days of public smoking, Auerbach held a one-man ceremonial cigar lighting on the bench. Rather than wait until the game's end, Red would light up at precisely the right moment, the exact spot when the other team had clearly given up or the Celtics were so firmly in control that it didn't matter, saying in so many puffs, "You're finished." The expression "Close, but no cigar" never applied here. Auerbach never missed it, never had to stub out a cigar because of a last-minute comeback in all his years of coaching.

At Madison Square Garden, when Red would lean forward, snap open his lighter and begin puffing, you could hear tens of thousands of teeth grinding together in frustration and envy as the cigar pronounced sentence on our foolish hope of ever beating the Celtics. (Knicks fans during the Ewing years may hold Michael Jordan's tongue in similar contempt.) We wanted our own White Owls, even if we were still in grammar school, and we wanted to be tapping the ashes into Sharman's big shoes. And so we gnashed and ground for many years until 1969 when the Knicks won their first title and I lit up my own victory cigar—a Dutch Masters, if I recall correctly. It was very good.

Years passed and with the wisdom of age and another NBA title for the Knicks, my hatred of the Celtics abated. As an omnivorous sports fan, I began to collect the list of Fat Lady moments that grew into the book you're now reading, and somewhere along the line I again found myself thinking of Red Auerbach's cigar; a scary flashback initially, but fascinating because somehow Red always

PROLOGUE

knew when the Fat Lady had indeed sung. When he lit up, the Fat Lady may as well have hopped onto the stage and belted her aria because the game was truly over. How did he know? Besides brilliant leadership, a deep knowledge of the game and a profound understanding of how to get the best out of his players, what secret did he have? Does the Fat Lady sing on a frequency only Red Auerbach can hear?

To learn the answer, I did the unthinkable: I called Red himself. He may have heard a hesitation in my voice, or he may have known my name from a 1950s-era list of pro-Knicks agitators, because it took him a few minutes to warm up. Once he did, though, I found the hated Red Auerbach to be an affable and generous man—of course—with the degree of crustiness earned by age and success.

"Why did you do it, light up?" I asked.

"I didn't like coaches up 20 points or down 20 points who continued coaching. They must do it for the exposure." Of course Red had the luxury of coaching grown professionals who didn't need supervision during garbage time, but I certainly agreed in principle. Also, smoking at the game was allowed in those days. Knicks coach Joe Lapchick smoked cigarettes on the bench, so Auerbach, a cigar smoker, lit up his relaxing victory cigar when the outcome was settled—a more seemly, almost gentlemanly habit, I had to admit, than chain-smoking through a tense game.

I asked if he had ever made a cigar mistake. The answer was never, although in one game, a late three-point play sent things into overtime and the cigar was quickly stashed away for later. Once the Cincinnati Royals handed out 5,000 cigars, all to be lit in celebration of a Royals' win, but, no surprise, the Celtics crushed the Royals that night. "I had my guys sky high," said Red.

Two of the greatest Celtics victories did not see a cigar lit during the game—when Havlicek stole the ball to ice the 1965 Eastern Division title against the Sixers, and when Larry Bird stole the ball and passed to Dennis

Johnson to finish off the Pistons in 1987. Both times the cigar was lit in the dressing room and was accompanied by champagne.

And so did Auerbach have some special knowledge of when the Fat Lady had sung? Not that I could tell. He had a lot of good sense and knew his sport and his athletes well enough to know what was possible, but he'd never been tested on other sports. Red may very well have been chomping a stogie when the ball skipped through Bill

Buckner's legs in the 1986 World Series or flicking off an ash when Roger Staubach launched the original Hail Mary pass. He was as mindful of the Fat Lady's whims as any coach or athlete, and maybe even more so, but his magic did not extend to telling the future.

Thank goodness that none of us can tell the future, and that the Fat Lady will continue to appear as long as games are played and people believe in the impossible.

The story of:
It Ain't Over 'til the
FAT LADY SINGS®

If you ask the people you're sitting with in the bleachers at Wrigley Field, or the folks next to you on the infield at Daytona, or the Chiefs' fans who've had season tickets with you since Arrowhead opened, where the phrase "It ain't over 'til the fat lady sings" came from, you'll get a wide range of answers.

While almost everyone associates the expression with the world of sports, no one, not even the historians and literary experts, are in agreement. Some credit the Fat Lady to the great Hall of Fame catcher Yogi Berra, but he only said, "It ain't over 'til it's over." Similar, but no Fat Lady. Opera lovers believe it dates back to some unknown spectator at an early Wagnerian opera in the days when gifted sopranos tended to be very robust women. I was once told by an expert that he was absolutely certain that the national anthem was once sung at the end of a baseball games, but my research failed miserably to prove this point.

I came close to an answer in the 1985 edition of The Concise Oxford Dictionary of Proverbs edited by J.A. Simpson, which attributes the saying to Ralph Carpenter, Texas Tech's sports information director, who declared, "The rodeo ain't over 'til the bullriders ride!" San Antonio sports editor Dan Cook then altered the phrase to "The opera ain't over 'til the fat lady sings."

A book called *Nice Guys Finish Seventh* by Ralph Keyes finally solves the puzzle. In a section called "The Inarticulate Decade" Keyes traces the Fat Lady back to the American South in the 1960s.

"Unlike the two decades preceding, the 1980s produced few memorable sayings. (Unless one considers "Go for the burn!" and "It's morning in America" memorable.) In fact, only one '80s slogan achieved quotebook status: "The opera ain't over till the fat lady sings." Where did this maxim come from? There is much confusion on that score. The most common opinion is that it sounds like Yogi Berra. I've also heard the saying attributed to W.C.Fields. Some associate it with big Kate Smith, whose rendition of "God Bless America" was once the theme song of the Philadelphia Flyers hockey team. A New York lawyer said he thought the line referred to a woman of ample girth who sang "The Star Spangled Banner" after Dodgers games ended at Ebbets Field. His wife was sure she had read it in a J.D. Salinger short story.

Here is how that saying actually came into being: During the 1978 National Basketball Association playoffs, the Washington Bullets took a commanding lead over the Philadelphia 76ers. Another victory would put them in the title game. Asked about their prospects, Bullets coach Dick Motta cautioned, "The opera ain't over till the fat lady sings."

The Bullets' coach never claimed to have coined this line. As Motta told reporters, after Washington had taken a 3-1 lead over the Spurs during an earlier series in San Antonio, he watched a late-night news story about the game on television. "This guy comes to the end of the story," Motta said with a laugh, "and he says on the sportscast, 'The opera ain't over until the fat lady sings.' " It didn't take long for this aphorism to make its way around the country. JR's daddy used the quip on Dallas. So did George Bush on the husting, countless sportscasters, endless political commentators, and sundry secondhand wits. When attributed to anyone at all, the line was most often attributed to Dick Motta. But didn't the sportscaster he got it from deserve credit?

The sportscaster was *San Antonio Express-News* columnist Dan Cook. Few people outside of San Antonio have heard of Cook. Among basketball fans Dick Motta was a household name. When coaching in the playoffs he commanded national attention. This is why Motta so often was thought to have coined the fat lady line. But Dan Cook was his source (and already gets credit for the line in some quote collections).

There's more to the story, however. Dan Cook may simply have been taking part in a great southern tradition: foisting off shopworn Dixieisms on unsuspecting Yankees as fresh merchandise. An obscure 1976 booklet called *Southern Words and Sayings* included this entry: "Church ain't out till the fat lady sings." Alvin Bethard of the Dupree Library in Lafayette, Louisiana, said that this was the way he'd always heard that saying while growing up in central Louisiana in the 1950s and 1960s. My poll of other longtime southerners confirmed that many were familiar with the saying long before Dick Motta gave it national exposure. San Antonio physician John Holcomb, 47, said he'd heard variations on this theme for 30 years or more, usually as "It ain't over till the fat lady sings." Television newscaster Robert Inman of Charlotte, North Carolina, recalled hearing that version when he was press secretary to Alabama Governor Albert Brewer in the late 1960s. Political reporter Bob Ingraham said he first heard the "opera" version while with the *Montgomery* (Alabama) *Advertiser* in the 1950s. Ingraham said he never was quite sure what this saying referred to, but thought that it "was tied to the perception of those like me who don't know much about opera that when the fat lady sings, the opera's about to end."

As so often happens, this old saying needed receptive ears before it could become familiar. For some reason, "The opera ain't over till the fat lady sings" defined America's mood in the '80s. Perhaps we were more desperate beneath the surface than our Reaganite merrymaking suggested. Slogans can do that: define eras. When the right one doesn't appear spontaneously or isn't said by the best person, we're not above nudging the process along. This isn't a modern phenomenom. Rewording and misattributing quotations to better suit their times is a pastime with a long, long history."

While I've heard that Fat Lady reference in the media and in sports on many occasions, being a tennis player, my favorite usage appeared in a *New York Times* article from September, 1997. John Newcombe, the famous Australian tennis star and captain of their Davis Cup team, down 2-0 to the Americans in a best of five format had this to say: "We're down, we're in trouble, but the fat lady hasn't called for a limo yet."

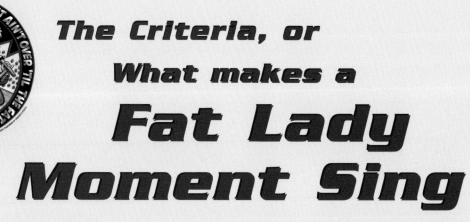

The Criteria, or What makes a Fat Lady Moment Sing

When I began to research this book, I visited *The Sporting News* library in St. Louis, hoping (or not, I guess) to find any similar books about great sports finishes. I expected a shelf full of them—any sports fan worth his peanuts has a list of his favorites, the Hail Mary passes, the buzzer beaters, the last-minute comebacks. But there weren't any such books. There were books about the greatest games and memorable moments, but nothing about the big finishes that make people talk around the coffee machine the next morning. So began my journey to find the 100 greatest Fat Lady finishes of all time. Applying common sense criteria in the beginning, I identified some 176 events, a number that included all of the obvious ones (Doug Flutie's Hail Mary pass, "The Giants Win the Pennant!", "Havlicek Stole the Ball"), as well as some not so obvious ones. When it came to boiling the list down to 100, though, I needed some guidelines, for no other reason than to eliminate my own biases. In other words, all 100 could not be Yankees games.

1. Magic

There were more rules beyond allowing a few teams other than the Yanks. First, and by far the most important criterion, was the presence of a magical moment, something not really explicable and certainly not in the play book. The Immaculate Reception—Franco Harris's catch and run off a deflected pass in the 1972 AFC divisional playoff with five seconds remaining to give the Pittsburgh Steelers a 13–7 win over the Oakland Raiders—is a perfect example. So too was Lew Worsham's sinking a wedge on the last hole for an eagle to defeat Chandler Harper by one stroke at the 1953 World Championship of Golf. Or how about Kirk Gibson limping up to the plate for the Dodgers to win a

World Series game against one of baseball's best all-time relievers, Dennis Eckersley? So to start with, a Fat Lady moment is about magic.

2. Its Own Icon

Second, somewhere close to magic, is the name reverence given to those very special moments that eclipse the event itself. The Franco Harris catch is the Immaculate Reception. Others you'll find in this book are the Homer in the Gloamin', the Shower of Sparks, the Shot Heard Around the World, the Catch, the Drive, the Heidi Game, the Miracle on Ice, and on it goes.

3. Greatest Athletes

Wherever possible, I looked to include events featuring the greatest athletes of all time. Muhammad Ali, arguably the best known worldwide person in the 20th century, had many great fights, including the Thriller in Manilla against Joe Frazier, but a great fight is not a Fat Lady moment. After much debate, I elected to include Ali's knockdown of the seemingly invincible George Foreman to our list of 100. Michael Jordan, Magic Johnson, Larry Bird, Ted Williams, Jack Nicklaus and Joe Louis all have highlighted moments; Hank Aaron, Joe DiMaggio, Babe Ruth and Dr. J do not.

4. At the Very End

Ideally, a Fat Lady appearance occurs at the end of games, just as the clock is winding down, or as the last shot, hit or stroke is to be played. Last-at-bat home runs are big favorites: Pittsburgh's Bill Mazeroski against the Yankees in the 1960 World Series; Carlton Fisk of the Red Sox against the Reds in 1975; Joe Carter of the Blue Jays off of Phillies reliever Mitch Williams in 1993; and of course Kirk Gibson of the Dodgers against the Athletics in 1988. But game-winning homers aren't the whole story. There's Julio César Chávez's knockdown of Meldrick Taylor at 2:58 of the last round, and Jake LaMotta's stunning comeback against Laurent Dauthuille in their 1950 middleweight title fight in the world of boxing. Basketball has the buzzer beater-Ernie Calverley sinking a 55-foot prayer for Rhode Island in the 1946 NIT; Indiana's Keith Smart and N.C. State's Lorenzo Charles both winning the NCAA title with last-second buckets; and maybe the greatest basketball game ever, when Duke topped Kentucky in the Regional final on Christian Laettner's miraculous turnaround jumper. The Hail Mary pass is a staple of classic football moments, from the original delivered by the Cowboys' Roger Staubach to Drew Pearson against the Vikings, to Doug Flutie's winning bomb to his Boston College roommate Gerard Phelan that came on the last play of a regular season game at the Orange Bowl. But football games can be won a few ways, including Tom Dempsey's record-setting 63-yard field goal and the remarkable five-lateral-finish to the 1982 Cal-Stanford game.

5. One Game

Individual performances, regardless of how outstanding they were, or the greatest games ever played do not rise to the level of a Fat Lady moment. Don Larsen's World Series does not qualify because the outcome was never in doubt. We also stayed away from a series of remarkable games: The New York Mets' defeat of the invincible Baltimore Orioles in the 1969 World Series or the Toronto Maple Leafs coming back from a three-game deficit in the 1941 Stanley Cup finals do not make our cut for this very reason. Neither does the Yankees' 1996 World Series victory over the Atlanta Braves; down 2–0 in games, heading on the road to face a brilliant pitching rotation, the Yankees roared back to win in the next four games.

6. Upset

While you might argue that an upset of great proportion—like the 1969 Amazin' Mets—would otherwise qualify as an individual event, an upset, would not be considered just because it was an upset, unless the outcome was continually in doubt. That's why, for example, the New York

Jets' victory of the Baltimore Colts which gave the AFL a credibility it had lacked previously does not appear in this text—the Jets victory was that decisive. On the other hand, Villanova's incredible upset of Patrick Ewing's Georgetown team in the 1985 NCAA final (the Perfect Game) does make our list because everyone watching was constantly waiting for the bubble to burst.

7. Event Importance

Our approach also revolved around big-time teams playing in playoff-type atmospheres, rather than unknown athletes or lesser-known teams playing a regular season game. In this regard, the astonishing 92-yard pass play with 16 seconds remaining from UTEP's quarterback Billy Stevens to Bob Wallace to defeat Utah in a 1965 game in Salt Lake City does not appear, nor does a field goal by Willy Merrick, his first kick ever, made with 10 seconds remaining to lead Marshall past Youngstown State, 31–28 in 1992.

8. Limit On Participation

Just how many times could we mention Michael Jordan and Joe Montana, two great athletes whose greatness had much to do with their uncanny ability to hit the clutch shot or make the pressure play in the closing moments of a big game? Jordan appears twice, in the 1982 NCAA final and again in the 1998 NBA Finals, when he cans an 18-footer following his own steal. Montana is likewise limited to two mentions, the 1978 Cotton Bowl and the pass deep into the back of the end zone to tight end Dwight Clark, (the Catch), leading San Francisco to a 28–27 over Dallas in the 1981 NFC Championship Game.

Have there been more than 100 great Fat Lady moments in sports? Absolutely. Just during the months we put together this book there have been a few, and they'll keep happening as long as people play games. If we missed any of your favorites, we hope we'll catch them in a future Fat Lady book.

Chapter 1
VICTORIES SNATCHED FROM THE JAWS OF DEFEAT

*B*ottom of the ninth. The home team down three. Two out; bases loaded with the big bat coming up to the plate. This is the moment we all dream of as fans and as players, but usually the result is heartbreak; a pop fly, a weak grounder, or, following the Mighty Casey's famous example, a strikeout. On rare occasion, though, a trailing team or player comes up with something that defies logic. When the whole game is on the line, it takes special players and teams to hit the chip-shot field goal with a second to go or sink the free throw. Here are 10 last-second miracles that happened before the Fat Lady got going.

THE LITTLE MIRACLE OF COOGAN'S BLUFF

On Aug. 11, 1951, the New York Giants were 13½ games behind the National League–leading Brooklyn Dodgers. To add insult to injury, a month earlier the Dodgers' manager, Charles Walter Dressen, had had the temerity to pronounce

Thomson's famous shot barely cleared the shallow wall in the Polo Ground's leftfield corner.

his crosstown rival DOA: After the Dodgers had taken a July 4 doubleheader from the Giants, Dressen had exulted: "We knocked them out. They won't bother us any more."

Reports of the demise of the Giants and their abrasive manager Leo Durocher were, it turned out, premature. Over the last month and a half of the '51 season, the Giants mounted a closing pennant drive as thrilling as any in baseball history. New York won 37 of its last 44 games (and 12 of its last 13) to force a three-game playoff series. The two teams split the first two games and now it came down to one game for the National League pennant.

By the ninth inning, the 34,320 fans in the Polo Grounds, located on a rise in northern Manhattan called Coogan's Bluff, feared the worst—Brooklyn led 4–1 and the Dodgers' pitching ace, Don Newcombe, had struck out the side the inning before.

A glimmer of hope appeared when New York's Alvin Dark and Don Mueller singled in the bottom of the ninth inning. After Newcombe got the Giants' Monte Irvin to pop out, Whitey Lockman slammed a double that scored Dark and sent Mueller racing to third base. Mueller injured his ankle as he slid into third and had to be carried off the field. Clint Hartung came in to run for Mueller.

With the score 4–2, Dressen chose to replace Newcombe with Ralph Branca to pitch to Bobby Thomson, who had been instrumental in the Giants' closing drive. From July 20, Thomson had batted .357—many of his hits leading to victories. Two days earlier, he had hit a homer off Branca. Clem Labine, also in the bullpen, had struck Thomson out the day before, but Dressen went with Branca, number 13. Now, as Thomson came to bat against Branca, Durocher pointed toward the leftfield wall only 279 feet away and urged him to hit a home run.

The count on Thomson reached 1 and 1. Rookie Willie Mays shook in the on-deck circle, possibly worried that he'd have to bat in such a clutch situation. On Branca's next pitch, Thomson swung and the ball shot toward the leftfield stands on a low trajectory, sinking a bit before it disappeared among

Brooklyn's Jackie Robinson (42) waited in the field to make sure Thomson touched all the bases.

"The Giants win the pennant!"
—Russ Hodges

the fans behind the short leftfield corner of the Polo Grounds. As the crowd roared over the Giants' dramatic 5–4 victory, Thomson rounded third and Durocher did a wild dance down the third base line. The radio broadcaster Russ Hodges, in a call that has become sports history, roared along with the crowd: "The Giants win the pennant! The Giants win the pennant! The Giants win the pennant! ... The Giants win the pennant, and they're going crazy!"

That the Yankees handled the Giants four games to two in the 1951 World Series has faded behind this home run, a shot that, to many, has come to represent all the drama, triumph and tragedy of baseball.

New York Giants 5, Brooklyn Dodgers 4

Brooklyn	AB	R	H	RBI	New York	AB	R	H	RBI
Furillo rf	5	0	0	0	Stanky 2b	4	0	0	0
Reese ss	4	2	1	0	Dark ss	4	1	1	0
Snider cf	3	2	2	0	Mueller rf	4	0	1	0
Robinson 2b	2	1	1	1	c Hartung	0	1	0	0
Pafko lf	4	0	1	1	Irvin lf	4	1	1	0
Hodges 1b	4	0	0	0	Lockman 1b	3	1	2	1
Cox 3b	4	0	2	1	Thomson 3b	4	1	3	4
Walker c	4	0	1	0	Mays cf	3	0	0	0
Newcombe p	4	0	0	0	Westrum c	0	0	0	0
Branca p	0	0	0	0	a Rigney	1	0	0	0
Totals	34	4	8	3	Noble c	0	0	0	0
					Maglie p	2	0	0	0
					b Thompson	1	0	0	0
					Jansen p	0	0	0	0
					Totals	30	5	8	5

*One out when winning run scored.
a Struck out for Westrum in eighth.
b Grounded out for Maglie in eighth.
c Ran for Mueller in ninth.

Brooklyn	1	0	0	0	0	0	0	3	0—4
New York	0	0	0	0	0	0	1	0	4—5

IT'S MAGIC

T he big fella was missing.

At least that's what the Lakers were saying about Kareem Abdul-Jabbar, their dominating 7'2" center.

Abdul-Jabbar was supposed to be back in Los Angeles, nursing the ankle he sprained in Game 5 of the 1980 NBA Finals against the Philadelphia 76ers.

Of course, the Sixers—down three games to two against L.A.—had the uneasy feeling that they were being conned and, come game time, the big fella would be in the lineup.

That he hadn't shown up yet in Philadelphia with his teammates didn't persuade the Sixers that he couldn't arrive at the last minute in a private jet.

But the reality was Abdul-Jabbar was waiting for his teammates some 3,000 miles away at his Bel Air, Calif. home, his sore ankle propped up on pillows. He was waiting to join them for the seventh and final game of the series that would be needed after the 76ers beat a Lakers team without the big fella.

But that night L.A. came into Philadelphia's Spectrum with a unique game plan to confound the Sixers' expectations.

Magic Johnson played every position in the game, from center to point guard.

In place of the big fella, starting at center was Los Angeles' magnificent rookie guard, 6'8" Earvin (Magic) Johnson. And while Magic would be the Lakers' pivot on offense, L.A. was not so foolhardy as to think he could match up on defense against Philadelphia's 6'11½" center, Darryl Dawkins. So the Lakers' 6'11" Jim Chones would be assigned Dawkins.

If the Sixers thought they had a pigeon in the pivot, Johnson quickly disabused them of the notion. The 20-year-old Magic, who had forsaken his college career after his Michigan State team won the NCAA title in his sophomore year, passed and scored while filling in for the big fella—42 points, seven assists—and by God, he rebounded too, pulling down 15 boards. Oh, and don't forget the three steals and the one blocked shot.

Instead of confronting a toothless tiger, as they expected, the Sixers ran into a lean, mean, basketball-playing machine. Philadelphia got as close as 103–101, but then the Johnson-led Lakers went off on a 20–6 tear to win 123–107.

"Big Fella," said series MVP Johnson into the TV microphones, "I did it for you. I know your ankle hurts but I want you to get up and dance."

Julius Erving—Dr. J—would lead the Sixers to the NBA title in 1983.

> "I want you to get up and dance."
> —Magic Johnson

L.A. Lakers 123
Philadelphia 76ers 107

L. A.	min	fgm	fga	ftm	fta	r	a	pf	pts
Chones	43	5	9	1	1	10	3	2	11
Wilkes	42	16	30	5	5	10	2	4	37
Johnson	47	14	23	14	14	15	7	3	42
Nixon	40	1	10	2	2	3	9	3	4
Cooper	39	4	9	8	9	4	6	4	16
Landsberger	19	2	7	1	2	10	0	4	5
Holland	9	3	4	2	2	0	0	2	8
Byrnes	1	0	0	0	0	0	0	0	0
Total	240	45	92	33	35	52	27	22	123

Philadelphia	min	fgm	fga	ftm	fta	r	a	pf	pts
Erving	39	13	23	1	4	7	3	4	27
C. Jones	26	2	3	2	2	6	2	4	6
Dawkins	31	6	9	2	5	4	1	5	14
Hollins	26	5	13	3	4	1	6	4	13
Cheeks	40	5	11	3	3	2	8	2	13
B. Jones	29	4	8	0	0	9	1	4	8
Bibby	21	4	10	0	2	3	3	2	8
Mix	25	8	11	2	2	4	2	1	8
Spanarkel	1	0	0	0	0	1	0	0	0
Toone	1	0	0	0	0	0	0	1	0
Richardson	1	0	1	0	0	0	0	0	0
Total	240	47	89	13	22	36	27	27	107

Los Angeles	32	28	33	30—123
Philadelphia	29	31	23	24—107

THE ALMOST CHAMPION

When the great heavyweight champion Joe Louis fought Billy Conn on June 18, 1941, history was on his side. No light heavyweight champion had ever stepped up against the heavyweight champ and won. The numbers were behind the Brown Bomber as well; Louis weighed in at 199 and was at that point 52–1, with 25 knockouts, while Conn was 169, with a 57-10-1 record, with all of 10 knockouts.

But Conn—a cocky Irishman from Pittsburgh—bucked the tide of history and gave the 54,487 paying customers at New York's Polo Grounds the shock of their lives with the fight he waged against Louis that night.

Rather than buckling under Louis's early assault, as so many other of Louis's opponents had, Conn withstood the blows and administered plenty of his own.

Conn surprised Louis with his speed and elusiveness and by the 12th round he was landing at will, even wobbling Louis late in the round with a pair of hooks.

At that point, the scorecards showed Conn in the lead: 7–5, 7-4-1 and 6–6. The strategy was obvious. Conn would only have to win one of the remaining three rounds by simply outboxing the weary Louis, and back in Pittsburgh's saloons Conn's neighbors would be drinking to the health of a new heavyweight champion.

But Conn had other ideas. As Hype Igoe, writing in the *New York Journal American*, would observe:

> For 12 rounds, the nimble, feather-footed Pittsburgher was Joe Louis's master. Then some quirk in his fiery Irish brain told him he could actually walk out in the 13th and "stretch" the great Brown Panther.
>
> Gorgeous audacity! Cruel overconfidence!
>
> Conn, never known for his power, decided to go for the knockout.

Throughout the fight, Conn dominated the action.

"I guess I forgot he was still dangerous."
—Billy Conn

Conn fought only eight more times after this bout, retiring with a 63-12-1 record, including another loss to Louis.

As Conn set out to trade with Louis, he left himself open and the champion hit him with a short right to the jaw. When Conn wavered, Louis was clear-minded enough to take advantage of the shock his right fist had engendered. A series of punches had Conn reeling. Louis dropped him with a right to the chin.

As the referee, Eddie Joseph, counted ten, Conn was almost to his feet. Too late.

Louis was still champion and all that remained for Conn was to explain why he hadn't left well enough alone. As Billy told reporters: "Gee, I don't know how to coast. I'm Irish and must fight."

Then, as the reality of what he'd done sank in, Conn said, "Gee! I had it. How could I have made such a blunder? I guess I forgot he was still dangerous."

Heavyweight Championship

Round 1	Round 2	Round 3	Round 4	Round 5	Round 6
Louis	Louis	Conn	Conn	Louis	Louis

Round 7	Round 8	Round 9	Round 10	Round 11	Round 12
Even	Conn	Conn	Louis	Conn	Conn

Round 13
Louis, Winner by KO

(according to the *Chicago Tribune*)

ONE MORE

Bill Bevens pitched for the New York Yankees, and on Oct. 3, 1947, at Brooklyn's Ebbets Field, he was pitching about as well as a fellow with a slight wild streak could. Through eight and two-thirds innings, in the fourth game of the World Series between the Yankees and the Brooklyn Dodgers, Bevens had not allowed a hit; a feat even more remarkable when you consider that Bevens had gone 7–13 on a team that finished 97–57.

If he could retire the final batter, Bevens would go into the record books as the first pitcher in World Series history to toss a no-hitter.

One more batter, and it would be over.

The batter was reserve infielder Cookie Lavagetto, who came to the plate as a pinch hitter for Dodgers second baseman Eddie Stanky.

There were two men on base at the time, both there on walks issued by Bevens—the second was an intentional pass ordered up by Yankees manager Bucky Harris after the Dodgers' slow-footed Al Gionfriddo stole only his third base of the year, and this one as a pinch runner. Lavagetto, who'd had all of 18 hits that year, stepped into the box.

The Yankees led 2–1, Brooklyn's only run having scored in the fifth inning when Bevens walked Spider Jorgensen and Hal Gregg—two of the 10 walks he issued on this day—and then watched as Stanky moved the runners up with a sacrifice bunt and Pee Wee Reese's grounder scored Jorgensen.

Now Lavagetto dug in, peering out at Bevens as 33,443 of the Dodgers' faithful at Ebbets Field rooted for him to break Bevens's spell. The swarthy Lavagetto, a righthanded batter who choked up on his bat to help him make contact, swung at Bevens's first pitch and missed.

But on Bevens's next delivery, Lavagetto sent the ball soaring high to the rightfield wall at Ebbets. Yankees outfielder Tommy Henrich raced back, hoping to spear the ball. No such luck. The ball was hit too deep. It struck the wall and caromed off. Henrich retrieved it and relayed it to George McQuinn at first. McQuinn threw to the plate, but it was too late.

Two Dodgers had come across to score.

Lavagetto's hit had broken up Bevens's no-hitter and beaten the Yankees 3–2.

The Dodgers had won a ball game with only one hit, a heartbreaking development for Bill Bevens, a pitcher who'd been just an out away from making history. The Yankees eventually won the Series in seven games, and Bevens would never play in another major league game after the Series, neither would Lavagetto.

Brooklyn Dodgers 3, New York Yankees 2

New York	AB	R	H	RBI
Stirnweiss, 2b	4	1	2	0
Henrich, rf	5	0	1	0
Berra, c	4	0	0	0
DiMaggio, cf	2	0	0	1
McQuinn, 1b	4	0	1	0
Johnson, 3b	4	1	1	0
Lindell, lf	3	0	2	1
Rizzuto, ss	4	0	1	0
Bevens, p	3	0	0	0
Total	33	2	8	2

*Two out when winning run scored.
a Walked for Gregg in seventh.
b Ran for Furillo in ninth.
d Ran for Reiser in ninth.
e Doubled for Stanky in ninth.

Brooklyn	AB	R	H	RBI
Stanky, 2b	1	0	0	0
e Lavagetto	1	0	1	2
Reese, ss	4	0	0	1
Robinson, 1b	4	0	0	0
Walker, rf.	2	0	0	0
Hermanski, lf.	4	0	0	0
Edwards, c	4	0	0	0
Furillo, cf.	3	0	0	0
b Gionfriddo	0	1	0	0
Jorgensen, 3b	2	1	0	0
Taylor, p	0	0	0	0
Gregg, p	1	0	0	0
a Vaughan	0	0	0	0
Behrman, p	0	0	0	0
Casey, p	0	0	0	0
c Reiser	0	0	0	0
d Miksis	0	1	0	0
Total	26	3	1	3

New York	1	0	0	1	0	0	0	0	0—	2
Brooklyn	0	0	0	0	1	0	0	0	2—	3

Bill Bevens only logged 40 career wins; this World Series game was the last major league game he ever pitched.

"Don't bother writing it ... nobody will believe it."
—heard in the press box at Yankee Stadium

Cookie Lavagetto choked up on the bat, sacrificing power for control. He had only 40 career home runs.

THE ICE BOWL

Football is a cold weather sport.

But it ran to extremes on Dec. 31, 1967, when the Packers and the Cowboys went at it for the NFL title on the tundra of Lambeau Field in Green Bay, Wis.

The temperature at daybreak was –16° below zero, and by game time it had warmed up to 13 below.

Both teams came well prepared. Green Bay pass catcher Boyd Dowler packed a pair of little cotton gloves. Throughout the game, he'd slip them on during timeouts, and then stick them under his belt when play resumed.

The wind chill was reportedly –50° when Starr scored.

Other players braved the frigid day dressed in sweatshirts, thermal underwear and woolen socks. It was an afternoon more suited for arctic exploring than football.

In what would be Vince Lombardi's last year as Packers coach, Green Bay was shooting for an unprecedent third consecutive league championship. Lombardi and the fear and devotion he inspired in his players had, after five NFL titles, become legend. Before 50,861 shivering, fans the Packers charged onto the field, determined to do Lombardi proud.

Before the game started, Clint Murchison, the millionaire owner of the Dallas team, had predicted, "It is too cold for the Green Bay passing game, and we will win with our running."

But 1967 had been a bad year for the experts when it came to figuring out Green Bay. Considered too old to keep up with the NFL's youngbloods, the Packers had made it to the title game and now proved wintry conditions would not deter their aerial assault. On Green Bay's first drive, Packers quarterback Bart Starr completed four of five passes, the last of them for eight yards and a touchdown to Dowler.

When Starr threw a second touchdown pass to Dowler giving Green Bay a 14–0 lead, the Packers' faithful began to envision a rout.

Wrong.

Despite the frozen field and the lack of traction it offered, Dallas and its running game battled back. In the fourth quarter, with the ball at midfield, Cowboys halfback and future coaching great Dan Reeves took a lateral and then lofted a perfect pass to Lance Rentzel, who caught it alone on the 20 and went on to score. Dallas went ahead 17–14.

The Packers' last chance came with 4:54 left in the game.

"The ball was on the 32," recalled Packers lineman Jerry Kramer later, "and I was thinking, 'Well, maybe this is the year we don't pull it off, that it will all end here.' But I know that every guy made up his mind that we were going to go down swinging."

The game came down to Green Bay at the Cowboys' one-yard line, third down, no time outs, 16 seconds remaining. Lombardi's Packers had only two options: try a field goal to tie the game, or run a play from scrimmage and risk losing. The Cowboys' defensive line was awesome, anchored by Bob Lilly and Jethro Pugh, with Lee Roy Jordan behind them at linebacker.

Other coaches may have done the safe thing and gone for the tie. But Lombardi wasn't that kind of coach. Lombardi bid for the victory.

"This game was our mark of distinction."

—Green Bay tackle Bob Skoronski

"The Sneak" is judged by many to be the most exciting moment in NFL history.

Lombardi said to run it and Starr made the call: He would carry the football behind Kramer on a play called 31 Wedge. If Kramer and center Ken Bowman got the job done, Starr would see daylight. This was the Packers' last chance to prove themselves to the man who'd led them to greatness. Failure was unthinkable today.

Starr took the snap. Kramer and Bowman bulled aside Pugh (though many claim Kramer was offside) and Starr slid into the end zone and the history books.

Coach Vince had made his last stand in Green Bay and what a beauty it was.

Green Bay Packers 21
Dallas Cowboys 17

Dallas	0	10	0	7—17
Green Bay	7	7	0	7—21

GB	Dowler (8, pass from Starr); Chandler (kick)
GB	Dowler (43, pass from Starr); Chandler (kick)
Dallas	Andrie (7, recovered fumble); Villanueva (kick)
Dallas	Villanueva (21, field goal)
Dallas	Rentzel (50, pass from Reeves); Villanueva (kick)
GB	Starr (1, run); Chandler kick
Attendance 50, 861	

Statistics of the Game

	Dallas	Green Bay
First downs	11	18
Rushing yardage	92	80
Passing yardage	100	115
Return yardage	43	44
Passes	11-26-1	14-24-0
Punts	8-39	8-29
Fumbles lost	1	2
Yards penalized	58	10

1988 World Series—Game One
Los Angeles Dodgers vs. Oakland A's

October 15, 1988

THE NATURAL

And so it came down to the Los Angeles Dodgers' last at bat.

The Dodgers trailed the Oakland Athletics 4–3 in Game 1 of the 1988 World Series. No one gave the overachieving Dodgers much of a chance to beat the Bash Brothers, Mark McGwire and Jose Canseco, and the rest of the talented Oakland squad. And if they were to rally against the A's now, they would have to do it against Dennis Eckersley, who, after 11 respectable seasons as a starter, had suddenly become the game's best reliever. Eckersley led the league that year in saves with 45, and had given up only five homers all season.

Finding a way to win would be no easy task for the Dodgers.

Indeed, when Eckersley retired the first two Dodgers batters in the bottom of the ninth inning at Dodger Stadium, Los Angeles' chances seemed slim to nonexistent. But when Eckersley walked Mike Davis, it brought the gimpy guy to center stage.

That was Kirk Gibson, who was hobbled by a strained ligament in his right knee and a severely strained hamstring in the left leg. Gibson had been the leader of some great Detroit Tigers teams in the '80s and though he had made his name as a baseball player, he had a rough-edged, unshaven grit that hearkened back to his football days at Michigan State. Gibson was a throwback, and the fans loved him for his all-out way of playing.

In the trainer's room, Gibson, who had taken injections of cortisone and Xylocaine for the sprained ligament in his right knee earlier in the day, had been watching the game on TV when he heard Dodgers broadcaster Vince Scully say: "The man who has been the spearhead of the Dodgers offense throughout the year, who saved them in the League Championship Series, will not see any action tonight, for sure. [Gibson] is not even in the dugout."

At that point, Gibson slipped into his uniform top and left the trainer's room for the dugout. Though he had not been expected to play, with the Dodgers down to their final out he suddenly appeared as a pinch hitter for pitcher Alejandro Pena.

The Dodger Stadium crowd of 55,933 rose to its feet, and stayed upright, as Gibson fouled off three offerings from Eckersley and then Davis stole second base. The pain was evident on Gibson's face.

As the count on Gibson ran to 3 and 2, the tension mounted.

Now Eckersley threw a slider, down, but too fat on the center of the plate.

"It was dumb," Eckersley later told reporters. "It was the one pitch he could pull for power."

Gibson retired after the 1995 season with 255 career home runs.

Gibson's dramatic home run reminded many of Roy Hobbs's fictional blast in Bernard Malamud's The Natural.

> ## "He hit the dogmeat out of it."
> —Dennis Eckersley

Gibson drove the baseball five rows up into the rightfield bleachers. Dodgers win 5–4.

The moment the ball rocketed off Gibson's bat, he raised his arm and held it aloft until he reached first base, pumping it up and down as he came around towards second, then third, towards manager Tommy Lasorda, who had leapt out of the dugout when the ball cleared the wall. His right leg dragging, Gibson came around to score, and with one shot, his only appearance in the Series, seemed to take all the air out of the vaunted A's, who never recovered, losing three of the next four. Oakland's can't-miss championship was gone.

L. A. Dodgers 5, Oakland Athletics 4

Oakland	AB	R	H	RBI	Los Angeles	AB	R	H	RBI
Lansford, 3b	4	1	0	0	Sax, 2b	3	1	1	0
Henderson, cf	5	0	2	0	Stubbs, 1b	4	0	0	0
Canseco, rf	4	1	1	4	Hatcher, lf	3	1	1	2
Parker, lf	2	0	0	0	Marshall, rf	4	1	1	0
Javier, lf	1	0	1	0	Shelby, cf	4	0	1	0
McGwire, 1b	3	0	0	0	Scioscia, c	4	0	1	1
Steinbach, c	4	0	1	0	Hamilton, 3b	4	0	0	0
Hassey, c	0	0	0	0	Griffin, ss	2	0	1	0
Hubbard, 2b	4	1	2	0	M. Davis, ph	0	1	0	0
Weiss, ss	4	0	0	0	Belcher, p	0	0	0	0
Stewart, p	3	1	0	0	Heep, ph	1	0	0	0
Eckersley, p	0	0	0	0	Leary, p	0	0	0	0
Total	**34**	**4**	**7**	**4**	Woodsen, ph	1	0	0	0
					Holton, p	0	0	0	0
					Gonzalez, ph	1	0	0	0
					Pena, p	0	0	0	0
					Gibson, ph	1	1	1	2
					Total	**32**	**5**	**7**	**5**

Oakland	0	4	0	0	0	0	0	0	0—4		
Los Angeles	2	0	0	0	0	0	1	0	0	2—5	

HAIL MARY

F rom the sideline, Boston College quarterback Doug Flutie watched with a feeling of helplessness.

Out there on the playing field, his Miami counterpart, a

6'5" sophomore named Bernie Kosar, was engineering a 79-yard scoring drive that appeared to sink Flutie and his BC teammates on this November day in 1984.

For when Miami's Melvin Bratton pounded into the end zone from one yard out, the touchdown gave Miami a 45–41 lead, leaving the 5'9¾" Flutie with a mere 28 seconds to rally his team.

Flutie was a quarterback whose size—or lack of it—had always been an issue with the so-called experts.

Too small to play Division I football, those geniuses had insisted when Flutie first materialized at the Chestnut Hill campus of Boston College.

But Flutie had proven his detractors very wrong. As a scrambling quarterback with a powerful arm, Flutie became the first 10,000-yard passer in major-college history.

And even on this unsunny Saturday afternoon in the Orange Bowl, against college football's defending national champion, Flutie once again had been a force, throwing for more than 400 yards against big bad Miami.

But now, as the clock ticked down, even Flutie appeared overmatched. It was third down and Flutie's Eagles were reduced to their last chance.

Six seconds were left on the clock and the football was 64 yards away from the goal line.

Flutie called a BC play designed for the situation: Trips Right, Red 55. The formation the Eagles set up in had three BC receivers positioned on the far right side of the field. At the snap, they would race toward the end zone, hoping that—miracle of miracles—Flutie could get the ball to one of them. In the event that the ball appeared in their vicinity and defensive traffic prevented them from making the catch, the receivers were under orders to tip the ball up into the air—tip it on the chance that it might settle into another Eagle's arms.

As Flutie faded back, Miami's Jerome Brown chased him out of the pocket and to the quarterback's right. Flutie improvised, circling back and around before he let fly. As the ball soared more than 60 yards, Flutie's roommate and favorite receiver, Gerard Phelan, had broken free of Hurricanes defensive back Darrell Fullington. Fullington leaped to knock the ball down but was nudged off balance by his teammate, Reggie Sutton. The ball shot past their upraised arms and into the hands of Phelan.

As Phelan gathered in the Hail Mary pass, he fell to the ground. In the end zone. Touchdown. Ball game. Another miracle performed by Douglas Richard Flutie, the little quarterback who could.

Boston College 47
University of Miami 45

Boston	14	14	3	16–47
Miami	7	14	10	14–45

BC	Martin 33 pass from Doug Flutie (Snow kick)
BC	K. Bell 5 run (Snow kick)
Miami	Bratton 2 run (Cox kick)
Miami	W. Smith 10 pass from Kosar (Cox kick)
BC	Doug Flutie 9 run (Snow kick)
Miami	Williams 8 pass from Kosar (Cox kick)
BC	Phelan 10 pass from Doug Flutie (Snow kick)
Miami	Bratton 2 run (Cox kick)
Miami	FG Cox 19
BC	FG Snow 28
BC	FG Snow 19
Miami	Bratton 52 run (Cox kick)
BC	Strachan 1 run (Snow kick)
Miami	Bratton 1 run (Cox kick)
BC	Phelan 48 pass from Doug Flutie (no conversion attempted)

Statistics of the Game

	B.C.	Miami
First downs	30	32
Rushes-yards	34-155	33-208
Passing yards	472	447
Return yards	88	128
Passes	34-46-0	25-38-2
Punts	3-32	1-45
Fumbles-lost	2-1	5-1
Penalties-yards	7-50	8-55
Possession	32:44	27:16

Left: Flutie's creative play extended into both the CFL and the NFL.

"You get on the same frequency with Doug and somehow things happen."
—Receiver Gerard Phelan

TEDDY BALLGAME'S FAVORITE HIT

Maybe everyone could tell it was the last carefree summer for a while and tried to make it stretch forever, because the 1941 baseball season was so remarkable that people still remember it. Atop the memories of that year is Ted Williams's .406 batting average, which remains as the last time anyone hit over .400 for a season. For all the great moments Williams had that historic year, though, his favorite—in fact his favorite hit of his entire legendary career with the Boston Red Sox—was in a game that didn't even count in the standings: the 1941 All-Star Game.

The Splendid Splinter at spring training in 1941.

Regarded as possibly the best All-Star Game ever, the 1941 game at Briggs Stadium in Detroit began with a different hero. The AL held a 2–1 lead going into the top of the seventh, when Arky Vaughan of the Pittsburgh Pirates broke things open with a two-run home run, giving the NL a 3–2 lead, and then followed in the eighth with another two-run homer.

Down 5–2, the AL fought back in the eighth. The DiMaggio brothers put together a run when Joe doubled and Dom knocked him in with a single, but that was as far as the rally went. The Americans went into the bottom of the ninth still down 5–3, facing the Cubs' dominating pitcher, Claude Passeau.

The first out came quickly on a pop-out by Frankie Hayes of the Athletics. Kenny Keltner of the Indians then beat out an infield hit. With a little sliver of hope now alive, the Americans dug in. Joe Gordon of the Yankees singled and when the Senators' Cecil Travis walked, suddenly the bases were loaded and Joe DiMaggio, the Yankee Clipper, was up. The season would end with DiMaggio leading the league in RBIs and total bases, but this time up he didn't stroke one of his typical ropes into the outfield; instead he slapped a hard grounder that looked like a sure double-play ball. Travis wasn't giving up, though. As the Cubs' Billy Herman made the force at second, Travis came in hard and Herman threw wide to first. Keltner scored and now it was 5–4, with Ted Williams at the plate.

A year from that afternoon in Detroit, Ted Williams would be in the Naval Air Corps, but July 8, 1941 was all about baseball. Williams stood in with two on and two out against Passeau, who had struck him out in the eighth. The count ran to 2 and 1 when Passeau threw a fastball waist high. Williams swung for the fences and pulled the ball deep to right, a ball that would keep going until it hit off the facade for a home

> ## "It was the kind of thing a kid dreams about."
> —Ted Williams

Joe DiMaggio was at home plate to meet Williams when he came around to score.

run and a 7–5 American League victory. As Williams said, "It was the kind of thing a kid dreams about and imagines himself doing when he's playing those little playground games we used to play in San Diego. Halfway down to first, seeing that ball going out, I stopped running and started leaping and jumping ... I've never been so happy, and I've never seen so many happy guys."

Joe DiMaggio and Bob Feller carried Williams off the field and Del Baker, manager of the Tigers, even kissed Williams on the head. Williams has called it "the most thrilling hit of my life," and it was the most thrilling of many a baseball fan who saw it, as well.

American League 7, National League 5

National League	AB	R	H	RBI
Hack, Chicago, 3b	2	0	1	0
Lavagetto, Bklyn., 3b	1	0	0	0
Moore, St. Louis, lf	5	0	0	1
Reiser, Brooklyn, cf	4	0	0	0
Mize, St. Louis, 1b	4	1	1	0
McCormick, Cinn., 1b	0	0	0	0
Nicholson, Chicago, rf	1	0	0	0
Elliot, Pittsburgh, rf	1	0	0	0
Slaughter, St. Louis, rf	2	1	1	0
Vaughan, Pittsburgh, ss	4	2	3	4
Miller, Boston, ss	0	0	0	0
Frey, Cincinati, 2b	1	0	1	0
Herman, Brooklyn, 2b	3	0	2	0
Owen, Brooklyn, c	1	0	0	0
Lopez, Pittsburgh, c	1	0	0	0
Danning, New York, c	1	0	0	0
Wyatt, Brooklyn, p	0	0	0	0
a Ott, New York	1	0	0	0
Derringer, Cincinnati, p	0	0	0	0
Walters, Cincinnati, p	1	1	1	0
c Medwick, Brooklyn	1	0	0	0
Passeau, Chicago, p	1	0	0	0
Total	**35**	**5**	**10**	**5**

American League	AB	R	H	RBI
Doerr, Boston, 2b	3	0	0	0
Gordon, New York, 2b	2	1	1	0
Travis, Washington, 3b	4	1	1	0
J. DiMaggio, New York, cf	4	3	1	1
Williams, Boston, lf	4	1	2	4
Heath, Cleveland, rf	2	0	0	0
D. DiMaggio, Boston, rf	1	0	1	1
Cronin, Boston, ss	2	0	0	0
Boudreau, Cleveland, ss	2	0	2	1
York, Detroit, 1b	3	0	1	0
Foxx, Boston, 1b	1	0	0	0
Dickey, New York, c	3	0	1	0
Hayes, Philadelphia, c	1	0	0	0
Feller, Cleveland, p	0	0	0	0
b Cullenbine, St. Louis	1	0	0	0
Levi, Chicago, p	1	0	0	0
Hudson, Washington, p	0	0	0	0
d Keller, New York	1	0	0	0
Smith, Chicago, p	0	0	0	0
e Keltner, Cleveland	1	1	1	0
Total	**36**	**7**	**11**	**7**

*Two out when winning runs were scored.
a Batted for Wyatt in third.
b Batted for Feller in third.
c Batted for Walters in seventh.
d Batted for Hudson in seventh.
e Batted for Smith in ninth.

National League	0	0	0	0	0	1	2	2	0—5
American League	0	0	0	1	0	1	0	1	4—7

THE IMMACULATE RECEPTION

The Oakland Raiders may have believed it was nothing but dumb luck, but the Pittsburgh Steelers and 50,000 of their crazed fans at Three Rivers Stadium had to think they were part of a miracle on Dec. 24, 1972. The nearly religious name the decisive play has come to be known by—the Immaculate Reception—tells just how important and how remarkable one play is to the devout Steelers faithful.

Starting at his own 20, Steelers quarterback Terry Bradshaw tried to get the team within field goal range. After five plays and 40 yards, he threw a pass intended for running back John (Frenchy) Fuqua.

As Fuqua reached for it, he collided at the Oakland 35 with Raiders safety Jack (Assassin) Tatum. The ball bounced off Tatum's body, and popped backward seven yards, at the

The Immaculate Reception was so amazing that it was replayed over and over on television, and, as seen here, diagrammed in Monday's papers.

It was the American Conference semifinal game. The Steel Curtain defense of Pittsburgh, with Mean Joe Green, Jack Ham and L.C. Greenwood had held the Raiders until Ken Stabler, whom coach John Madden had put in for Daryle Lamonica at quarterback, took a 30-yard run into the end zone to edge into a 7–6 lead in the final minute of play.

very moment that rookie Steelers running back Franco Harris came chugging by.

As Fuqua would tell reporters later, "I saw the ball and thought I could catch it, but felt someone hit me from behind. Next thing I knew Franco went roaring past me and I wondered what the hell was going on."

> # "I wasn't even supposed to be out there."
> —Franco Harris

Terry Bradshaw (left) and Franco Harris (right) both made the Hall of Fame. Bradshaw still leads the Steelers in passing yards and passing touchdowns, while Harris leads the franchise in rushing and touchdowns scored.

Harris snatched the ball off his shoe tops and began running with it toward the goal line.

"I wasn't even supposed to be out there," Harris said. "I thought Terry was in trouble, having to scramble, so I better get out there if he had to throw to me. But he threw it deep."

Harris took the ball 42 yards for a touchdown that gave Pittsburgh a 13–7 victory with five seconds left.

Tatum claimed the ball never hit him and the officials did something they'd never done before—they consulted television replays to confirm their decision. Madden didn't dispute it, though, and the Steelers went on to the AFC Conference Game, where they lost to Miami. The Immaculate Reception, though, was the moment when Franco Harris and the Steelers '70s dynasty launched forward to greatness.

Divine intervention? Probably not, but don't say that in Pittsburgh.

Pittsburgh Steelers 13
Oakland Raiders 7

Pittsburgh	0	0	3	13	—13
Oakland	0	0	0	7	—7

Pitt	FG Gerela, 18
Pitt	FG Gerela 29
Oak	Stabler 30, run (Blanda, kick)
Pitt	Harris 60, pass from Bradshaw (Gerela, kick)
Attendance	50,350

Statistics of the Game

	Steelers	Raiders
First Downs	13	13
Rushing Yardage	36-108	31-138
Passing yardage	144	78
Passes	11-25	12-30
Interceptions By	2	1
Punts	7-48	7-45
Fumbles Lost	0	2
Yards Penalized	5	16

KORDELL AIRS

IT OUT

Rocket Left Victory was how Colorado designated the play.

It was the Buffaloes' version of the Hail Mary pass, saved for those last-gasp occasions when football miracles are called for.

On this day—Sept. 24, 1994—there was no question that Colorado was in the kind of jam that cried for something on the order of divine intervention. But the Buffaloes were not in Lourdes, France. They were in Ann Arbor, Mich., playing before 100,000 rabid Wolverines fans blasting the famous Michigan fight song, and they would have to depend on a mere mortal to answer their prayers.

That man was Colorado quarterback and future Pittsburgh Steeler Kordell Stewart. The situation was thus:

Both teams had been undefeated going into the game. Coach Gary Moeller's Michigan team had beaten Notre Dame and at 2–0 were already talking national championship. Colorado fans were saying the same thing though. Bill McCartney, Colorado's coach who later left the sideline to lead the Christian men's group, the Promise Keepers, didn't dissuade them. Buffaloes running back, future first-round draft pick Rashaan Salaam, scored from one-yard out with 2:16 to go. Michigan led 26–21 but couldn't run out the clock, giving Colorado the ball back with 15 seconds to go. A pass from Stewart to Michael Westbrook moved the ball to the Colorado 36, then Stewart spiked the ball to save time for one final play. Only six seconds remained.

The play that Stewart called Rocket Left Victory put receivers Michael Westbrook, Blake Anderson and Rae Carruth wide left and James Kidd off to the right.

At the snap, Stewart dropped back seven steps, looked downfield and then let the ball fly. The pass soared 73 yards in the air. Six Michigan defenders were massed inside the five-yard line, ready to reject Stewart's missile and slam it to the turf.

Even Colorado quarterback Kordell Stewart wasn't sure he could throw the ball all 73 yards to the end goal.

"We work against that play all of the time. It's not a miracle."

—Michigan coach Gary Moeller

Though he grew up outside of Detroit as a Michigan fan, receiver Michael Westbrook ended the Wolverines national title hopes with this catch.

One of those defenders, free safety Chuck Winters, managed to get a hand on the ball, but so did Colorado's Anderson. The ball floated towards the end zone, where the 6'4", 210-pound Westbrook jumped and snatched it off the back of Wolverines cornerback and future New England Patriot Ty Law and fell into the end zone. As his joyous teammates piled on top of Westbrook, and as Stewart fell to his knees and kissed the grass, the officials signaled the touchdown that gave Colorado a shocking last-second victory, 27–26. The massive crowd at Michigan Stadium fell silent.

The Buffaloes of Colorado had soared into legend on Rocket Left Victory.

As he lay on the grass, Westbrook shouted up to the heavens: "Never give up. Never give up!"

Colorado Buffaloes 27
Michigan Wolverines 26

Colorado	7	7	0	13—27
Michigan	0	9	17	0—26

Colo.	Salaam 2 run (Voskeritchian kick)
Mich.	FG, Hamilton, 33
Colo.	Westbrook 27 pass from Stewart (Voskeritchian kick)
Mich.	Biakabutuka 4 run (pass failed)
Mich.	Wheatley 5 run (Hayes pass from Collins)
Mich.	FG, Hamilton, 20
Mich.	Toomer 65 pass from Collins (run failed)
Colo.	Salaam 1 run (Voskeritchian kick)
Colo.	Westbrook 64 pass from Stewart (no attempt)

Statistics of the Game

	Colorado	Michigan
First downs	23	21
Rushes-yards	43-217	41-157
Passing yards	294	258
Total offense	511	415
Return yards	29	5
Passes	21-32-1	17-24-0
Punts	5-41-0	6-35-8
Fumbles-lost	4-3	1-1
Penalties-yards	10-102	9-68

Chapter 2
BUZZER BEATERS

*I*n any sport where there's a clock, there's a buzzer to be beaten. Basketball, the highest-scoring sport to use a clock, has a long history of memorable buzzer beaters; in fact, the challenge is to pick the best, given that a single year of March Madness in the NCAA tournament usually features a few great ones. Football plays the clock, too. Timeouts are hoarded, pass routes designed to take receivers out of bounds and Hail Mary passes lofted up toward the end zone in hope of a game-winning miracle. Hockey teams pull their goalie to add an extra skater for the last minute of play and while that last-second goal doesn't happen often, it's scored enough to make it a real possibility every time. Whatever the sport, buzzer beaters are the quintessential Fat Lady moments.

MICHAEL

Was Michael mortal?

That was the question that the 1998 NBA Finals, pitting Michael Jordan's Chicago Bulls against the Utah Jazz, raised.

Jordan and Dennis Rodman (91), both in their final game as Chicago Bulls, contained Utah's Karl Malone.

At 35, His Airness at times had looked fallible against the Jazz. Not only had he missed a crunch-time jump shot in Game 5, but there were moments when he appeared to show his age, moments when he looked fatigued, moments when those standards of Jordan excellence seemed to be slipping.

When the Bulls arrived in Salt Lake City for Game 6 of their championship series, Chicago led in games, 3–2. But a Delta Center crowd was revved up for home court heroics after Utah had stolen away home court advantage by beating Chicago in Game 5 at the United Center. The 19,911 partisan fans fully expected the Jazz to tie the series and take it to a climactic Game 7.

But on this night, Jordan—the alltime leading playoff scorer—was determined to squelch the Jazz right here, right now. With Scottie Pippen limited to 26 minutes because of back spasms, Michael took it upon himself to be the engine of the Bulls' championship machine.

As the game clock ticked down, even with Jordan's dominating performance, the Bulls were chasing Utah. Jordan had missed five straight shots from outside when Utah's sterling guard, John Stockton, hit a three-point shot with 41.9 seconds remaining. Stockton's three gave the Jazz an 86–83 lead and sent the crowd into a frenzy.

Jordan narrowed the lead to 86–85 on a driving layup with 37.1 seconds and set up as memorable a finish as fans of Jordan's would have.

On the next offensive set, the Jazz put the ball in the hands of their main man, Karl (the Mailman) Malone, the broad, high-scoring All-Star forward with an interest in 18-wheel trucks and no NBA titles. Malone didn't deliver this night. Jordan sneaked along the baseline and stole the ball from him.

"When I got the ball, I looked up and saw 18.6 seconds

left," Jordan said later. "And I felt like we couldn't call a timeout; it gives the defense an opportunity to set up. It was a do-or-die situation."

At do-or-die, nobody in the history of the game had been any better than Michael.

As he brought the ball upcourt, he juked the capable Jazz defender Bryon Russell. As Russell lurched off-balance, Jordan squared away from behind the key and let fly.

The shot dropped softly through the hoop, Jordan's 45th point of the game, in 44 minutes, to seal the title, the Bulls' sixth during Jordan's career. For Jordan, who would announce his (second, and final) retirement before the 1999 season, it would be the final shot of his career—and a fitting exit.

"I think it's the best performance ever by Michael Jordan at a critical moment in a critical situation," said Bulls coach Phil Jackson.

Michael Jordan's last shot.

Chicago Bulls 87, Utah Jazz 86

Chicago	Min	fgm	fga	ftm	fta	r	a	pf	pts
Pippen	26	4	7	0	0	3	4	2	8
Kukoc	42	7	14	0	0	3	4	3	15
Longley	14	0	1	0	0	2	0	4	0
Jordan	44	15	35	12	15	1	1	2	45
Harper	29	3	4	2	2	3	3	2	8
Rodman	39	3	3	1	2	8	1	5	7
Burrell	10	0	1	0	0	0	0	0	0
Wennington	4	1	1	0	0	0	0	1	2
Kerr	24	0	0	0	0	0	3	3	0
Buechler	8	1	1	0	0	2	1	1	2
Total	240	34	67	15	19	22	17	23	87

Utah	Min	fgm	fga	ftm	fta	r	a	pf	pts
Russell	37	2	5	3	4	4	2	2	7
Malone	43	11	19	9	11	11	7	2	31
Keefe	14	1	3	0	0	1	0	1	2
Hornacek	37	6	12	4	4	6	0	0	17
Stockton	33	4	10	1	2	3	5	4	10
Carr	26	4	7	1	2	3	0	4	9
Eisley	15	1	1	1	1	2	3	1	3
Morris	16	1	3	0	0	2	1	4	2
Anderson	16	2	4	1	1	1	1	0	5
Foster	3	0	0	0	0	0	0	1	0
Total	240	32	64	20	25	33	19	19	86

Chicago	22	23	16	26—87
Utah	25	24	17	20—86

"I never doubted myself."
—Michael Jordan

THE BULL RAGES

It had taken Jake LaMotta eight years and 89 bouts to finally get a shot at the middleweight title.

The previous year, on June 16, 1949, the Bronx Bull, as LaMotta was known, had knocked out Edith Piaf's favorite pugilist, France's Marcel Cerdan of France, to become the middleweight champion of the world.

Yet here it was, a little more than a year later, on Sept. 13, 1950, and an uninspired LaMotta appeared on the verge of losing his title to another Frenchman, Laurent Dauthuille, in only his second title defense.

Dauthuille had outboxed LaMotta, refusing to be lured into the brawl that The Bull had tried to bait him into. When LaMotta lay against the ropes, playing possum, Dauthuille wouldn't fall in with him. He continued to do what had worked for him in an earlier nontitle victory over LaMotta in '49 and again on this night: he boxed, boxed, boxed.

The result was not pretty for LaMotta fans. By the middle rounds, LaMotta's left eye was nearly swollen shut and his lackadaisical attitude prompted the referee, Lou Handler, to scold the champ for his lack of effort.

By the 15th and final round, Dauthuille seemed a sure-fire winner. The unassuming challenger led on the judges' cards by scores of 72–68, 74–66 and 73–67, and gave no evidence early in the final round of losing a grip on his game.

Suddenly, with time running out, LaMotta caught Dauthuille flush with a left hook that turned the Frenchman's legs rubbery. LaMotta tore after the challenger, driving Dauthuille across the ring with a succession of hooks.

Dauthuille tried to clinch but the furious LaMotta was having none of that. He forced Dauthuille into the ropes and, with a final hook, knocked him onto the canvas.

Dauthuille ended up with his head resting on the bottom rope, and was counted out with only 13 seconds left in the fight.

The Bronx Bull had gored the matador.

Never a pretty fighter LaMotta was immortalized by Martin Scorsese's classic film Raging Bull.

Dauthuille goes down. LaMotta racked up a record of 83-19-4 before retiring in 1954.

"Viva La France!"
—Dauthuille's cornerman Harry Raskin
at the start of the 15th round

Middleweight Championship

The cards at the point of LaMotta's knockout of Dauthuille

Referee Lew Hander	8–6	Dauthuille
Judge Jack Asprey	7-6-1	Dauthuille
Judge Joe Lenahan	7-3-4	Dauthuille

BIRD DOGGIN'

The bashing, hard-edged Pistons and the elegant, pedigreed Celtics did not play nice when they faced each other, and Game 5 of the 1987 Eastern Conference final was no exception. With the series tied at two games apiece, Detroit's Bill Laimbeer and Boston's Robert Parish set the tone, tangling on court, with Parish throwing punches. The Pistons appeared to be on the verge of stealing the fifth game when Isiah Thomas hit a jumper that gave the Pistons a 107–106 lead with 17 seconds left.

At the other end of the Boston Garden parquet, Larry Bird tried to regain the lead for the Celtics. But his baseline drive was knocked away by the Pistons' Dennis Rodman.

The deflected ball went out of bounds off Celtics guard Jerry Sichting, giving Detroit possession with five seconds left.

On the Detroit bench, Pistons coach Chuck Daly was waving and screaming for a timeout. But neither Thomas nor the other Pistons saw Daly's frantic gestures.

Meanwhile, Thomas prepared to inbound the basketball from the sidecourt. As he did, Bird geared up to defend against the Pistons' Joe Dumars. Speed was not featured among Bird's Hall of Fame talents, but intelligence was. Just as Thomas was about to release his pass, Bird began "cheating" towards the intended target of the pass, Detroit's Laimbeer.

As Bird later told reporters: "I saw Laimbeer standing there and I was going to foul him real quick. But then I saw that the ball was kind of lobbed up there."

So instead of fouling Laimbeer, Bird went for the steal.

In a near-repeat of Havlicek's famous play against the Sixers in 1965, Bird stole the pass and Celtics announcer Johnny Most got the chance to echo his call of 22 years ago.

"As soon as I got it," Bird said, "I was going to shoot. I was counting four seconds in my head and then I turned around and saw DJ cutting down the lane."

DJ was Dennis Johnson, the Celtics guard. As Bird intercepted the pass and Johnson cut to the basket, Bird seized the opportunity and hit Johnson with the pass for the layup to win the game, 108–107, amidst bedlam in the small, sweaty and euphoric Boston Garden.

Dennis Johnson and Bird combined to steal the conference title from their fierce rivals.

Right: Larry Bird's 21,791 points are second on the Celtics' all-time scoring list to John Havlicek.

"We lucked out."

—Larry Bird

Boston Celtics 108
Detroit Pistons 107

Detroit	fgm	fga	ftm	fta	pts
Mahorn	2	3	0	0	4
Dantley	10	15	5	5	25
Laimbeer	7	20	2	4`	1416
Dumars	2	5	0	0	4
V. Thomas	6	16	5	8	17
Johnson	8	13	4	4	20
Salley	3	8	1	2	7
Rodman	7	7	0	0	14
Green	0	0	0	0	0
Total	**45**	**87**	**17**	**23**	**107**

Boston	fgm	fga	ftm	fta	pts
McHale	8	9	4	4	20
Bird	12	25	12	12	1236
Parish	3	10	5	6	11
D. Johnson	5	13	8	10	18
Ainge	5	12	0	0	12
Daye	2	3	3	5	7
Vincent	1	4	2	2	4
Sichting	0	1	0	0	0
Roberts	0	0	0	0	0
Kite	0	1	0	0	0
Total	**36**	**78**	**34**	**39**	**108**

Detroit	29	27	29	22—107
Boston	38	20	28	22—108

THREE-PEAT

In 1993 the Chicago Bulls sought to become a basketball dynasty by winning their third straight NBA title.

In the history of the league only two teams had ever done that—the Minneapolis Lakers, who had won three consecutive crowns from 1952–54 and the Boston Celtics, who had won eight straight titles from 1959–66. All that stood between the Bulls and their three-peat was the Phoenix Suns, Chicago's opponent in the championship series, and their MVP forward, the outspoken Charles Barkley.

The Bulls led the series three games to two, sparked as usual by Michael Jordan, the greatest player in the game. But Chicago was playing Game 6 on Phoenix's home court, and against a team that had won two of the last three games in the series, including a triple-overtime thriller and a hard-to-come-by road win at Chicago Stadium.

After one more season with the Bulls, Paxson retired.

With 38.1 seconds left, the Suns held a slender 98–96 lead. A Phoenix basket would likely put the game out of reach for the Bulls and jeopardize their three-peat. The Suns ran the clock down, then Dan Majerle shot an air ball, and the Bulls took possession with 14.1 seconds left. Chicago was still alive.

Bulls coach Phil Jackson called a timeout. As the teams came out of their huddles, everybody in the arena expected the Bulls to trust their chances to Jordan, who had averaged 41 points (a Finals record), 8.5 rebounds and 6.3 assists per game.

Indeed, the inbounds pass ended up with Jordan, who passed the ball to Scottie Pippen in the front court. Jordan then cut past Pippen, looking for a return pass, but he was blanketed on defense by Phoenix's scrappy guard Kevin Johnson.

That forced Pippen to unload to forward Horace Grant along the left baseline. Grant had misfired on his last nine shots, so he passed the ball to John Paxson, who was lingering back of the three-point line like a secret weapon.

Paxson caught the ball. Two years before, he had hit five jumpers down the stretch in the final game of the Bulls' first title series, but since then he'd had knee surgery and B.J. Armstrong had taken most of his minutes. Could Paxson, now a role player, provide Jordan-like heroics? He sent the ball rotating towards the basket.

"It seemed like the ball was in the air for about an hour," said Phoenix coach Paul Westphal.

When Paxson's three-point shot descended, it was right on target. His three-pointer gave the Bulls a 99–98 lead. Grant blocked Johnson's jumper as time expired to give the Bulls their third straight NBA title.

"Pax," said Jordan, "is a heartbreaker. He's had a way of breaking other teams' hearts by hitting that jumper in the clutch ever since he's been here. When I saw him with the ball and a good look at the basket, I knew it was going in."

"He never hits shots that clutch in our driveway games."

—Jim Paxson, John Paxson's brother

Chicago Bulls 99
Phoenix Suns 98

Chicago	min	fgm	fga	ftm	fta	reb	a	pf	pts.
Grant	33	0	5	1	2	7	3	5	1
Pippen	43	10	22	3	7	12	5	3	23
Cartwright	26	1	3	0	0	4	1	5	2
Armstrong	41	6	10	2	2	0	4	5	18
Jordan	44	13	26	4	6	8	7	3	33
Paxson	22	3	4	0	0	1	1	1	8
S.Williams	22	2	7	1	3	7	1	3	5
Tucker	7	4	4	0	0	0	1	1	9
King	2	0	1	0	0	0	1	0	0
Total	240	39	82	11	20	39	24	26	99

Phoenix	min	fgm	fga	ftm	fta	reb	a	pf	pts.
Barkley	44	7	18	7	10	17	4	5	21
Dumas	22	3	8	2	2	3	1	2	8
West	20	1	2	2	4	4	1	5	4
K.Johnson	46	6	14	7	7	5	10	3	19
Majerle	46	7	17	5	6	8	2	3	21
Miller	14	1	4	2	2	2	0	1	4
Ainge	30	3	6	1	1	3	2	0	9
Chambers	12	4	10	1	1	5	0	2	12
F.Johnson	6	0	3	0	0	0	0	0	0
Total	240	32	82	30	36	47	20	21	98

Chicago	37	19	31	12—99
Phoenix	28	23	28	19—98

GET SMART

Basketball is a rhythm game. Ask any shooter. When it's going right, the ball is an extension of the hand and the player releases it without a second thought. Instinctively. When that happens—and the shots are falling—your basketball-shooting man is, as they say, "in the zone."

The night did not start that way for Keith Smart when his

Indiana University team played Syracuse in the NCAA championship game in 1987, at the Superdome in New Orleans. And Indiana coach, the voluble and controversial Bob Knight, loved and feared by his players, was not known for his patience.

Maybe it was a matter of early-game jitters. Or else a case of Smart trying too hard to impress all those friends and neighbors who had made it to the Superdome from just down the road in Baton Rouge, where he had been a fry cook at McDonald's after graduating from high school.

Whatever the reasons, Smart—a rare junior college transfer for Indiana—was cold as ice against Syracuse in the first half, and Knight sat him on the bench a while, hoping to settle him down.

But still Smart struggled. Again in the second half, Knight benched him for 4½ minutes. But down the stretch, with Indiana trailing 61–56 and 7:22 left in the game, Smart began to find his rhythm.

As *Sports Illustrated* would report: "Smart's spectacular leaping bank shots and layups tied the game at 61 and 63 and put Indiana ahead 67–66. And following [Syracuse guard Sherman] Douglas's own enthralling fake-behind-the-back-pass, driving layup that returned the lead to Syracuse at 68–67, Smart deadlocked the contest once more at 70 before he missed a baseline jumper that would have tied it at 72 with 39 seconds left."

Instead, Syracuse's Howard Triche nudged the lead to 73–70 when he hit the front end of a one-and-a-bonus free throw. But when Triche missed the bonus, Smart drove for a basket that cut the lead to 73–72.

Bob Knight's tough coaching style made him very controversial and influential.

Another missed foul shot, this one by Syracuse freshman Derrick Coleman, gave the Hoosiers one last chance to salvage the game.

The play Knight would draw up was for the team's leading scorer, Steve Alford, who'd made seven three-point shots and led the team with 23 points against Syracuse. But Alford didn't get the chance. Disobeying Knight was tantamount to mutiny and freelancing on the Hoosiers squad was virtually unknown. Yet somehow the ball landed in the hands of Indiana's Daryl Thomas, who passed it to Smart in the left corner.

Smart—a man now locked in the zone—launched again, this time a 16-foot jumper that dropped through the net, bringing a roar from the record-breaking crowd of 64,959 and bringing Knight his third NCAA championship as Indiana won 74–73.

Keith Smart delivers the winning basket from the corner.

Indiana 74
Syracuse 73

Syracuse	min	fgm	fga	ftm	fta	r	a	pf	pts
Triche	32	3	9	2	4	1	1	4	8
Coleman	37	3	7	2	4	19	1	2	8
Seikaly	34	7	13	4	6	10	1	3	18
Monroe	32	5	11	0	1	2	3	1	12
Douglas	39	8	15	2	2	2	7	3	20
Brower	9	3	3	1	3	1	0	3	7
Thompson	17	0	2	0	0	3	1	0	0
Total	200	29	60	11	20	38	14	16	73

Indiana	min	fgm	fga	ftm	fta	r	a	pf	pts
Calloway	14	0	3	0	0	2	1	3	0
Thomas	40	8	18	4	7	7	1	1	20
Garrett	33	5	10	0	0	10	0	4	10
Alford	40	8	15	0	0	3	5	2	23
Smart	35	9	15	3	4	5	6	2	21
Meler	4	0	0	0	1	1	0	0	0
Eyl	13	0	0	0	0	1	1	2	0
Smith	1	0	0	0	0	0	0	1	0
Hillmarr	20	0	1	0	0	2	6	2	0
Total	200	30	62	7	12	31	20	17	74

Syracuse	33	40—73
Indiana	34	40—74

Attendance-64,959

"Coach Knight wasn't going to let us quit."
—Keith Smart

DEMPSEY AND THE LONG KICK

It was 1970 and placekickers like Tom Dempsey were going out of fashion. Dempsey was an old-school straight-on kicker rather than one of the side-wheeling soccer-influenced booters that had begun to infiltrate NFL rosters. Only four years earlier, in 1966, Garo Yepremian, a side-wheeler from Cyprus playing for the Detroit Lions, had beaten Norm Van Brocklin's Minnesota Vikings with a last-minute field goal. That prompted the Dutchman, when asked what should be done about these newfangled kickers, to reply: "Tighten the immigration laws."

While Dempsey was a conventional placekicker, he was hardly typical. He had been born without toes on his right foot and without a right hand. To accommodate his foot, the 6'1", 264-pound Dempsey was permitted to wear a special square-toed shoe. Still, even with the flat-edged shoe, Dempsey was an erratic kicker, hitting only five out of 15 attempts in his second season.

On Nov. 8, 1970, the 23-year-old Dempsey was playing for the New Orleans Saints in a game against the Lions, and watching from the sideline as the Lions edged ahead 17–16 with 18 seconds left, on Errol Mann's 18-yard field goal.

That didn't leave the Saints much time to mount a drive. Following the kickoff, New Orleans started its offensive series from its 28 yard line with eight seconds left. That gave quarterback Billy Kilmer one shot to move the ball upfield. He hit Al Dodd with a 17-yard pass with two seconds left in the game, stopping the clock. No one had apparently noticed that Dodd never got both feet in bounds before going out of bounds.

New Orleans Saints coach J.D. Roberts called for Dempsey to try an improbable 63-yard field goal.

Nobody in NFL history had ever kicked a field goal that far. The record, set on Sept. 27, 1953, by the Baltimore Colts' Bert Rechichar, was 56 yards.

Dempsey's holder, Joe Scarpati, told the kicker that he would set the ball down a yard deeper than usual to give him more time to lay into the pigskin. On the snap, the ball spiraled to Scarpati. The Lions barely rushed. Scarpati set it down as Dempsey stepped forward and kicked. The ball sailed to the goalpost and just cleared the bar.

"I knew I could kick the ball that far, but whether or not I could kick it straight that far kept running through my mind," said Dempsey. He later told a newsman he

After the kick Cowboys president Tex Schramm complained about Dempsey's special shoes but he quickly recanted under fire.

> ## "He could stand there and kick it 200 times and not hit it that sweet again."
> —Lions assistant coach Bill McPeak

only knew the kick was good, by inches, when the referee's hands shot up and the crowd roared. "It's quite a thrill," he said. "I'm still shook up."

The Lions, who had been nine-point favorites, were shook up too. Joe Schmidt, the Lions coach, said, "It was a [expletive] miracle ... It's like winning the Masters with a 390-yard hole in one on the last shot."

Lightning never hit again the same way for Dempsey. After being cut by the Saints that summer, he went on to spend nine more seasons with the Eagles, Rams, Oilers and Bills, never making a kick farther than 54 yards.

New Orleans Saints 19
Detroit Lions 17

Detroit	0	7	7	3—17
New Orleans	3	3	3	10—19

New Orleans	FG Dempsey, 29
Detroit	Farr 10, run (Mann, kick)
New Orleans	FG Dempsey, 27
Detroit	Sanders 2, pass from Munson (Mann, kick)
New Orleans	FG Dempsey, 8
New Orleans	Barrington 3, run (Dempsey, kick)
Detroit	FG Mann, 18
New Orleans	FG Dempsey, 63

Statistics of the Game

	Saints	Lions
First downs	15	18
Rushing yardage	131	135
Passing yardage	141	143
Return yardage	42	51
Passes	15-28	13-25
Interceptions by	2	0
Punts	6-44	3-31
Fumbles lost	0	3
Yards penalized	124	31

MR. SMITH'S
DARK CLOUD

For 21 years, Dean Smith had coached the University of North Carolina basketball team, a long period in which Smith often came close but never managed to win an NCAA championship.

John Thompson led Georgetown to the NCAA title two years later. He retired in 1999.

As a result, Smith had developed a reputation as a coach who "couldn't win the big one."

Never mind that he had taken the Tar Heels to the NCAA final three times and to the Final Four on three other occasions. Without a championship, a cloud hung over Smith's head.

In 1982 Smith had still another chance to win it all. This time his Tar Heels were matched in the NCAA final against a Georgetown University team led by seven-footer Patrick Ewing and guard Eric (Sleepy) Floyd. Georgetown coach John Thompson was as formidable as his team; a tall, burly man, Thompson was a brilliant leader who put great emphasis on shaping and educating his players, and was the first African-American to coach a team to the Final Four.

UNC was not without its own complement of stars—James Worthy, Matt Doherty, Sam Perkins and a freshman named Michael Jordan.

In a closely contested game, Smith elected to go to his famed four-corners offense—a delay strategy since outlawed by the 45-second clock—as his Tar Heels led 57–56 with 5:32 to go.

The crowd booed the deliberate pace but Georgetown was not deterred. As the last minute ticked down, the Hoyas had edged ahead 62–61 and needed only a defensive stop in the final 32 seconds to keep Smith from getting the NCAA-championship monkey off his back.

But Georgetown failed on defense. Tar Heels guard Jimmy Black located the 6'5" Jordan standing free in front of the Carolina bench, with an open shot from 16 feet. Jordan sank it to put UNC ahead 63–62 with

> ## "If I had a rubber band, I'd have brought it back."
> — Fred Brown

Michael Jordan's jumper with 15 seconds to go turned out to be the game winner.

15 seconds left, enough time for the Hoyas to nail down a game-winning shot.

But a strange thing happened. Georgetown guard Fred Brown had the basketball and, he thought, a bead on an open man, teammate Eric Smith, running towards him. Unfortunately, that man wasn't Smith, but UNC's James Worthy, who had snuck between Brown and Smith. Worthy took the pass, and with it, Georgetown's hopes for a title.

North Carolina had finally won an NCAA title and Dean Smith at last had silenced his critics.

North Carolina 63, Georgetown 62

Georgetown	min	fgm	fga	ftm	fta	r	a	pf	pts
E. Smith	35	6	8	2	2	3	5	5	14
Hancock	8	0	2	0	0	0	0	1	0
Ewing	37	10	15	3	3	11	1	4	23
F. Brown	29	1	2	2	2	2	5	4	4
Floyd	39	9	17	0	0	3	5	2	18
Spriggs	30	0	2	1	2	1	0	2	1
Jones	10	1	3	0	0	0	0	0	2
B. Martin	5	0	2	0	0	0	0	1	0
G. Smith	7	0	0	0	0	0	0	1	0
Total	200	27	51	8	9	22	16	20	62

N. Carolina	min	fgm	fga	ftm	fta	r	a	pf	pts
Doherty	39	1	3	2	3	3	1	0	4
Worthy	38	13	17	2	7	4	0	3	28
Perkins	38	3	7	4	6	7	1	2	10
Black	38	1	4	2	2	3	7	2	4
Jordan	34	7	13	2	2	9	2	2	16
Peterson	7	0	3	0	0	1	1	0	0
Braddock	2	0	0	0	0	0	1	1	0
Brust	4	0	0	1	2	1	1	1	1
Total	200	25	47	13	22	30	14	11	63

N. Carolina	31	32—63
Georgetown	32	30—62

1992 NCAA East Regional Final
Duke vs. University of Kentucky

March 29, 1992

BUZZER

BEATER

It was college basketball played at a skill level that stole your breath away.

As Duke and Kentucky battled to the wire in the NCAA East Regional championship game in Philadelphia's Spectrum on March 29, 1992, both teams were hitting better than 60% of their shots from the floor.

But through 40 minutes of regulation and all but the final 2.1 seconds of a five-minute overtime, one player stood out as the perfect offensive machine. Duke's 6'11" Christian Laettner had sunk all nine of his field goal attempts and gone a flawless 10 for 10 from the free throw line.

Yet for all that, Laettner had not been able to halt the banked driving shot that Kentucky's 6'2" senior guard Sean Woods lofted over Laettner's outstretched arms to give Kentucky a 103–102 lead with those 2.1 seconds remaining.

As Woods's shot scored, Duke quickly called a timeout and hurried to the sideline, where Blue Devils coach Mike Krzyzewski told his players, "First of all, we're going to win. Okay?"

Easier said than done. But Coach K had a play in mind, and now he diagrammed the X's and O's that would be Duke's last chance against Kentucky.

The play started with the ball in the hands of Blue Devils forward Grant Hill at the far baseline. From there, Hill fired a pass 75 feet from where he stood without a Kentucky player harrassing him.

That was the defensive strategy of Wildcats coach Rick Pitino, who apparently decided that his players would better serve farther up the court, in a kind of prevent defense. But the ball nonetheless managed to land in Laettner's hand as he stood back of the foul line.

In those 2.1 ticks, Laettner managed to fake left, dribble right, swivel left and put up a 17-foot jump shot that fell through the hoop just before the final buzzer sounded.

The ball fell through and broke Kentucky's heart.

It left even Hill struggling for the words to convey the wham-bam climax.

"If you're asking for a way to describe what happened, you're asking the wrong person. I'm just shocked."

Through all of Duke's incredible run of seven Final Four appearances in nine years and two NCAA titles, this game stands out as the one to remember them by.

The Blue Devils went on to win the NCAA title, and Grant Hill (far left), would go on to stardom in the NBA. Mike Krzyzewski (center), continues to coach Duke.

Duke 104
Kentucky 103

Kentucky	fgm	fga	ftm	fta	pts.
Mashburn	11	16	3	3	28
Pelphrey	5	7	3	3	16
Martinez	2	4	0	0	5
Woods	9	15	2	2	21
Farmer	2	3	4	6	9
Feldhaus	2	6	1	2	5
Brown	6	11	3	5	18
Ford	0	2	0	0	0
Timberlake	0	0	1	2	1
Riddick	0	0	0	0	0
Braddy	0	1	0	0	0
Total	37	65	17	23	103

Duke	fgm	fga	ftm	fta	pts.
Lang	2	2	0	1	4
Davis	3	6	7	10	13
Laettner	10	10	10	10	31
Hurley	6	12	5	6	22
T. Hill	6	10	5	5	19
G. Hill	5	10	1	2	11
Parks	2	2	0	0	4
Clark	0	0	0	0	0
Total	34	52	28	34	104

Duke	50	54—104
Kentucky	45	58—103

"We're going to win."
—Duke Coach Mike Krzyzewski

NOTRE DAME UNRAVELS UCLA'S STRING

For weeks beforehand, all anyone could talk about was the upcoming bout between Notre Dame's Fighting Irish and the UCLA Bruins. That both teams were undefeated was only the tip of the iceberg. Notre Dame's No. 2 ranking was outdone only by UCLA, who had been ranked first in college basketball since 1968, with seven straight championships to back them up. Furthermore, with each game they played, UCLA was setting the NCAA record for consecutive wins, a record it first established at Notre Dame's Athletic and Convocation Center, where the Bruins defeated the Irish to reach 61 in a row. The last time UCLA coach John Wooden had landed his team in the L column was back in 1971, dropping a road game to Notre Dame, 89–82. Framed on all sides by confrontations with the Irish, the 88-game string of victories seemed destined to be ended in South Bend.

On Jan. 19, 1974, a crowd of 11,343 gathered to witness the historic matchup, with hundreds of thousands more at home riveted to their television sets. Anticipating a terrific clash of strength, skill and wits, disappointed spectators watched as the first half shaped up much like any of UCLA's past 88 starts. Future Trail Blazers and Celtics great Bill Walton, playing in

UCLA coach John Wooden took the Bruins to one more title, in 1975, then retired. Under his leadership, UCLA won 10 NCAA titles in 12 years.

an elastic corset after missing three games due to a back injury, was giving an outstanding performance, leading the Bruins to a 17-point lead, and establishing a 43–34 margin at intermission.

The second half continued in similar fashion, and with 3:32 remaining UCLA was out in front 70–59. But when the Irish returned to the court, after a timeout called by Notre Dame coach Digger Phelps, something had definitely changed. The Irish suddenly had the stride and touch it had been missing all game, while the Bruins seemed to be tripping over their own shadows.

Running a press, the Irish scored with 3:07 on the clock when 6'9" center John Shumate sank a hook shot over an unrested Walton. Then, moments later, stealing the inbounds pass, Shumate earned another two points, cutting the Bruins lead to seven. Managing to hold on to the inbounds pass, Tommy Curtis got the ball as far as midcourt before he lost it to freshman sensation Adrian Dantley who trotted to the UCLA hoop for the easy basket, making it a five-point game.

Again Curtis brought the ball upcourt, but this time he needed no help turning it over, handing the Irish yet another scoring opportunity on his traveling violation. Earning his 22nd and 23rd points of the night, Notre Dame junior Gary Brokaw's field goal dropped to bring the score to 70–67. The UCLA comedy of errors rolled on as the Bruins lost possession again, when Dave Meyers, on his way to the basket, got called for steps. Earning the high-scorer spot for the game, Brokaw hit another jumper to make it a one-point game.

On the other side of the court, UCLA star senior Keith Wilkes, trying to stop Notre Dame's momentum, drove hard to the basket and fouled Brokaw, committing the Bruins' fifth consecutive turnover. With under a minute to play, the Irish took possession of the ball. Notre Dame set up the play

"Winners do the talking. Losers keep quiet."
—John Wooden

to Shumate, but he was quickly double-teamed, leaving junior guard Dwight Clay uncovered. Brokaw dished to Clay, who put up a long jumper and in an explosion of cheers, earned the first and only Irish lead, 71–70.

As the final 21 seconds ran down, the Bruins, having shot 70% through the first half, missed six consecutive attempts, going scoreless in the last three minutes of the game. With a final score of 71–70, the Irish handed the Walton Gang the first loss of their varsity career and ended the longest winning streak in the history of college basketball.

Notre Dame remained undefeated for a week, losing 94–75 in an away game against UCLA.

UCLA 70, Notre Dame 71

UCLA	fgm	ft	fta	pts
Wilkes	6	6	7	18
Trgovich	3	1	1	7
Walton	12	0	0	24
Curtis	3	3	4	9
Meyers	5	0	2	10
Lee	0	2	2	2
Johnson	0	0	0	0
Total	29	12	16	70

Notre Dame	fgm	ft	fta	pts
Brokaw	10	5	7	25
Clay	2	3	4	7
Shumate	11	2	4	24
Dantley	4	1	1	9
Novak	0	0	0	0
Paterno	2	0	0	4
Hartin	1	0	0	2
Total	30	11	16	71

UCLA	43	27—70	
Notre Dame	34	37—71	

CALVERLEY'S DESPERATION SHOT

In 1946, Rhode Island State was not the purist's idea of the way basketball should be played. The Rams were a run-and-gun team at a time when the game tended to be played at waltz tempo. Rhode Island coach Frank Keaney, who also happened to be a chemistry professor at the school, had invented the fast break back in the '30s and this year's model was one of his finest ever to wear Keaney Blue, a light blue dye he had created in the lab and which became the school color. Their smallish team, including a 5'11", 145-pound center—yes, center—named Ernie Calverley, who also had a heart murmur, flew up and down the court, shooting the ball with a trigger-happy mentality. As a result, they had averaged 78 points per game, an absurdly high total for that era, before shot clocks and three point-ers. Still, they'd won 18 of 20 that year, and the season before had made it to the semifinals of the National Invitational Tournament at Madison Square Garden, where they lost to DePaul and the great George Mikan, 97–53.

In contrast, Bowling Green, the team the Rams would meet in the first round of the '46 NIT averaged only 63 points per game. And that was with 6'11½" Don Otten, a legitimate big man—a rarity in an age of clumsy pivot men. Bowling Green had lost the NIT final game the season before to DePaul.

In those days, as pro basketball was just beginning to form, the NIT was at least the equal of the NCAA tourna-ment and New York's Madison Square Garden was the acknowledged home of basketball. For this game, 18,458 squeezed in, a then record crowd for basketball at the Garden, with a healthy number of Rhode Island State fans.

Bowling Green, though favored to win, had a hard time corralling Calverley, son of a Rhode Island lace maker, and his Rhode Island State teammates. Sportswriter Dick Young

called Calverley, a two-time All-American, "the boney Sinatra of the court." As Louis Effrat of *The New York Times* would note of the March 14, 1946 game:

> *Rhode Island State's fire-horse type of play—the Rams never stopped driving—puzzled the Falcons no little. Otten's tremendous height, however, kept them [Bowling Green] very much in the game, his rebound tap-ins were unstoppable and principally because of him Bowling Green trailed by only one point, 35–34, at halftime.*

Towards the end of the second half, Otten, who had scored 31 points, fouled out. The Rams tied the game 68–68, but with three seconds left, Bowling Green had the lead, 74–72.

Rhode Island State took a timeout. Then the Rams' Bob Shea inbounded the ball to Calverley, who turned and fired from beyond the half-court line: a two-hander that sailed 55 feet ... incredibly, into the basket, never even touching the rim. Calverley's shot tied the game at 74–74 and sent it into overtime. Radio broadcaster Marty Glickman has called "The Shot" as it was later dubbed, "still the most exciting moment in my broadcasting experience."

The Rhode Island State fans and players were ecstatic. In the five-minute overtime, Calverley, who ended up with 16 points, did not score. But, as Effrat would report, "Ernie gave his club just about everything else—poise, speed, steadiness, incredibly perfect passes and a fiery will to win."

Win they did. Rhode Island beat Bowling Green 82–79 in overtime.

And in the end, it was Calverley, the 5'11" center, that the fans and coach Frank Keaney carried off the floor.

Officials at Madison Square Garden painted an x on the court where Calverley had let fly, to commemorate the most famous basketball shot of the time.

"I never thought it was going to actually go in."
—Ernie Calverley

Rhode Island 82
Bowling Green 79

Rhode Island	G	F	P
Hole, lf	5	1	11
Palmieri	1	1	3
Nichols, rf	9	3	21
Calverley, c	6	4	16
Shea, lg	7	3	17
Sclafani, rg	1	2	4
Allen	3	4	10
Total	**32**	**18**	**82**

Bowling Green	G	F	P
Kublak, lf	5	0	10
Plinke	1	0	2
Schwab	0	0	0
Dudley, rf	3	1	7
Martin	3	0	6
Conroy	0	0	0
Otten, c	11	9	31
Knierim, lg	2	0	4
Dunham	2	0	4
Inman, rg	5	5	15
Total	**32**	**15**	**79**

The phrase "sudden death" strikes some as too downbeat a term for sports, but no other words fully capture the risk of settling contests with the next score. Although the substitute—"sudden victory"—may celebrate the triumph, it doesn't speak to the long road every athlete takes to come so close to victory. Indeed, sudden death admits that most athletes have devoted their lives to get to within one basket, one goal, one point, of winning, and that losing does hurt, no matter how good a sport one may be. Rest assured, the Fat Lady shines upon winners and losers alike.

Chapter 3
SUDDEN DEATH
VICTORIES

1981 NFC Championship Game
Dallas Cowboys vs. San Francisco 49ers

January 10, 1981

THE CATCH

The stakes were high: The winner would go to Super Bowl XVI.

But right up to the final seconds, you couldn't say whether that National Football Conference champion would be the Dallas Cowboys or the San Francisco 49ers.

It was that kind of seesaw game, the lead shifting from one team to the next as they knocked heads in San Francisco's Candlestick Park on Jan. 10, 1981.

But with 4:54 left in the game and the ball at the 49ers' 11, it looked as though once again the Cowboys would blow San Francisco out of the playoffs ... as they had done in three previous playoffs. Dallas led 27–21, and there were 89 yards of football real estate for San Francisco to navigate.

But that's when 49ers quarterback Joe Montana rallied his forces. Noting that the Cowboys remained in their nickel defense—four linemen, two linebackers and five defensive backs—Montana shifted the emphasis from pass to run, relying on halfback Lenvil Elliott, a 30-year-old castoff from Cincinnati. Elliott got six yards on a draw play and, after Montana hit Freddie Solomon for six yards and a first down at the 23, Elliott swept right for 11 yards to the 49ers' 34 and then swept left for seven more yards. The 49ers were on the move.

After an offside penalty, Montana completed a five-yard curl pass to fullback Earl Cooper, just before the two-minute warning. The 49ers kept driving. With 58 seconds left, Montana had his team at the Cowboys' six-yard line and had 49ers coach Bill Walsh whispering in his ear to go with a play called Sprint Right Option.

The first option on the play would be Solomon. But if Solomon were covered, the second option would be 49ers tight end Dwight Clark, 6'4", 210 pounds, cutting across the end zone, right to left, then reversing himself and breaking back right.

As Montana rolled to his right, he was hotly pursued by Cowboys linemen Ed (Too Tall) Jones, Larry Bethea and a blitzing D.D. Lewis. Solomon was covered, but Clark appeared to be open at the back of the end zone.

On the run Montana fired. The ball was thrown high. Clark leapt into the air, thinking: "Oh no, I can't go that high."

But, as he later would say, "Something got me up there. It must have been God or something."

Clark pulled the ball in for the touchdown that gave San Francisco a 28–27 victory, a catch that would propel them on to a Super Bowl victory against Cincinnati.

A catch that would be forever chiseled in the memory of 49ers' fans.

San Francisco went on to best the Cincinnati Bengals in the Super Bowl and established their dynasty.

"I thought, Oh no, I can't go that high."
—Dwight Clark

Dwight Clark pulls down "The Catch."

| San Francisco 49ers | | | | 28 |
| Dallas Cowboys | | | | 27 |

Dallas	10	7	0	10—27
San Francisco	7	7	7	7—28

S.F.	Solomon 8 pass (Wersching, kick)
Dallas	Septien FG 44
Dallas	Hill 20 pass from White (Septien, kick)
S.F.	Clark 26 pass from Montana (Wersching, kick)
Dallas	Dorsett 5 run (Septien, kick)
S.F.	Davls 2 run (Wersching, kick)
Dallas	Septien FG 22
Dallas	Cosbie 21 pass from White (Septien, kick)
S.F.	Clark 6 pass from Montana (Wersching, kick)

Statistics of the Game

	Dallas	S.F.
First downs	16	26
Rushes yards	32-115	31-127
Passing yards	135	266
Return yards	13	29
Passes	16-24-1	22-35-3
Sacks by	4-38	3-20
Punts	6-39	3-36
Fumbles lost	4-2	3-3
Penalties yards	5-39	7-106
Time of Possession	32:57	27:03

Attendance-80,525

Gabby Hartnett played 19 seasons with the Cubs, and later as a manager spoke in favor of integration in the major leagues.

"That home run took all the fight out of us. It broke our hearts."
—Paul Waner

THE HOMER IN THE GLOAMIN'

Cubs general manager Bill Veeck had built a new scoreboard for Wrigley Field in 1937 and personally planted the ivy on the outfield walls that same year. But there were no lights at Wrigley Field in 1938—owner Phil Wrigley had dismissed Veeck's suggestion to install them back in 1934, saying they were a fad. Wrigley's shortsighted decision inadvertently paid off in 1938, with one of baseball's most dramatic finishes.

Through the thick of summer 1938, the Chicago Cubs had been trying to overtake the Pittsburgh Pirates, but the Pirates were always just a step beyond. As the season wound down to its final days, Chicago, under player-manager Gabby Hartnett, was finally in position to wrest first place from the Pirates. On Sept. 28, as Pittsburgh and Chicago met head-on at Wrigley Field, the Cubs trailed the Pirates by a mere half-game in the standings. The outcome that afternoon would be crucial.

The Pirates scored three runs in the sixth inning off Chicago pitcher Clay Bryant to lead the Cubs 3–1. But Chicago came roaring back to tie the score in the bottom of the inning on doubles by Hartnett and Rip Collins and a bunt single by Billy Jurges.

In the eighth, when the Pirates scored two runs, again the Cubs answered back. Collins opened the bottom of the eighth with a single, Jurges walked and former Yankee Tony Lazzeri hit a pinch-hit double, scoring Collins and advancing Jurges to third. Stan Hack then walked and Billy Herman drove in the tying run with a single.

By the ninth inning, though, evening was descending on Wrigley Field, and a real threat existed that the game would have to be called on account of darkness. Should that happen, the game would have to be rescheduled the next day as part of a doubleheader, a troubling prospect for the wornout Cubs pitching staff.

When Chicago relief pitcher Charley Root held the Pirates scoreless in the ninth, the Cubs knew they were battling not just Pittsburgh hurler Mace Brown—they were racing time. With each pitch, the threat of the game being called grew.

Brown retired Phil Cavarretta, the first Cubs batter in the bottom of the ninth. The shadows lengthened. Brown retired the next man, Carl Reynolds. It grew darker.

Up came Hartnett. With the count 2-0, he hit a line drive that soared into the leftfield bleachers. The 34,465 jubilant Cubs fans swarmed onto the Wrigley Field turf, forcing Hartnett to fight his way through the mob. The homer sent the Cubs into first place and Chicago would go onto win the pennant.

Just under fifty years later, on August 8, 1988, the first night game was played at Wrigley Field. (The Cubs won that one, too.)

Chicago Cubs 6, Pittsburgh Pirates 5

Pittsburgh	AB	R	H	RBI	Chicago	AB	R	H	RBI
L. Waner, cf	4	0	2	0	Hack, 3b	3	0	0	1
P. Waner, rf	5	0	2	0	Herman, 2b	3	0	0	1
Rizzo, lf	4	1	1	1	Demaree, lf	3	0	0	0
Vaughan, ss	2	2	1	0	Cavarretta, rf	5	0	0	0
Suhr, 1b	3	2	1	0	Reynolds, cf	5	0	1	0
Young, 2b	2	0	0	0	Hartnett, c	4	2	3	1
a Manush	1	0	1	0	Collins, 1b	4	3	3	1
Thevenow, 2b	0	0	0	0	Jurges, ss	3	1	1	0
Handley, 3b	4	0	2	3	Bryant, p	2	0	1	0
Todd, c	4	0	0	0	Russell, p	0	0	0	0
Klinger, p	4	0	0	0	b O'Dea	1	0	0	0
Swift, p	0	0	0	0	Page, p	0	0	0	0
Brown, p	0	0	0	0	French, p	0	0	0	0
					Lee, p	0	0	0	0
Total	35	5	10	4	c Lazzeri	1	0	1	1
					d Marty	0	0	0	0
					Root, p	0	0	0	0
					Total	38	6	12	5

a Batted for Young in eighth.
b Batted for Russell in sixth.
c Batted for Lee in eighth.
d Ran for Lazzeri in eighth.

Pittsburgh	0	0	0	0	0	3	0	2	0—5
Chicago	0	1	0	0	0	2	0	2	1—6

THE RETURN OF THE RANGERS

For decades—five plus, but who was counting?—the New York Rangers had been denied the Stanley Cup; 54 years of ups and downs, painfully unrelieved by the glory and joy which comes with being the champions of the National Hockey League. But in 1994 long-suffering Rangers fans

Mark Messier scored four game-winning goals in the Rangers drive to the 1994 Stanley Cup.

accustomed to crushed dreams believed this was the year. With firebrand Mike Keenan as coach and former Edmonton Oilers great Mark Messier as captain, the Rangers polished off the New York Islanders and Washington Capitals in the first two rounds and now faced their cross–Hudson River rivals, the New Jersey Devils, for the conference title.

By Game 6, though, the favored Rangers were in trouble. Down 3–2 in the series, longtime followers of the team could make out the familiar sound of choking from the Rangers' direction. But Messier would have none of it. Before the game at New Jersey's Brendan Byrne Arena he had stolen a page from Joe Namath's book and guaranteed a Rangers victory; now, down 2–1 in the third period, it looked as if he'd have to deliver.

Deliver, he did. Messier tied the game at 2:48 of the third period, scored the game-winner at 12:12, and iced it with an empty-net goal at 18:15; a natural hat trick and one of the most thrilling one-man pressure performances in hockey history.

On to Game 7. The Rangers led 1–0 and the voice on the Madison Square Garden public address system announced "last minute to play." The Garden was poised for a victory celebration.

The Devils pulled goalie Martin Brodeur and as the clock ticked down, it didn't appear the gamble would pay off. Then, suddenly, New Jersey's Claude Lemieux fired a shot off the pads of Rangers goalie Mike Richter. The loose puck skidded toward the stick of Lemieux's teammate, Valeri Zelepukin who with 7.7 seconds left in the game flicked the puck past Richter to tie the game 1–1.

The heartbreak of a 40-year odyssey came rolling over the Garden like a London fog. Would this be just another cruel turn in the Rangers' ongoing Stanley Cup chase? Had they raised themselves off the canvas, only to be knocked down at the bell?

Esa Tikkanen celebrates as the winning goal slips past Devils goalie Martin Brodeur.

The first overtime period passed with no score but it was a full 20 minutes of beautifully end-to-end played hockey. The tension in Madison Square Garden twisted further and further up into the second overtime. Early in the period, the puck was deflected into the Devils zone. Ranger Stephane Matteau and the Devils' Scott Niedermayer gave chase and Matteau got to it first. He skated around the New Jersey net and, at 4:24 of the second overtime, he beat Brodeur with a wraparound shot to give the Rangers a 2–1 victory that sent them to the Stanley Cup finals. On television, Rangers announcer Howie Rose cried over and over, "Matteau! Matteau!" Up in high seats, the crowd screamed, "We want the cup! We want the cup!" And after the Rangers beat the Canucks in seven games in the finals, New York finally had the Stanley Cup back. Thanks in no small part to Mark Messier and Stephane Matteau.

New York Rangers 2
New Jersey Devils 1

New Jersey	0	0	1	0	0—1
N.Y. Rangers	0	1	0	0	1—2

First Period: No scoring

Second Period: 1) NY, Leetch 6 (Graves, Messier), 9:31. Penalty-Lemieux, NJ (interference), 12:13.

Third Period: 2) NJ, Zelepukin 5 (Lemieux, Richer), 19:52. Penalty-Kovalev, NY (elbowing), 6:32.

First Overtime: No scoring

Second Overtime: 3) NY, Matteau 6, 4:24.

Goalies- New Jersey, Brodeur
New York, Richter

CLUTCH HOMER

It was a routine double-play ball off the bat of Pirates batter (and future Yankee manager) Bill Virdon, but as Yankees shortstop Tony Kubek stooped to field the ball, it struck a pebble, flew up and slammed into Kubek's larynx. Kubek dropped to the ground, badly injured, and was removed by stretcher from the field.

The freak bounce opened the gates for a Pittsburgh rally in the bottom of the eighth inning of the crucial seventh game of the 1960 World Series—a five-run rally capped by Hal Smith's three-run home run that gave the Pirates a 9–7 lead. Freak is the operative word here. Despite the tied series and the Pirates' lead, the Yankees had outscored Pittsburgh by 29 runs, powered by Bobby Richardson's 12 RBIs and Mickey Mantle's three home runs. The Pirates simply had no business being three outs away from a World Series win, their first since 1925.

The Pirates' optimism proved premature, though, as manager Danny Murtaugh brought in relief pitcher Bob Friend to close down the Yankees. Friend was tagged for singles by Richardson and Dale Long and, when Friend was replaced by Harvey Haddix, it got no better. After Haddix got Roger Maris to foul out, Mantle drove in Richardson with a single. Yogi Berra, up next, hit a sharp grounder to first baseman Rocky Nelson. Nelson fielded the ball and stepped on first for the second out of the inning, and then swiped the glove at Mantle, as the Mick, bad knees and all, slid back into the bag, just ahead of the tag. But as Nelson was doing that, Gil McDougald, running for Long, crossed the plate, tying the game at 9–9.

Haddix got the final out of the inning when New York's Bill Skowron grounded out.

Bill Mazeroski, the brown-haired, brown-eyed second baseman of the Pirates, led

Second baseman Mazeroski's nickname was "No Touch" for his ability to quickly turn the double play.

> ## "I only wish my dad had been alive to see it."
> —Bill Mazeroski

A six-time all-star, Mazeroski also played on the great Pirates' team of the early '70s with Clemente and Stargell.

haired, brown-eyed second baseman of the Pirates, led off the ninth inning against Yankees reliever Ralph Terry.

With the count 0 and 1, Mazeroski hit the next pitch 402 feet over the leftfield brick wall at Forbes Field as Berra, the regular Yankees catcher who had been put in leftfield as a substitute, just watched the ball go by. Pittsburgh won the game 10–9, and their first World Series in 35 years. Forbes Field has been demolished, but a plaque still stands, along with a piece of the outfield wall, on the campus of the University of Pittsburgh commemorating Mazeroski's home run.

Pittsburgh Pirates 10, New York Yankees 9

New York	AB	R	H	RBI	Pittsburgh	AB	R	H	RBI
Richardson, b	5	2	2	0	Virdon, cf	4	1	2	2
Kubek, ss	3	1	0	0	Groat, ss	4	1	1	1
DeMaestri, ss	0	0	0	0	Skinner, lf	2	1	0	0
d Long	1	0	1	0	Nelson, 1b	3	1	1	2
e McDougald, 3b	0	1	0	0	Clemente, rf	4	1	1	1
Maris, rf	5	0	0	0	Burgess, c	3	0	2	0
Mantle, cf	5	1	3	2	b Christopher	0	0	0	0
Berra, lf	4	2	1	4	Smith, c	1	1	1	3
Skowron, 1b	5	2	2	1	Hoak, 3b	3	1	0	0
Blanchard, c	4	0	1	1	Mazeroski, 2b	4	2	2	1
Boyer, 3b, ss	4	0	1	1	Law, p	2	0	0	0
Turley, p	0	0	0	0	Face, p	0	0	0	0
Stafford, p	0	0	0	0	c Cimoli	1	1	1	0
a Lopez	1	0	1	0	Friend, p	0	0	0	0
Shantz, p	3	0	1	0	Haddix, p	0	0	0	0
Coates, p	0	0	0	0	**Total**	31	10	11	10
Terry, p	0	0	0	0					
Total	40	9	13	9					

a Singled for Stafford in third.
b Ran for Burgess in seventh.
c Singled for Face in eighth.
d Singled for DeMaestri in ninth.
e Ran for Long in ninth.

New York	0	0	0	0	1	4	0	2	2—9	
Pittsburgh	2	2	0	0	0	0	0	5	1—10	

1975 World Series—Game Six
Boston Red Sox vs. Cincinnati Reds

October 21, 1975

FISK AND THE FOUL POLE

Fans were already calling the 1975 World Series between the Boston Red Sox and the Cincinnati Reds one of the best ever. The teams were stocked with Hall of Fame talent: the Red Sox featured a pitching staff led by cigar-smoking Cuban Luis Tiant and the quirky lefthander Bill Lee, had Fred Lynn, Jim Rice, Carl Yastrzemski in the field, and Carlton Fisk behind the plate. For the National League, Cincinnati's Big Red Machine was at its peak, with Johnny Bench, George Foster, Ken Griffey, Joe Morgan, Tony Perez,

Fisk's urging the ball fair is still judged to be one of baseball's most memorable moments.

and Pete Rose. The first five games had more than their share of great performances and drama. Tiant shut out the Reds 6–0 in Game 1; Bench and Griffey headmanned an eighth inning Reds comeback in Game 2; and Game 3 went

to Cincinnati after a controversial noncall of interference in the 10th inning keyed a 6–5 extra-inning Reds win. Tiant won his second, Game 4, by a score of 5–4 to tie the series, at two, but Cincinnati's Perez hit two homers in Game 5 to give the Reds a 5–1 win and a 3–2 lead in games.

So it was on Oct. 21, 1975, that the Cincinnati Reds sought to clinch the World Series against the Red Sox at Fenway Park in Boston.

The Sox jumped out to a 3–0 first-inning lead when Lynn hit a three-run home run into the right centerfield bleachers. But Cincinnati stormed back, scoring three runs in the fifth inning when Griffey drove in two runs with a triple and then scored on Bench's single.

In the seventh inning, Cincinnati increased its lead when Foster's double drove in two more runs to make the score 5–3. An inning later, Cesar Geronimo nicked Tiant, the Red Soxs starter, for a solo home run, driving the 34-year-old Bosox pitcher to the showers and depriving him of his third win of the series.

Gloom settled over the misshapen ballpark off Kenmore Square. Cincinnati had a commanding 6–3 lead through seven and a half innings.

But the night, it turned out, was young.

In the Red Sox half of the eighth, with two runners on, Cincinnati pitcher Rawley Eastwick threw a fastball to pinch hitter Bernie Carbo that Eastwick meant to put on the inside corner. But the pitch was out and up. Carbo, who'd already had a pinch hit homer in Game 2, hit it up and out, into the centerfield seats to tie the game 6–6. The game went into extra innings, where neither team broke through for three frames.

Four hours after the game had started, at 12:33 a.m., as the game went into bottom of the 12th inning, Red Sox catcher Carlton Fisk, nicknamed Pudge, a native New Englander dear to all Boston fans, came up. With a rapt tele-

"This is some kind of game."
—Pete Rose to Carlton Fisk
while at the plate

Carlton Fisk hit only 10 homers in the 1975 season, but with a .331 average.

vision audience, even at this late hour, watching across America, Fisk hit a sinker from Pat Darcy to deep leftfield. As the ball soared along the leftfield line, Fisk watched, mesmerized, jumping up and down as he waved at the ball to stay fair.

Coming down on its long arc, the baseball hit the leftfield foul pole, giving the Red Sox a 7–6 victory and a place in the collective sporting memory of the country. The Reds won Game 7 to take the series, but Game 6 is the one everyone remembers. Still regarded as one of the most exciting baseball games ever, Game 6 of the 1975 Series helped turn televised postseason baseball into the spectacle it is today.

Boston Red Sox 7, Cincinnati Reds 6

Cincinnati	AB	R	H	RBI	Boston	AB	R	H	RBI
Rose, 3b	5	1	2	0	Cooper, 1b	5	0	0	0
Griffey, rf	5	2	2	2	Drago, p	0	0	0	0
Morgan, 2b	6	1	1	0	R. Miller, ph	1	0	0	0
Bench, c	6	0	1	1	Wise, p	0	0	0	0
T. Perez, 1b	6	0	2	0	Doyle, 2b	5	0	1	0
G. Foster, lf	6	0	2	2	Yastrzemski, lf	6	1	3	0
Concepcion, ss	6	0	1	0	Fisk, c	4	2	2	1
Geronimo, cf	6	1	2	1	Lynn, cf	4	2	2	3
Nolan, p	0	0	0	0	Petrocelli, 3b	4	1	0	0
Chaney, ph	1	0	0	0	Evans, rf	5	0	1	0
Norman, p	0	0	0	0	Burleson, ss	3	0	0	0
Billingham, p	0	0	0	0	Tiant, p	2	0	0	0
Armbrister, ph	0	1	0	0	Moret, p	0	0	0	0
C. Carroll, p	0	0	0	0	Carbo, lf	2	1	1	3
Crowley, ph	1	0	1	0	**Total**	41	7	10	7
Borbon, p	1	0	0	0					
Eastwick, p	0	0	0	0					
McEnany, p	0	0	0	0					
Driessen, ph	1	0	0	0					
Darcy, p	0	0	0	0					
Total	50	6	14	6					

Cincinnati	0	0	0	0	3	0	2	1	0	0	0	0—6
Boston	3	0	0	0	0	0	0	3	0	0	0	1—7

1958 NFL Championship Game
Baltimore Colts vs. New York Giants

December 28, 1958

THE *GREATEST* GAME EVER PLAYED

Pro football in the late '50s was popular, but baseball was definitely the national pastime when the Baltimore Colts came to frigid Yankee Stadium to face the New York Giants for the NFL championship on Dec. 28, 1958. By the end of the game, though—the first sudden death football game ever played and the first championship game broadcast live on television—America began to reconsider its love affair with baseball. Only an amazing event could change America so deeply, and this game was indeed that amazing.

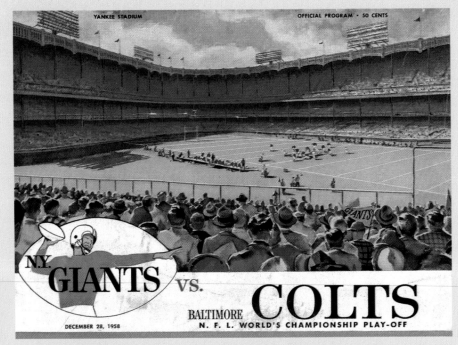

A rare program from one of sports' most legendary games.

The upstart Giants, who made the title game by beating the powerful Cleveland Browns three times in the season, took an early 3–0 lead after a long carry by running back Frank Gifford and a field goal by Pat Summerall. Despite the Giants'

quick lead, the day seemed to belong to the heavily favored Colts. Led by slope-shouldered Johnny Unitas, his running backs Lenny Moore and Alan (the Horse) Ameche, and Hall of Fame receiver Raymond Berry, the Colts grabbed control of the field. A fumble recovery by Baltimore's Big Daddy Lipscomb set up the first touchdown, scored by Ameche; the second was a 15-yard strike from Unitas to Berry.

The Colts appeared to have the game locked up as they marched again down the field in the third quarter. With first-and-goal at the Giants' three-yard line, all Baltimore had to do was punch the ball in, but the Giants' defense, led by linebacker Andy Robustelli, dug in. On the fourth down, instead of going for the easy field goal that would have made it 17–3, the Colts went for the kill. It was a mistake. New York's Cliff Livingston tackled Ameche on the five and the Giants had the ball and the momentum.

Now the Giants moved the ball. The key play of the drive was a completion from quarterback Charlie Conerley to Kyle Rote, who fumbled as he was tackled. New York's Alex Webster scooped up to ball and took it to the Colts one-yard line. Mel Triplett scored on the next play and it was 14–10. New York kept control into the fourth quarter, and took a 17–14 lead early in the quarter on a 15-yard connection between Conerley and Gifford. The next time the Giants took the ball, the Colts' defense stopped them. Gifford was brought down a foot short of a first down on a third down run and the Giants were forced to punt.

With just over two minutes to go, Unitas grabbed the reins.

"It's the greatest thing that ever happened."

—Raymond Berry

He drove the Colts from their own 14 to the Giants 13, mostly with passes to Berry, whose poor eyesight and slow feet were no obstacle today. With seven seconds remaining, Baltimore's Steve Myhra kicked a 20-yard field goal to tie the game at 17 and send it to sudden death.

Though the Giants won the toss, they couldn't advance the ball, falling just inches short of a first down on a quarterback option play, and Unitas took over again. Starting at their own 20, the Colts slammed down the field. When Ameche finally rammed the ball across from the one-yard line, the Colts claimed the title with a 23–17 win, and the NFL claimed millions of new fans, many of whom had never seen a football game, let alone one so perfect in its combination of great play and unexpected fortune.

Baltimore Colts 23
New York Giants 17

Baltimore	0	14	0	3	6—23
New York	3	0	7	7	0—17

Baltimore Scoring- Touchdowns: Ameche 2 (2. 1, plunges), Berry (15, pass from Unitas). Conversions: Myhra 2. Field Goal: Myhra (20).
New York Scoring- Touchdowns: Triplett (1. plunge), Gifford (15, pass from Conerley). Conversions: Summerall 2, Field Goal: Summerall (36)

Statistics of the Game

	Colts	Giants
First downs	27	10
Rushing yardage	138	88
Passing yardage	322	178
Passes attempted	40	18
Passes completed	26	12
Passes intercepted by	0	1
Punts	4	6
Av. dist. of punts, yds	51	48
Fumbles lost	2	4
Yards penalized	62	52

THE WILD THING'S BLOWN SAVE

Not since the New York Yankees of 1977 and 1978 had any team repeated as World Series champs. And now, after knocking on the door for so long, the Toronto Blue Jays were trying to follow up their championship season of 1992 with another one. Never mind that in this era of revolving-door personnel the Blue Jays of 1993 included a dozen new players: for Toronto fans, they were still the same Jays.

Early on in Game 6 of the 1993 World Series against the Philadelphia Phillies, the defending champs appeared to be a lock to repeat. Leading the series three games to two, the Jays had their pitching ace, Dave Stewart, cruising along with a 5–1 lead after six innings.

But then in the seventh inning—disaster struck in Toronto's SkyDome. Stewart was rocked for a three-run homer by Lenny Dykstra. And before the Blue Jays' hurlers

Williams had such a hot hard-to-control fastball that players sometimes refused to face him during his years in the minors.

that followed Stewart could retire the side, Philadelphia had added two more runs—a five-run inning that gave the Phillies a 6–5 lead.

And that's how the game stood going into the bottom of the ninth as Philadelphia's closing relief pitcher Mitch Williams took the mound.

Williams defined quirky relievers in the '90s. Nicknamed the Wild Thing, Williams lived up to his moniker with not only his blazing intensity, but also unpredictable swings between unhittable fire and absolute junk. As entertaining and occasionally overpowering as Williams was, managers and fans of the Rangers, the Cubs, and now the Phillies had lost years of their lives wondering whether the man on the mound would strike out the side or give up a home run. Earlier in the series, in Game 4, Williams had blown a 14–10 lead and afterward received three telephoned death threats. But here was a chance for him to mitigate that earlier misspent evening. Shut down the Blue Jays here and now, and send this series to Game 7, and he would be A-OK again with Phillies fans.

Easier said than done. Williams walked the first batter, Ricky Henderson, but got the next man, Devon White, to fly to left. Up came Paul Molitor, who lined a single to center, advancing Henderson to second. That brought up Blue Jays rightfielder Joe Carter, who had gone hitless in his previous seven at bats.

The count on Carter went to 2 and 2. Then Williams shook off his catcher Darren Daulton and delivered a slider, down and in. Carter swung and the ball rose towards the leftfield wall, soaring over it at the 379-foot mark and landing in the Blue Jays bullpen. At 11:39 that night, before 52,195 fans in the SkyDome, Joe Carter had won the World Series for Toronto 8–6, and Mitch Williams became one of baseball's biggest goats. The Wild Thing was released by the Phillies, and his career was effectively over the next season.

Joe Carter was one of the game's most productive hitters with men in scoring position.

"We were hoping he would come in."
—Ricky Henderson on Mitch Williams

Toronto Blue Jays 8, Philadelphia Phillies 6

Philadelphia	AB	R	H	RBI		Toronto	AB	R	H	RBI
Dykstra, cf	3	1	1	3		R.Henderson, lf	4	1	0	0
Duncan, dh	5	1	1	0		White, cf	4	1	0	0
Kruk, 1b	3	0	0	0		Molitor, dh	5	3	3	2
D. Hollins, 3b	5	1	1	1		Carter, rf	4	1	1	4
Batiste, 3b	0	0	0	0		Olerud, 1b	3	1	1	0
Daulton, c	4	1	1	0		l Griffin, pr-3b	0	0	0	0
Eisenreich, rf	5	0	2	1		R. Alomar, 2b	4	1	3	1
M. Thompson, lf	3	0	0	0		T. Fernandez, ss	3	0	0	0
a Incaviglia, ph, lf	0	0	0	1		Sprague, 3b-1b	2	0	0	1
Stocker, ss	3	1	0	0		Borders, c	4	0	2	0
Morandini, 2b	4	1	1	0		**Total**	33	8	10	8
Total	35	6	7	6						

a- hit sacrifice fly for M. Thompson in the 7th.
l-ran for Olerud in the 8th.

Philadelphia	0	0	0	1	0	0	5	0	0—6
Toronto	3	0	0	1	1	0	0	0	3—8

SUDDEN DEATH
STANLEY CUP

Going into Game 7 of the 1950 Stanley Cup finals at Detroit's Olympia, the third straight season the Red Wings, powered by the great Gordie Howe, had fought their way to the NHL's final showdown, the long-suffering Detroit team understood that after a mere 60 minutes of hockey they would either be taking champagne baths or would leave the arena empty handed for the third straight time. With Howe out due to a near fatal concussion he'd gotten on March 28, though, the champagne seemed far away.

Having fought their way back from a 3–2 series deficit, The New York Rangers had the momentum as the two teams squared off for the seventh and decisive game. Play was rough from the opening face-off; neither team managed to muster a shot on goal through the first five minutes of play. But 11:14 into the first period, with Red Wings leftwinger Ted Lindsay in the penalty box for high-sticking, Rangers defenseman Allan Stanley, converted New York's momentum into a 1–0 lead over Detroit.

With the game becoming more and more rough, Detroit's Marty Pavelich quickly joined Lindsay in the box for slashing. Taking advantage of the 5-on-3, Ranger Tony Leswick slapped one past goalie Harry Lumley to put the Wings in the hole by two. Before the first period came to a close, New York skated a player short twice, but the Rangers defense held tight and the Red Wings couldn't score.

Five minutes into the second period, Detroit finally got a power play they could deliver on. Called for interference, Stanley watched helplessly from the penalty box as the Red Wings evened the game, scoring goals only 21 seconds apart. The first of the two Detroit scores came at 5:09 when Red Kelly, stealing the puck from Alex Kaleta, dished to Pete Babando, who slipped it past Rangers goalie Chuck Rayner. Then, at 5:30, a high, hard 20-foot shot found the New York net as Frank Eddolls screened Rayner. Six minutes later the Rangers went out ahead again when Buddy O'Connor made good on Nick Mickoski's rebound. But the lead was short-lived. With just over four minutes remaining in the second period, Red Wing Jimmy McFadden beat his

As Gordie Howe's linemate on the Production Line of the 1940s and '50s, Ted Lindsay drove the team with aggressive play. He spent 157 total minutes in the penalty box during the 1949–50 season.

> ## "Boy, it took us a long time to win the Cup, but it was sure worth it."
> —Harry Lumley

New York goalie Chuck Rayner watches the puck slip past him in Game 7.

man to the puck as it came off the boards behind the New York goal and firing from an impossible angle, ricocheted the puck off Rayner's left skate and into the net.

What followed was 20 minutes of hard-hitting, penalty-ridden, stalemate hockey. After the dust had settled and the third period was complete, the score remained 3–3. The Stanley Cup would be won with sudden death for the first time ever. The first overtime period passed with no score. Then, 8:31 into the second sudden death period, with the crowd of 13,000 still jammed into the Olympia, Babando scored his second goal of the night, delivering the Stanley Cup to the overjoyed—and overdue—Detroit Red Wings.

Detroit Red Wings   4
New York Rangers   3

N.Y. Rangers	2	1	0	0	0-3
Detroit Red Wings	0	3	0	0	1-4

First Period: 1) NY Stanley 2 (Leswick) PPG 11:14; 2) NY Leswick 2 (O'Connor, Laprade) PPG 12:18.
Penalties- Pavelich DET (holding) 6:12; Laprade NY (roughing), Lindsay DET (roughing, slashing) 8:18; Pavelich DET (slashing) 11:27; O'Connor NY (tripping) 12:42; Slowinski NY (tripping) 19:14.

Second Period: 3) DET Babando 1 (Kelly, Couture) PPG 5:09; 4) DET Abel 6 (Dewsbury) PPG 5:30; 5) NY O'Connor 4 (Mickoski) 11:42; 6) DET McFadden 2 (Peters) 15:57.
Penalty- Stanley NY (interference) 3:56

Third Period: No Scoring.
Penalty- Kyle NY (hooking) 0:24; Dewsbury DET (holding) 1:33.

First Overtime Period: No Scoring.
Penalties- None.

Second Overtime Period: 7) DET Babando 2 (Gee) 8:31.
Penalties- None.

Goalies: New York Rayner; DET-Lumley

PETTY LARCENY

At 47 years of age, Richard Petty was not too old to still savor a race among the good ol' boys.

When he turned up in Daytona Beach, Fla., on July 4, 1984, for the $387,300 Firecracker 400 he was shooting for his 200th career Grand National victory.

With two laps to go, the popular Petty, in a Pontiac Grand Prix, had just seen Cale Yarborough, in a Chevrolet Monte Carlo, snatch the lead from him when, coming out of the fourth turn, a yellow flag went up.

The caution flag had been thrown just after he and Yarborough zipped across the finish line. By NASCAR rules, that enabled both drivers to race the final lap back to the flag while the other drivers were obliged to hold their positions.

For Petty and Yarborough, the race was on.

Going into the third turn, Yarborough shot beneath Petty and into the lead. But his car wouldn't stay low, which let Petty dive low and pull alongside Yarborough as the cars emerged from the turn.

Now they were coming up on the lapped cars of Ken Ragan and David Pearson, and Petty began edging towards the outside wall as Yarborough's and Petty's cars began bumping at more than 200 mph.

"I had the draft of three or four cars running up in front of us," said Petty. "I thought they were going to be detrimental to begin with because I thought they were going to keep me from running beside [Yarborough]. But I was able to run right behind those cars and pick up a little bit of the draft, which kept me up with him until we caught up with them. Then when we pulled over, I had the draft of the inside car and the outside car because I was in the middle.

"Cale and I touched a couple of times, not enough to really upset the cars but it did affect the cars. The last bam that happened squirted me out in front a little bit so it worked out to my advantage."

Indeed, Petty had beaten Yarborough to the finish line and the yellow flag and, ultimately, to victory.

"I knew what he was going to do. I knew where he was going to do it," said Petty. "I knew what I was going to try to do and I pulled it off."

It was Petty larceny that brought Richard the checkered flag as he finished in 2:19:59 at an average speed of 171.204 mph.

Firecracker 400

	Driver	Car	Laps	Time
1.	Richard Petty	Pontiac Grand Prix	160	2:19:59
2.	Harry Gant	Chevrolet Monte Carlo 36	160	
3.	Cale Yarborough	Chevrolet Monte Carlo SS	160	
4.	Bobby Allison	Buick Regal	160	
5.	Benny Parsons	Chevrolet Monte Carlo SS	160	
6.	Bill Elliot	Ford Thunderbird	160	
7.	Terry Labonte	Chevrolet Monte Carlo SS	159	
8.	Dale Earnhardt	Chevrolet Monte Carlo SS	159	
9.	Neil Bonnet	Chevrolet Monte Carlo SS	159	
10.	Joe Ruttman	Chevrolet Monte Carlo SS	157	
11.	Tym Richmond	Pontiac Grand Prix	157	
12.	Geoff Bodine	Chevrolet Monte Carlo SS	157	
13.	Phil Parsons	Chevrolet Monte Carlo SS	157	
14.	Tommy Ellis	Chevrolet Monte Carlo SS	157	
15.	Ricky Rudd	Ford Thunderbird	156	
16.	Trevor Boys	Chevrolet Monte Carlo SS	156	
17.	David Pearson	Chevrolet Monte Carlo SS	156	
18.	Dave Marcis	Pontiac Grand Prix	156	
19.	Jody Ridley	Chevrolet Monte Carlo SS	155	
20.	Rusty Wallace	Pontiac Grand Prix	155	

With the traditional champagne spraying about, Petty celebrates his record victory.

" ... I pulled it off."
—Richard Petty

Harry Gant took second when Yarborough headed to the pits, apparently thinking the race was over. Yarborough finished third.

CHARLIE HUSTLE VERSUS FOSSE

No matter what the sport, All-Star games are usually played with a degree of restraint. After all, it's merely a showcase: a few hours that afford the fans a chance to see the game's best bumping up against one another. But the 1970 baseball All-Star Game, played at Cincinnati's new $45 million Riverfront Stadium before 51,838, including President Richard Nixon, would be an exception to the rule. The five Reds on the squad—Pete Rose, Tony Perez, Johnny Bench, Jim Merritt and Wayne Simpson—surely wanted to show off

Rose's competitive spirit—headfirst slides and all—led to 4,256 career hits.

in front of the home crowd as the Big Red Machine began to gel in the early 1970s.

The American League, which had lost 12 of the previous 13 midsummer classics, appeared on the verge of improving its luck, leading 4–1 going into the bottom of the ninth.

But suddenly National League bats came alive. San Francisco's Dick Dietz opened the inning by slamming a home run off the AL's Catfish Hunter to narrow the lead to 4–2. Then Bud Harrelson of the Mets and Hall of Famer Joe Morgan of Houston singled, prompting American League manager Earl Weaver to bring in Fritz Peterson of the Yankees to pitch to Willie McCovey of the Giants.

Wrong move. McCovey knocked in Harrelson with a single to make it 4–3. Another pitching change brought Mel Stottlemyre of the Yankees in for Peterson. A sacrifice fly off of Stottlemyre by the legendary Roberto Clemente of Pittsburgh tied the game 4–4.

And that's how it stood as the National League came to bat in the bottom of the 12th.

In that inning California Angels pitcher Clyde Wright got the first two batters—Joe Torre, who later managed the Yankees to World Series titles, and Clemente out. But then Cincinnati's Pete Rose, known as Charlie Hustle, singled and then advanced to second on a single by Billy Grabarkewitz of Los Angeles.

That brought Jim Hickman of the Cubs to bat. Hickman cracked a 1 and 0 pitch for a single to center. Slick-fielding by Amos Otis of the Royals scooped the ball up in center and, as Rose rounded third, fired to catcher Ray Fosse of the Indians at the plate.

Fosse and Rose had met for the first time the night before the game. The two had had dinner together and even went back to Rose's house to talk baseball. But Rose was not one for sentiment, especially after striking out in the bottom of the ninth to kill the National League's comeback rally as he did. When Rose saw Fosse blocking the plate he did not break stride or try to get cute with a hook slide. Fosse was just as tough; he could have conceivably stepped aside and swept the tag as Rose slid by, but Fosse decided to block the plate. Goaded by a passionate hometown crowd rooting on

"We each did what we thought we had to do to make the play."
—Ray Fosse

As Cubs manager Leo Durocher looks on, Pete Rose bears down on home plate, and Ray Fosse.

one of their favorites, Charlie Hustle went hellbent-for-leather at Fosse, barreling into the catcher. In the collision that followed, Fosse was driven backward into a somersault and Rose touched home plate for the game-winning run.

Rose, who simply would not slack off, All-Star Game or not, would end up with a swollen left knee and Fosse with a severely bruised left shoulder. Rose, of course, would go on to set the record for most hits in a career, and play well into his 40's.

That evening, the first time a national television audience saw Riverfront Stadium, marked the beginning of the Reds' dynasty. Both men would survive the seismic shock of their collision, but Fosse would have shoulder problems for the last eight years of his career.

National League 5, American League 4

NL	AB	R	H	RBI	AL	AB	R	H	RBI
Mays, cf	3	0	0	0	Aparicio, ss	6	0	0	0
G Perry, p	0	0	0	0	Yastrzemski, 1b	6	1	4	1
McCovey, 1b	2	0	1	1	F Robinson, lf	3	0	0	0
Osteen, p	0	0	0	0	Horton, lf	2	1	2	0
Torre, ph	1	0	0	0	Powell, 1b	3	0	0	0
Allen, 1b	3	0	0	0	Otis, cf	3	0	0	0
Gibson, p	0	0	0	0	Killebrew, 3b	2	0	1	0
Clemente, rf	1	0	0	1	Harper, pr	0	0	0	0
Aaron, rf	2	0	0	0	B Robinson, 3b	3	1	2	2
Rose, lf	3	1	1	0	Howard, lf	2	0	0	0
Perez, 3b	3	0	0	0	Oliva, rf	2	0	1	0
Grabarkewitz, 3b	3	0	1	0	D Johnson, 2b	5	0	1	0
Carty, lf	1	0	0	0	Wright, p	0	0	0	0
Hickman, 1b	4	0	1	1	Freehan, c	1	0	0	0
Bench, c	3	0	0	0	Fosse, c	2	1	1	1
Dietz, c	2	1	1	1	Palmer, p	1	0	0	0
Kessinger, ss	2	0	2	0	McDowell, p	0	0	0	0
Harrelson, ss	3	2	2	0	A Johnson, ph	1	0	0	0
Beckert, 2b	2	0	0	0	J Perry, p	0	0	0	0
Gaston, cf	2	0	0	0	Fregosi, ph	1	0	0	0
Seaver, p	0	0	0	0	Hunter, p	0	0	0	0
Staub, ph	1	0	0	0	Peterson, p	0	0	0	0
Merritt, p	0	0	0	0	Stottlemyre, p	0	0	0	0
Menke, 2b	0	0	0	0	Alomar, 2b	1	0	0	0
Morgan, 2b	2	1	1	0	**Total**	44	4	12	4
Total	43	5	10	4					

American League	0	0	0	0	0	1	1	2	0	0	0	0—4
National League	0	0	0	0	0	0	1	0	3	0	0	1—5

Chapter 4
COMEBACKS

Comebacks may be the most exciting part of watching sports. Right before your eyes, someone down 5–1 in the fifth set of a Grand Slam tennis match fights their way back to victory; a golfer charges from four strokes down with six holes to play. Once the comeback starts, it can seem to take on a life of its own. One good play follows another; the other team makes a mistake; almost always something unbelievable happens and before you know it, the team that was down four touchdowns in the fourth quarter is lining up for the winning extra point. Some comebacks are so awesome that the fans of the team that is behind turn off their televisions or leave the ballpark. But the true fan stays until the bitter end, knowing that the Game Ain't Over 'Til the Fat Lady Sings.

U.S. Open Championships
Tom Jennings vs. Dick Lane

September 4, 1977

BILLIARDS' BIGGEST COMEBACK

Anyone who's ever played pocket billiards knows that it's a sport of streaks, but Tom Jennings took that to an extreme at the 12th Annual U.S. Open championships in Dayton, Ohio, in 1977. The dark-haired, moustachioed Jennings went into the Open as the reigning champion, a victory that had turned heads given his track record. Since the tournament was run as a double elimination (as soon as a player lost two matches he was out) and prior to his victory in 1976, Jennings had played in four U.S. Opens without winning a single match. With that 0–8 tournament record on his shoulders, Jennings had surprised everyone by holding on to take the title in 1976, and as only one man, the famous Steve Mizerak, had ever repeated, few gave Jennings a chance to win in 1977.

To start the tournament, the players were split into two brackets. Usually 32 players entered the tournament, but this year's tournament featured only 16, so the players were more closely matched, and play was more conservative than usual when it began. That Jennings was a long shot was made clear after the first match, when he lost to Tom (the Cat) Kollins, 150–135. To keep his title, Jennings would now have to win seven matches in a row, a feat tricky enough at this level of play, but hard to imagine under tournament pressure.

Dick Lane continues as an active professional billiards player.

Jennings forged ahead. His next match was his best of the tournament, as he crushed Tom Reid 150–38 in only three innings. Maybe the big win stoked his confidence, as Jennings now reeled off four straight wins to reach the finals of his bracket, where he would have to beat Joe Balsis two times to advance to the finals. Though Balsis had looked strong so far, Jennings did what he had to do and took Balsis 150–54 and 150–43 to earn a berth in the finals.

The man he was facing, Dick Lane, had shot well in his early matches, including a run of 111 balls against Mike Carella in his bracket final. The overall final was to be played to 200 balls and it was expected to be close, but this was a day for surprises. After 19½ innings, Lane led 196–42 and had a run of 64 balls going. Just four more balls and Lane would be the champion. To top it off, he was shooting a break shot. Lane seemed to have it wrapped up.

But he missed the break.

Lane was known to be a very methodical, analytical player who took his time between shots. Jennings had had to sit for long stretches and watch his opponent run table after table. Whether Jennings had been imagining himself somewhere else or planning his comeback, he dove into the opening with a new game, running off 71 balls and closing the gap to 196–113.

The two now traded 10 innings of mostly safeties, but Jennings was hot now and brought himself to within 16, at 197–171 after 30. After Lane lost one ball on a foul, a tough combination came up for Jennings. He still had 29 to make versus four for Lane. He took the chance, nailed the shot and ran through the final 28 he needed to win, finishing the most amazing comeback in straight pool history and holding on to his crown for one more year.

U.S. Open Championship

	W-L	High Run	Innings	Money Won
Tom Jennings	7–1	71	165	$5,000
Dick Lane	4–2	111	109	$2,100
Mike Carella	4–2	68	92	$800
Joe Balsis	3–2	71	82	$800
Bob Vanover	3–2	113	80	$500
Bill Stigall	2–2	73	92	$400
Scott Kitto	2–2	63	57	$300
Mark Beilfuss	2–2	57	102	$300
Nick Varner	1–2	76	34	$250
Tom Kollins	1–2	57	39	$250

Jenning's Three inning match against Tom Reid was the best of the tournament.

1986 ALCS—Game Five
Boston Red Sox vs. California Angels

October 12, 1986

ONE PITCH AWAY

Nineteen-eighty-six was supposed to be the California Angels' year. Stocked with high-priced talent by their owner, former cowboy singer Gene Autry, the Angels roared into the American League Championship Series behind manager Gene Mauch. Most famous for managing the Philadelphia Phillies 1964 team, a team that lost 10 straight to hand the

Dave Henderson was an important part of Boston's thrilling run in 1986.

pennant to the Cardinals, Mauch was often considered the greatest manager never to own a World Series ring.

But this was to be his year and Oct. 12, 1986 was sup-

posed to be the day he finally won the pennant. Everything was pointing to it. In the sixth inning of Game 5, with the Angels leading the series 3–1, California had a runner on first when Bobby Grich hit a towering fly ball to left center that chased centerfielder Dave Henderson back to the wall. As Henderson reached the warning track, he leaped into the air and appeared to have made a gem of a catch, but as he descended his wrist struck the top of the wall, the ball squirted out of his glove and over the fence for a home run. The Angels took a 3–2 lead.

When they added two more runs in the seventh, the Angels looked like they would be the American League champion. Back in the clubhouse the champagne was set out for the celebration.

Even when Boston's Bill Buckner opened the ninth with a single, there seemed no cause for alarm. Angels' pitcher Mike Witt, who'd won 18 games, had scattered seven hits through eight innings and still appeared strong enough to finish the game. But then the next Boston batter, Don Baylor, laid into a Witt curveball and drove it over the leftfield fence to narrow the Angels' lead to 5–4.

Witt got Dwight Evans for the second out and, to ensure victory, Angels manager Mauch brought in lefthander Gary Lucas to pitch to Rich Gedman. Lucas promptly hit the batter with his first pitch. Mauch made another change, bringing in Donnie Moore, whose journeyman career had finally stabilized that year, to face, of all people, Henderson. With two strikes, Henderson cracked a two-run home run over the leftfield fence to give Boston a 6–5 lead. Even though California rallied in the bottom of the ninth to tie the game 6-6 and send it into extra innings, the Red Sox

> ## "All of a sudden, everything there was just gone."
> —Dave DeCinces

Brian Downing watches Henderson's shot as it reaches the centerfield bleachers at Anaheim Stadium.

scored again in the 11th to win the game 7–6. The Angels still had a 3–2 lead in the series, but not for long. The Red Sox won the next two games back in Boston and the American League pennant.

Gene Mauch would never manage a team to the World Series and Donnie Moore, largely because he was never allowed to forget the home run he gave up to Henderson, committed suicide in 1989.

Boston Red Sox 7, California Angels 6

Boston	AB	R	H	RBI	California	AB	R	H	RBI
Boggs, 3b	5	0	1	0	Burleson, 2b	2	0	0	0
Barrett, 2b	5	0	0	0	Wilfong, 2b	3	0	2	2
Buckner, 1b	4	0	1	0	Schofield, ss	5	0	1	0
Stapleton, 1b	1	1	1	0	Downing, lf	3	0	0	1
Rice, lf	5	1	1	0	DeCinces, 3b	5	1	2	0
Baylor, dh	4	2	1	2	Grich, 1b	5	1	1	2
Evans, rf	5	0	1	0	Jackson, dh	5	0	1	0
Gedman, c	4	2	4	2	Hendrick, rf	3	0	1	0
Armas, cf	2	0	0	0	White, rf	2	1	1	0
Henderson, cf	2	1	1	3	Boone, c	3	1	3	1
Owen, ss	2	0	0	0	Jones, pr	0	1	0	0
Greenwell, ph	1	0	1	0	Narron, c	0	0	0	0
Romero, ss	2	0	0	0	Pettis, cf	3	1	1	0
Total	42	7	12	7	**Total**	39	6	13	6

Boston	0	2	0	0	0	0	0	0	4	0	1—7
California	0	0	1	0	0	2	2	0	1	0	0—6

BAD LUCK
BOSOX

Ever since they traded Babe Ruth to the Yankees in 1919, the Boston Red Sox hadn't won a World Series, but with a three games to two lead in the 1986 Fall Classic, things were looking very, very good. In fact, after their miraculous comeback in the ALCS against the Angels, as they won three straight to snatch away the pennant, it seemed that fate was ready to lift the Curse of the Bambino. But things aren't always what they seem.

The Sox took a 3–2 lead into the seventh inning of Game 6 at New York's Shea Stadium, but when Roger Clemens came out of the game with finger trouble, Calvin Schiraldi took the mound for the Sox and the Mets eked out the tying run. No one scored in the ninth, but Boston's Dave Henderson clubbed an 0-and-1 fastball over the leftfield fence off the Mets' Rick Aguilera in the top of the tenth and the Red Sox scored another when Wade Boggs doubled and came around on a single by Marty Barrett. Boston 5, New York 3.

Bob Stanley's wild pitch to Mookie Wilson allowed the tying run to score.

Given Boston's history of near-epic misfortune, Red Sox fans should have known better than to chill the champagne.

Schiraldi appeared up to the job for Boston when he got Wally Backman to fly out to left and Keith Hernandez to fly deep to center.

Maybe it was the sight of the Shea Stadium scoreboard flashing, WORLD CHAMPION BOSTON RED SOX, but something brought the Mets bats to life. Successive singles by Gary Carter, Kevin Mitchell and Ray Knight narrowed the Red Sox lead to 5–4 and all of Boston began to squirm.

Out came Schiraldi, to be replaced by Bob Stanley, who promptly uncorked a wild pitch past catcher Rich Gedman that allowed Mitchell to score the tying run.

The damage seemed to be staunched when Stanley got Mookie Wilson to hit a routine ground ball up the first base line to Red Sox first baseman Bill Buckner.

Buckner, with nearly 2,500 hits and a years of stalwart play at first for the Dodgers, the Cubs and the Red Sox, had his name coming up among Hall of Fame candidates. Now that his career was running down, he had been playing on two painfully damaged legs. Boston manager John McNamara chose to keep him in, though, despite his decreased mobility. Buckner set his glove down, but the ball rolled under it and on through his legs. Knight came around to score the winning run for New York.

One out away from being world champs for the first time since 1918, the Red Sox suddenly found themselves in a series deadlocked at three games apiece, but somehow it felt as if they'd lost already. Even with a 3–0 lead going into the sixth, the Red Sox couldn't hold on and the Mets took Game 7, 8–5. Game 6, and with it the whole series, had slipped through the Red Sox' fingers. The Curse of the Bambino still stands.

"There's nothing to say."
—Bill Buckner

New York Mets 6, Boston Red Sox 5

Boston	AB	R	H	RBI	New York	AB	R	H	RBI
Boggs, 3b	5	2	3	0	Dykstra, cf	4	0	0	0
Barrett, 2b	4	1	3	2	Backman, 2b	4	0	1	0
Buckner, 1b	5	0	0	0	Hernandez, 1b	4	0	1	0
Rice, lf	5	0	0	0	Carter, c	4	1	1	1
Evans, rf	4	0	1	2	Strawberry, rf	2	1	0	0
Gedman, c	5	0	1	0	Aguilera, p	0	0	0	0
Henderson, cf	5	1	2	1	Mitchell, ph	1	1	1	0
Owen, ss	4	1	3	0	Knight, 3b	4	2	2	2
Clemens, p	3	0	0	0	Wilson, lf	5	0	1	0
Greenwell, ph	1	0	0	0	Santana, ss	1	0	0	0
Schiraldi, p	1	0	0	0	Heep, ph	1	0	0	0
Stanley, p	0	0	0	0	Elster, ss	1	0	0	0
Total	42	5	13	5	Johnson, ss	1	0	0	0
					Ojeda, p	2	0	0	0
					McDowell, p	0	0	0	0
					Orosco, p	0	0	0	0
					Mazzilli, rf	2	1	1	0
					Total	36	6	8	3

Boston	1	1	0	0	0	0	1	0	0	2—5		
Mets	0	0	0	0	2	0	0	1	0	3—6		

I'VE GOT A HORSE RIGHT HERE

He has just a long shot chance," said owner Jack Amiel of his entry into the 77th Kentucky Derby, a three-year-old colt named Count Turf. A $14.60-dollar-odds long shot to be precise. On the day of the Kentucky Derby, Count Turf's record for 1951 was anything but sterling, scoring in only one of his 10 appearances. His jockey, Con McCreary, despite having ridden Calumet Farm's Pensive to victory in the '44 Derby, was still looking to cement his comeback, with only four wins since quitting the circuit for most of the previous year. Battle Morn, the hands-down favorite at 12–5, was to be ridden by

Count Turf was the 63rd Kentucky-bred horse to win the Derby.

veteran jockey Eddie Arcaro, a four-time Derby winner. Seven-for-nine on the year at Churchill Downs after having won the day's third race atop Kentucky Colonel, Arcaro and Battle Morn seemed a mortal lock in the seventh.

Under the excited gaze of 100,000 spectators, the gates opened for the Kentucky Derby, $1.3 million of their money riding on the outcome of the 1¼ mile contest, a single-race world record. First out of the stalls were Phil D, a $31.20-for-$2 "fielder," and Greentree Stable's Hall Of Fame and Nora Mikell's Repetoire, winner of four of his four stakes in the year. Running in the middle of the pack was Count Turf with Battle Morn in 18th and second choice Mameluke bringing up the rear.

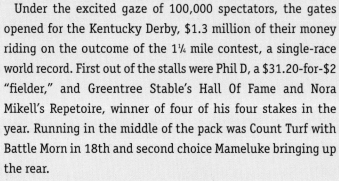

Going into the backstretch Phil D, Hall Of Fame and Repetoire held their place at the front. Overtaking five riders, Count Turf had moved into sixth, just over a length behind Counterpoint and long shot Royal Mustang. Hanging back in 15th place, Arcaro and Battle Morn were still nowhere to be seen.

Entering the far turn, Repetoire's jockey Peter McLean, let the eager colt run to the head of the pack. McCreary, continuing to work Count Turf forward, found his way to the No. 4 spot and the crowd's enthusiasm surged. As the riders came around the bend and into the stretch, the spent Repetoire faded quickly. Biding his time carefully, McCreary now gave Count Turf his legs and made for the lead. Seven lengths behind him, Arcaro, having fought his way to the 10th spot, made his move. But, he only made it as far as sixth, when Battle Morn backed off, after nearly tripping on the heels of Emil Denemark's Ruhe. Count Turf, however, quickly passed Repetoire, Hall Of Fame and then Phil D to take the lead in the final stretch.

> "I think every race is written in a book, and this was in the book, because everything happened right."
> —Con McCreary

The $98,050 jackpot for Count Turf was the Derby's biggest cup to that point.

At the finish, Count Turf came in the winner by four lengths. Long shot Royal Mustang, placed at a hefty 53–1 payoff, brought even more cheers from the boisterous crowd. Eighth choice Ruhe, a head behind Royal Mustang, took third. Accompanied by their elated, if surprised, owners, the three horses entered the winner's circle.

It wasn't until after the wreath of roses was presented to McCreary that trainer Sol Rutchick discovered Count Turf had won the Kentucky Derby with his rear right shoe loose.

Kentucky Derby

Starters	Jockeys	P.P.	Time	Value
Count Turf	McCreary	9	2:05.4	$98,050
Royal Mustang	P.J. Bailey	16		
Ruhe	J.D. Jessop	10		
Phil D	York	18		
Fanfare	Brooks	5		
Battle Morn	Arcaro	11		
Anyoldtime	R.L. Baird	1		
Pur Sang	J. Adams	20		
Hall Of Fame	Atkinson	17		
Timely Reward	Stout	3		
Counterpoint	Gorman	2		
Repetoire	McLean	19		
King Clover	Bone	12		
Sonic	Boland	6		
Sir Bee Bum	Madden	13		
Snuzzle	Porch	14		
Fighting Back	W.L. Johnson	8		
Big Stretch	Dodson	15		
Golden Birch	Dwain	4		
Mameluke	Adair	7		

THE DRIVE

With 5:43 left to play in regulation, the Cleveland Browns had forged ahead of the Denver Broncos 20–13 on a 48-yard pass play from Bernie Kosar to Brian Brennan.

In Cleveland Stadium, 79,915 Browns' fans whooped it up, envisioning this as the climactic moment in a victory that would finally send their team to the Super Bowl as the American Football Conference champion.

Before the Broncos dramatic Super Bowl victory in 1998, "The Drive" was probably Denver's most cherished sports memory.

Who could blame them for their optimism? On Jan. 11, 1987 the Browns' hard-nosed defense, affectionately known as the Dawgs and led by cornerback Hanford Dixon, had only to shut down the Broncos one more time, twice at

most, and the glory that had been—those ghosts of Groza, Graham and Brown—would be revisited. As a city, Cleveland had weathered much in the previous 20 years, and Sundays spent rooting for the Browns were one of the few things folks there could brag about. All those crazy barking, dog-mask-wearing, fans who packed the Dawg Pound section in the end zone would be rewarded.

Oh yes, those Cleveland fans could taste victory, even more so when the Broncos fumbled the ensuing kickoff, forcing poor John Elway, the Denver quarterback, to start his offensive series mired at his two-yard line with a brisk wind from off of Lake Erie blowing in his face.

But for Elway, a quarterback with a reputation for late-game heroics, this would be business as usual. The son of a college football coach, Elway had been raised on the game's X's and O's and had never met a dire situation from which he did not believe a victory could be extracted.

So never mind those lunatic Cleveland fans at the back of the end zone throwing dog biscuits onto the field—a ritual blessing for the Dawgs of Cleveland defense. Never mind the wind or the score. Elway was about to go to work.

Quicker than you could say Paul Brown, the 6′3″, 210-pound Elway had the Broncos on the move. Elway ran, Elway passed, Elway kept making clutch third-down plays.

Now it was third-and-one, with 39 seconds left. Elway

Elway was no stranger to big finishes; he was the quarterback of the Stanford squad that lost to University of California in the five-lateral shocker in 1982.

dropped back and fired a bullet to Mark Jackson angling across from the left side into the end zone. Touchdown, extra point! The game was tied 20–20 on a vintage Elway-engineered drive.

"It was the greatest drive I've ever been involved with," said Elway. "We just came out fighting and clawing and got the job done."

The overtime was a mere formality. The shaken Browns' defense, the pride of those biscuit-throwing loonies in the Dawg Pound, was no longer an obstacle.

In overtime Elway took his team 60 yards to the Cleveland 15, then told Broncos placekicker, Rich Karlis, "It's like practice."

Karlis kicked a 33-yard field goal to win the game 23–20.

Denver Broncos 23
Cleveland Browns 20

Denver	0	10	3	7	3—23
Cleveland	7	3	0	10	0—20

Clev.	Fontenot 6 pass from Kosar (Moseley, kick)
Denver	FG Karlis 19
Denver	Willhite 1 run (Karlis, kick)
Clev.	FG Moseley 29
Denver	FG Karlis 26
Clev.	FG Moseley 24
Denver	Brennan 48 pass from Kosar (Moseley, kick)
Denver	Jackson 5 pass from Elway (Karlis, kick)
Denver	FG Karlis 33

Statistics of the Game

	Broncos	Browns
First downs	22	17
Rushing	6-149	4-100
Passing	225	256
Total Return Yardage	83	142
Passes	22-38-1	18-32-2
Sacks by	2-19	1-3
Punts-average	7-38	6-43
Penalties-Yards	6-39	9-76
Fumbles-Lost	2-0	3-1
Time of Possession	34:05	31:43

CASPER'S COMEBACK

On this final day of the U.S. Open—June 19, 1966—Arnie and his Army were charging through the Olympic Country Club in San Francisco. With a seven-stroke lead on Billy Casper, Arnold Palmer had stormed through the first nine holes in 32 strokes, and it seemed a foregone conclusion that he would win the Open and maybe even break the scoring record of 276 strokes set in 1948 by Ben Hogan. All the redoubtable Palmer had to do was shoot even par for the remaining nine holes and he would clock out at 274.

Trailing him, but paired with him, was Casper, known for his sure putting, but also for battles with his weight and depression. Two years earlier he had weighed 225 and found himself constantly sleepy and uneasy. Looking for reasons, he submitted to a battery of tests and learned that he was allergic to a long list of foods and chemicals. Now placed on an exotic hypoallergenic diet that included buffalo and bear meat, Casper found himself, for this U.S. Open leaner, and better prepared for what was to happen.

At the 10th hole, Palmer's victory drive hit a bump with a bogey. Six strokes up, but still nothing to worry about. A bogey at 13; it happens. Still five strokes up. The trouble kicked in at 15, where Palmer went for broke, drove for the hole and ended up in a bunker to take a 4, while Casper sank a long putt for a 2. The lead was four, and now counting. Staying true to his power game, Palmer again drove hard on the 16th, lost control and ended up with a 6. Playing his more conservative game, Casper birdied the hole and was now only down one shot. Palmer bogeyed 17 and Casper made par. The match was tied and when both made par on the 18th, the playoff between Casper and Palmer was scheduled for the next day. Arnold Palmer had completely self-destructed.

At the start of the playoff, Palmer was again red-hot through the first nine holes—his score of 33 was two under par and two better than Casper. But the back nine virus that undermined his game the day previous struck again. On the par-4 430-yard 11th hole, Palmer hit his second shot from the rough to the left of the green and then blew a four-foot putt. While Casper was birdieing the 11th in three strokes, Palmer took a 5. His two stroke lead was gone. The match was dead even again.

On the 191-yard par-3 13th, Palmer made par but Casper did better. Casper shot into the lead when he sank a 40-foot putt for a birdie. When the ball toppled into the cup, he raised his hands triumphantly above his head.

From that point on, Palmer never could regain his touch and Casper held together like glue. He finished with a one-under-par 69 while Palmer was three over at 73.

"I've been hoping and praying for this for a long time," said Casper, a devout Mormon who tithed 10% of all his golf earnings. "At no time did I give up here, even after I was seven strokes down yesterday. When Palmer slipped, I slipped inside the door he left ajar."

U.S. Open

Out			
Par	543	444	434-35
Casper	543	454	325-35
Palmer	543	344	334-33

In			
Par	444	343	544-35-70
Casper	434	243	653-34-69
Palmer	454	354	744-40-73

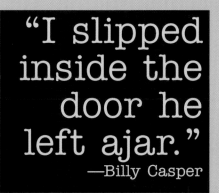

At the 13th, Casper took the lead for good with a birdie.

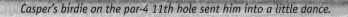

Casper's birdie on the par-4 11th hole sent him into a little dance.

HARVARD BEATS YALE
29-29

In the Ivy League, Harvard versus Yale is a long and storied rivalry, the equivalent of Army versus Navy, Michigan versus Ohio State, USC versus UCLA. In New Haven and in Cambridge it is simply referred to as the Game. On Nov. 23, 1968, old and venerable Harvard Stadium was packed, the importance of the Game compounded by the fact that both teams entered it undefeated—each with identical records of 8–0.

Yale was led by quarterback Brian Dowling and a future Dallas Cowboys star, fullback Calvin Hill (father of basketball star Grant Hill), while Harvard was paced by the backfield of Ray Hornblower and Vic Gatto, both of whom would play hurt during this big game.

The game that was expected to be a hotly-contested battle quickly turned into an apparent Yale rout. The Eli jumped out to a 22–0 lead midway through the second quarter.

Harvard fought back behind reserve quarterback Frank Champi, but with 4:16 left in the game, Yale still had what appeared to be an insurmountable lead, 29–13, and its fans were chanting, "We're Number 1!"

Yet Harvard hadn't conceded the game to its rival. As offensive guard and future Oscar-winning actor, Tommy Lee Jones, would recall: "Going into the game, we heard a lot about Yale's defense. But I thought they'd be stronger. I wasn't impressed. We started beating them up late in the third quarter. They were getting tired, weak and dumb. And we weren't. So even when Yale went up 29–13, I felt we could catch up. I had the greatest faith in that [Harvard] team. I felt we could do anything."

Harvard would need a break or two if it ever was to catch Yale, and it got just that when Yale fumbled at the Harvard 14.

Yale's Kent Schmoke yanks down Harvard's Vic Gatto during the first quarter.

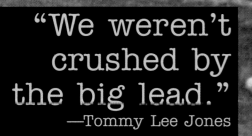

Pete Varney, (80) makes the catch in the end zone for the two-point conversion that tied the game 29–29.

Champi, a 5'11" junior from Everett, Mass., engineered a nine-play 86-yard drive that culminated in his 15-yard touchdown pass to Bruce Freeman. Harvard added the two-point conversion on Gus Crim's run. Yale 29, Harvard 21.

As expected, Harvard's Ken Thomas tried an onside kick, but to everyone's amazement, it worked. When Yale's Mike Bouscaren let the ball slip through his hands, Harvard's Bill Kelly jumped on it at the Yale 49.

Forty-two seconds to go. Enough time, it turned out, for Champi to scramble for 14 yards and Crim to ramble for 14 more. A face-mask penalty left Harvard with the ball at the Yale 6.

On the next play, Champi rolled right and fired a strike to Gatto in the left corner of the end zone. Then Champi calmly hit Pete Varney for the two extra points which climaxed a comeback so inspiring that the student paper, the Harvard Crimson, would headline: HARVARD BEATS YALE 29–29.

Yale 29, Harvard 29

Yale	7	15	0	7—29
Harvard	0	6	7	16—29

Yale	Dowling 3 run (Bayless, kick).
Yale	Hill 3 pass from Dowling (Bayless, kick).
Yale	Marting 5 pass from Dowling (Marting, pass from Dowling).
Harv.	Freeman 15 pass from Champi (kick failed).
Harv.	Crim 1 run (Szaro, kick).
Yale	Dowling 5 run (Bayless, kick).
Harv.	Freeman 15 pass from Champi (Crim, run).
Harv.	Gatto 8 pass from Champi (Varney, pass from Champi).
Attendance	40,280.

Statistics of the Game

	Yale	Harvard
First downs	19	17
Rushing yardage	251	118
Passing yardage	116	104
Return yardage	60	30
Passes	13-23	8-22
Interceptions By	0	1
Punts	3-36	8-36
Fumbles lost	6	1
Yards penalized	66	30

Dave Wottle

GOLD FOR THE GUY WITH THE CAP

A white golf cap was his trademark.

Dave Wottle, an unassuming collegian from Bowling Green University, became a familiar figure to stadium spectators at the 1972 Munich Olympics and to millions watching on television as he ran his heats in the 800-meter race while wearing the cap, qualifying ultimately for the finals.

For Wottle, reaching the finals was an accomplishment, given what he had to overcome to get that far. A month before

Wottle's cap became his trademark; he even forgot to take it off his head during the playing of The Star Spangled Banner.

the Sept. 2 gold medal race, Wottle suffered from tendinitis in his knees that was bad enough to limit his workouts and then forced him into a crash training program in the days leading up to the Olympic competition.

This was not exactly the prescribed routine for a world-class runner attempting to peak for the Olympics.

Worse—at least from the point of view of his coaches—was that Wottle, only recently married, had brought his bride to Munich. Aside from having physical problems, that made him, in the coaches' opinion susceptible to a loss of focus which an Olympic competitor should have.

"Coach [Bill] Bowerman asked me not to bring my bride to Munich," said Wottle. "He thought it might hurt my performance.

"She came along and is living away from the [Olympic] Village, but I see her every day. I think it's all up to the individual. Personally I was so anxious to get a medal that we decided to abstain from sex until my event was over."

Well, the event—the gold medal race—was one to which Wottle brought no great expectations. Indeed, as he fought his way into contention from the back of the pack, where he usually liked to run, and chased Kenyans Mike Boit and Robert Ouko and the favorite, the Soviet Union's Yevgeny Arzhanov, he hoped to sneak in for a third-place finish and a bronze medal.

Thirty meters from the finish he passed Ouko.

"Then I began running for the silver," Wottle said.

He moved into second place, past Boit, and figured that that was as good as it would get.

But then he realized that Arzhanov was slowing, and he turned on the jets.

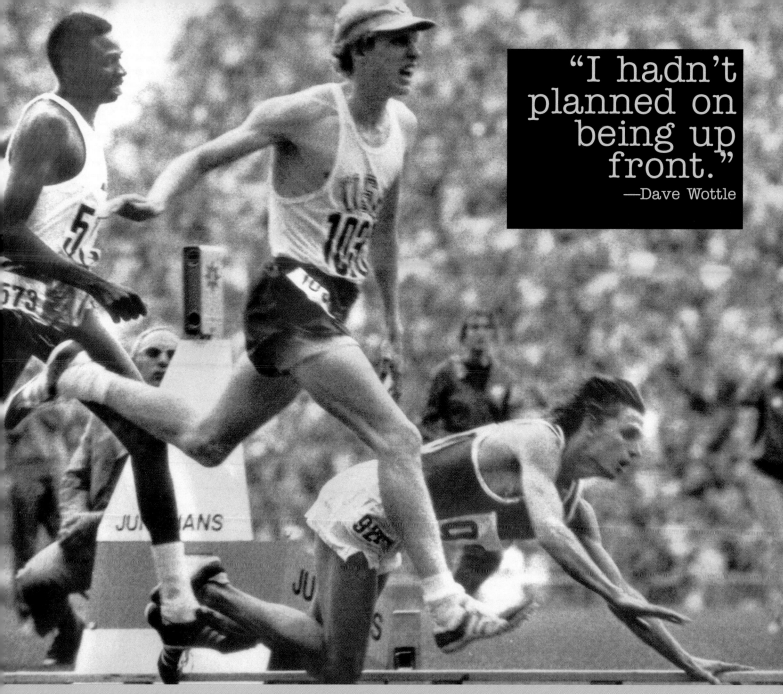

"I hadn't planned on being up front."
—Dave Wottle

Arzhanov's push to the line made him lose his balance, giving the race to Wottle.

With five meters to go, he found himself alongside the red-shirted Soviet runner.

At that point Arzhanov lost his balance as he lunged for the finish line and fell onto the synthetic red track. While both Arzhanov and Wottle would be timed in 1:45.9 seconds, it was Wottle who would hit the finish tape first, in the closest-ever 800-meter finish.

The man in the golf cap had defied injuries—and his honeymoon—to go gold.

Men's 5,000 Meters

1	David Wottle	USA	1:45.9
2	Yevgeny Arzhanov	SOV	1:45.9
3	Michael Boit	KEN	1:46.0
4	Franz-Josef Kemper	GER	1:46.5
5	Robert Ouko	KEN	1:46.5
6	Andrew Carter	GBR	1:46.6
7	Andrzej Kupczyk	POL	1:47.1
8	Dieter Fromm	GDR	1:48.0

MONTANA
IGNITES
THE IRISH

Senior quarterback Joe Montana had had a touch of flu in the week leading up to the 43rd annual Cotton Bowl—a game that pitted Montana's Notre Dame team against Houston.

If that wasn't handicap enough for the Irish's quarterback, there was a bit of weather to worry about too. Jan. 1, 1979, you see, turned out to be the coldest in Cotton Bowl history—a wind chill factor of –6°, with winds swirling from 15 to 30 mph. Cold enough for 39,500 ticket-holders to be no-shows.

After Kris Haines scored the tying touchdown, Joe Unis had to kick the winning extra point twice because of a Notre Dame penalty.

Not a great day to be a healthy quarterback, never mind one who'd belonged in sick bay earlier in the week. And given how Montana performed early in the game, it appeared he really did belong next to a bowl of chicken soup rather than in a huddle of 11 muscled-up football players.

At halftime the Cougars led 20–12 and Notre Dame coach Dan Devine, who had left the Green Bay Packers to coach in South Bend, would sit Montana down as the third quarter began and hope a sophomore backup, Tim Koegel, could get the Fighting Irish on track. No such luck. Houston broadened its margin to 34–12 by the end of the third quarter.

By then Devine had reinserted Montana, a last ditch hope that it might bring a pulse to the Irish attack. With only 7:32 remaining, the ghosts of George Gipp, Knute Rockne and the Four Horsemen—that Notre Dame mystique—hovered over the mostly deserted and damnably frigid Cotton Bowl and somehow set off the '79 squad. How else to explain what happened? With 7:32 to go, Notre Dame's Tony Belden blocked a punt that freshman Steve Cichy snatched out of the air and rambled 33 yards for a touchdown that cut Houston's lead to 34–20. Suddenly some of those 39,500 no-shows were wishing they were in their cold seats at the Cotton Bowl. They might have sensed that the legend of Joe Montana, arguably the game's greatest quarterback, was about to be born.

Montana, who had completed only six of 15 passes for 71 yards in the first half, drove the Irish on their next drive 61 yards in five plays, running for the final two yards for the touchdown. He then passed to Kris Haines for the two extra points. Houston 34, Notre Dame 28. The Notre Dame fight song echoed again through the stadium and the drums beat faster.

Notre Dame got the ball back when Houston was forced to kick, but when Montana fumbled with 1:50 left, that appeared to doom the Irish's chances.

Once again, though, Houston could not move the football.

"Let's do it."
—Joe Montana

Faced with a fourth-and-one at its own 29, and with a kicking game that had generated only 25 yards in ten punts, Cougars' coach Bill Yeoman chose to go for the first down. When Houston failed to make it, the Irish took over with less than half a minute and no timeouts remaining.

Montana scrambled for 11 yards, then passed for 10 more to Haines, who made the catch at the eight with only six seconds showing on the clock.

Two plays later, Montana fired low and outside to Haines in the right-front corner of the end zone: touchdown! Joe Unis kicked the extra point. And that was it—a 22-point fourth-quarter Houston lead up in smoke as the Fighting Irish behind Montana won 35–34 on the final play of the game.

The amazing leadership and talent of Joe Montana had fully blossomed on this cold, Texas day; his football heroics had only just begun.

Notre Dame 35, Houston 34

Notre Dame	12	0	0	23—35
Houston	7	13	14	0—34

N.D.	Montana 3 run (kick failed)
N.D.	Buchanan 1 run (pass failed)
Hou.	Adams 15 pass from Davis (Hatfield, kick)
Hou.	Love 1 run (Hatfield, kick)
Hou.	FG Hatfield 21
Hou.	FG Hatfield 34
Hou.	Davis 2 run (Hatfield, kick)
Hou.	Davis 5 run (Hatfield, kick)
N.D.	Cichy 33 return of blocked punt by Belden (Ferguson pass from Montana)
N.D.	Montana 2 run (Haines, pass from Montana)
N.D.	Haines 8 pass from Montana (Unis, kick)

Statistics of the Game

	Notre Dame	Houston
First downs	13	16
Rushing yardage	131	229
Passing yardage	163	60
Interceptions by	0	4
Passes	13-37	4-13
Punts	7-26	10-25
Fumbles lost	3	3
Yards penalized	74	39

THE BILLS
BUFFALO
THE OILERS

A team whose starting quarterback and star linebacker are not suited up because of injuries and whose best running back limps off the field with a hip injury is down 35–3 in the third quarter of a playoff game. Time to change channels? Maybe not. This same script had the Buffalo Bills going quietly into the night in 1993, but the Bills, led by thinking man's head coach, Marv Levy, and a backup quarterback with a hot hand, had other ideas.

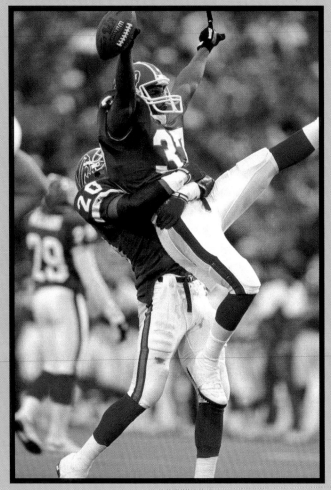

Bills safety Henry Jones lifts cornerback Nate Odomes, whose interception in overtime sealed the win for Buffalo.

Trailing the Houston Oilers by that 35–3 count in the American Football Conference wild-card game on the chilly, but clear afternoon of Jan. 3, 1993, the Bills did not give up. Without quarterback Jim Kelly and linebacker Cornelius Bennett, and with running back Thurman Thomas knocked out of the game, the Bills looked to backup quarterback Frank Reich to bring them back before an astonished crowd of Buffalo faithful at cold, windy Rich Stadium.

Reich had experience in improbable comebacks. In 1984, in college football's greatest comeback, he'd brought the University of Maryland back from a 31–0 deficit against Miami to a 42–40 victory. But when Houston safety Bubba McDowell intercepted a Reich pass early in the third quarter and ran it back 58 yards for the touchdown that made it 35–3, even hard-core Buffalo fans began to leave. As for Reich, he never gave up. At a time when the team's chances were, as Bills coach Marv Levy would put it, "about the same chance a guy has of winning the New York Lottery," Reich began to move his club. A 10-play 50-yard Buffalo drive climaxed with Thomas's replacement, Kenneth Davis, scoring from a yard out. That made it Oilers 35–10 with 8:52 left in the third quarter.

After recovering a squib kickoff, Buffalo scored again when Reich hit Bills wideout Don Beebe with a 38-yard aerial strike that made the score 35–17.

Reich then found Andre Reed with a 26-yard pass to make the score 35–24.

The Oilers, led by quarterback Warren Moon, suddenly couldn't do anything right. Two plays into Houston's next series, Bills safety Henry Jones intercepted a Moon pass. And four plays later, Reich threw another scoring pass to Reed, this time for 18 yards to narrow the gap to 35–31 with two minutes remaining in the third quarter.

The pace slowed down now that it was a game again. But then Buffalo scored again, in the fourth quarter, to go ahead

"It was a big choke by us. Collapse is too nice a word."

—Oilers cornerback Cris Dishman

38–35 on a Reich-to-Reed pass for a 17-yard touch-down with 3:08 remaining.

Just enough time, it turned out, for the Oilers to move down the field, and for Al Del Greco to boot a 26-yard field goal for Houston to send this game into overtime.

Houston won the coin toss and elected to receive. Its strategy backfired when Bills corner-back Nate Odomes intercepted another Moon pass, giving Buffalo the ball at the Houston 20. Two carries by Davis gained six yards and brought on Steve Christie at 3:06 of the overtime to kick a 32-yard field goal that completed the most amazing come-back in NFL history.

Said Reich, "Our defense was great, and my line was magnificent."

For that matter so was the Comeback Kid, Frank Reich, author of the biggest comebacks in both college and pro football.

Buffalo Bills 41, Houston Oilers 38

Houston	7	21	7	3	0—38
Buffalo	3	0	28	7	3—41

Hou.	Jeffires 3 pass from Moon (Del Greco, kick)
Buf.	FG Christie 36
Hou.	Slaughter 7 pass from Moon (Del Greco, kick)
Hou.	Jeffires 27 pass from Moon (Del Greco, kick)
Hou.	McDowell 58 Interception return (Del Greco, kick)
Buf.	Davis 1 run (Christie, kick)
Buf.	Beebe 38 pass from Reich (Christie, kick)
Buf.	Reed 26 pass from Reich (Christie, kick)
Buf.	Reed 18 pass from Reich (Christie, kick)
Buf.	Reed 17 pass from Reich (Christie, kick)
Hou.	FG Del Greco 26
Buf.	FG Christie 32

Statistics of the Game

	Houston	Buffalo
First Downs	27	19
Rushes-yards	22-82	26-98
Passing	347	268
Return Yards	65	17
Comp-Att-int	36-50-2	21-34-1
Sacked Yards Lost	4-24	3-21
Punts	2-25	2-35
Fumbles Lost	2-0	0-0
Penalties Yards	4-30	4-30
Time of Possession	37:39	25:27

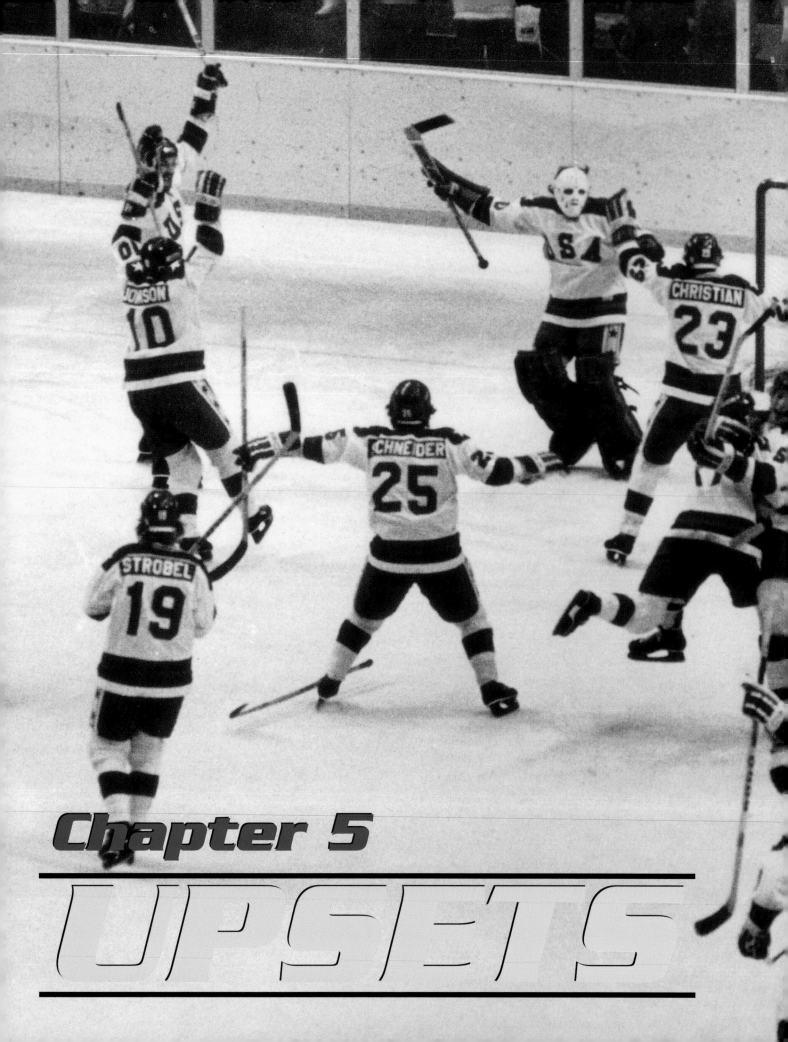

Chapter 5
UPSETS

M ost often in sports, the better team wins; still, the game needs to be played because, as we all know, miracles do happen. For every Celtics dynasty and Yankees juggernaut, there must be a Jack Fleck, who came from nowhere to beat Ben Hogan at the U.S. Open in 1955, or a U.S.A. hockey team that shocked the world and the U.S.S.R. hockey team in 1980 to win the gold medal. Upsets can take place for a great many reasons: the favorite may not play its best; the underdog can have the game of its life; fate can intervene in the form of extreme weather or a strange call by an official. Suddenly something amazing begins. A team or player that no one believed in starts to believe in themselves and then anything can happen. The Fat Lady loves upsets ...

Jennifer Capriati vs. Steffi Graf®

THE KID COMES UP BIG

Twice before Steffi Graf had won the gold medal in women's tennis at the Olympics—in 1984 when tennis was a demonstration sport and again in 1988. Now at the 1992 Barcelona Olympics she appeared to have a lock on another gold medal when Graf's opponent in the final turned out to be the 16-year-old American, Jennifer Capriati.

What other conclusion could you draw?

To begin with, Capriati had played Graf four times previously and not won any of those matches. What's more, in all of 1992, Capriati hadn't reached the finals of any tourna-

Though not pleased to lose the gold, Graf had already won gold twice in her career, when tennis was an Olympic demonstration sport.

ment. Once a rising young star in the sport, Capriati was already considered by some to be on the downside of her career. Then there was the hint of turmoil in the Capriati camp when several months earlier her coach, Pavel Slozil,

was fired, to be replaced by Jennifer's father, Stefano. Finally there was the pressure that young Capriati would be forced to deal with because of the white-hot attention that the Olympics drew. Who could expect a 16-year-old to cope?

But in the time leading up to the gold medal match, Capriati had been counseled by Manuel Santana, who'd won Wimbledon in 1966 and was an old family friend. Santana urged her to be patient, not to rush her shots.

For all his sage counseling, though, it looked as if form would hold when Graf, the second-ranked player in the world, went out and won the first set from Capriati 6–3. Business as usual, the experts figured.

But that was when Capriati, who'd joined the pro tour at the age of 14, set conventional wisdom on its ear. She won the next set 6–3, and kept the pressure on Graf in the third and final set. The key moment of the match came in the third set, 4–4 in games, when Graf double-faulted to leave her in a love–40 hole. She managed to get back to deuce, but Capriati's steady two-fisted backhands and a forehand on the line broke Graf's service.

As the crowd began to chant "U.S.A.!, U.S.A.!" Capriati went on to win 3–6, 6–3, 6–4.

"It was definitely one of my greatest matches in terms of fighting for everything, running down balls, and really grinding it out," said Capriati afterward.

When the national anthem was played as she stood on the awards stand, Capriati placed her hand over her heart and, with tears in her eyes, watched the American flag hoisted in her honor.

Women's Tennis Final

| Jennifer Capriati | USA | 3 | 6 | 6 |
| Steffi Graf | GER | 6 | 3 | 4 |

The gold medal at Barcelona was arguably the high point of Capriati's checkered career.

THE RELUCTANT WINNER

*T*he experts could have told you that the U.S.'s best prospects for a gold in the 100-meter dash at the 1952 Helsinki Olympics were not there at the starting line.

Gone was Arthur Bragg of Morgan State College, who'd pulled a muscle in the semifinals. Jim Golliday, the U.S. college champion considered the nation's best bet at the Olympic trials, never even got into the starting blocks because of an injury. And the speedy Andy Stanfield had decided to bypass the 100-meter race to concentrate instead on the 200 meters.

For the U.S., with those elite runners gone, it was left to a couple of unknowns—F. Dean Smith, who later became a stuntman in hundreds of films and TV shows, and Lindy Remigino, a 21-year-old Manhattan College student from Hartford—to go for gold.

Their chances, according to the experts, were slim and none.

Remigino? He had made it to the Olympic tryouts on the basis of his finishing fifth in the NCAA championship. Hardly a world-class credential.

The favorites in the 100 were 31-year-old Mac Bailey of Great Britain and 30-year-old Herb McKenley of Jamaica. McKenley, who held the world record in the 400 meters, had entered the 100 to practice his start for the 400.

But when the starter's gun sounded, it was Remigino who

flew out of the blocks, blazing down the straight-away. Bailey and McKenley came fast in pursuit and, 20 yards from the tape, had drawn to within a yard of the American upstart.

That was when the long-striding McKenley took it up another gear and closed on Remigino, both men hitting the finish line at virtually the same time. Remigino was convinced that McKenley had caught him and extended his hand in congratulation.

But wait ...

The judges examined a photo of the finish, saw that Remigino's right shoulder had reached the tape an inch ahead of McKenley's chest and declared the American the long shot winner.

Remigino could hardly believe it. In fact, he did not believe it. He told the judges he thought they had made a mistake, but they stuck to their decision.

At that point, Remigino turned to McKenley and is supposed to have said: "Gosh, Herb, it looks as though I won the darn thing."

That "darn thing" was maybe the greatest upset in Olympic history.

Men's 100-meter

1. Lindy Remigino	USA	10.4
2. Herbert McKenley	JAM	10.4
3. Emmanuel McDonald Bailey	GBR	10.4
4. F. Dean Smith	USA	10.4
5. Vladimir Sukharyev	SOV	10.5
6. John Treloar	AUS	10.5

right: From top, Sukharyev, McKenley, Remigino, Smith, Bailey and Trelor.

left: Remigino (981) just edges McKenley (295) of Jamaica and Bailey (second from left) of the U.K.

"Gosh, Herb, it looks as though I won the darn thing."
—Lindy Remigino

MIRACLE
ON ICE

They were young unknowns, hockey no-names. But that would change as coach Herb Brooks fine-tuned his patchwork U.S. hockey team for the 1980 Winter Olympics in Lake Placid, N.Y.

Nine of Brooks's charges were from the University of Minnesota, whose hockey team Brooks coached with the no-nonsense fervor of a Vince Lombardi. "The Anatollah of Ice Hockey" he was called.

Call him what you want. When Brooks gathered his 20 players—average age 22—he did not mince words. "Gentlemen," he said, "you don't have enough talent to win on talent alone."

The greatest talent in international hockey belonged to the Soviet Union. From 1956, the Russians had had a virtual monopoly on Olympic gold, and few expected them not to repeat in 1980. The only break in the Soviets' domination had been in 1960, at the Squaw Valley Olympics, when another American squad full of unknowns surprised the world to win the ice hockey gold.

Like the 1960 team, Brooks's boys made up for whatever talent they lacked with hustle and teamwork—a parlay that brought them surprising success.

In its opening game, Team U.S.A. salvaged a 2–2 tie with Sweden when Bill Baker whipped in a shot from 55 feet with 27 seconds remaining. Then came a string of victories—7–3 over Czechoslovakia, 5–1 against Norway, 7–2 over Romania and 4–2 against West Germany.

With each victory, excitement about the team intensified. Suddenly the hockey squad developed a following, and players like Ken Morrow, David Silk, Mark Johnson, and Mike Eruzione, along with goalie Jim Craig, became widely known.

All of that was well and good. But did these Americans really think they could butt heads with the Soviets? Not likely, according to the experts.

Nonetheless their chance came on Feb. 22, 1980, when the ragtag Americans went up against the best hockey team in the universe, amateur or professional—the U.S.S.R.

The Soviets' reputation didn't seem to matter that night; the Americans were not intimidated. By the second period they had driven the Soviets' primo goalie, Vladislav Tretiak, from the net with the score tied 2–2.

And even when Aleksandr Maltsev scored on a power-play goal at 2:18 of the second period to give the Soviets a 3–2 lead, the Americans refused to crack. In the third and final period, the miracle on ice began.

First Johnson gathered in a misplayed puck from a Soviet defender and slammed it past replacement goalie Vladimir Myshkin at 8:39 of the third period to tie the game 3–3.

Then less than a minute and a half later, Eruzione

Mike Eruzione's third period goal against Vladimir Myshikin won the game, but coach Herb Brooks had actually considered cutting Eruzione prior to the Olympics.

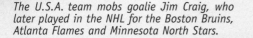

The U.S.A. team mobs goalie Jim Craig, who later played in the NHL for the Boston Bruins, Atlanta Flames and Minnesota North Stars.

scored on a 30-foot blast to give Team U.S.A. a 4–3 lead.

After that, it was nail-biting time as the Soviets swarmed the American zone time and again over the final 10 minutes, only to be turned back by goalie Craig.

"Do you believe in miracles?" TV broadcaster Al Michaels asked a delighted TV audience as the final seconds of the game ticked away.

But the gold wasn't locked. Two days later, Team U.S.A. had to come from behind in the third period to defeat the Finnish team 4–2 in the gold-medal game of the Olympic tournament, completing the improbable miracle they hadn't dared to imagine only weeks before.

Men's Hockey Semifinal

USA	2	0	2—4
USSR	2	1	0—3

First Period: 1) USSR, Krutov (Kasatonov), 9:12. 2) USA, Schneider (Pavelich), 14:03. 3) USSR, Makarov (A. Golikov), 17: 34. 4) USA, Johnson (Christian, Silk), 19:59. Penalty—Mikhailov, USSR, 3:25.

Second Period: 5) USSR, Maltsev (Krutov), 2:18. Penalties—Harrington, USA, :58; Craig, USA, 9:50; Lebedev, USSR, 17:08; Morrow, USA, 17:08.

Third Period: 6) USA, Johnson (Silk), 8:39. 7) USA, Eruzione (Pavelich, Harrington), 10:00. Penalty—Krutov, USSR, 16:47.

Goalies: USA, Craig. USSR, Tretiak, Myshkin

THE PERFECT GAME

Georgetown had the 7-footer Patrick Ewing ... and it had an in-your-face fullcourt press defense that made other teams quake in their shoes.

The Hoyas had held the opposition to a mere 39% from the floor, the lowest in the country. According to the wise men of college hoops, all of that meant there was no way coach John Thompson's Hoyas, 35–2, could lose the 1985 NCAA championship to Villanova. Too big, too strong, too damn good for Villanova, 24–10, that was the consensus about the Georgetown team, the defending NCAA champions who went into the title game on a 17-game win streak.

Villanova's Wildcats, on the other hand, hadn't even cracked the Top 20 in any poll in the nation and had finished third in the Big East, behind Georgetown and St. John's.

But Villanova coach Rollie Massimino told his players that if they played smart, and fearless—if they played perfect basketball—they had a chance to whup the Hoyas.

Smart-and-fearless meant not cracking under Georgetown's defensive pressure, and it meant working hard to get the good shot. No one could have guessed what a huge difference getting a good shot would make for the Wildcats.

In the first half, Villanova followed Massimino's game plan. Using Dwayne McClain and Harold Pressley to handle the ball against the press, 'Nova managed to cope with the Hoyas' defensive pressure. And once it got the ball past the midcourt line, the Wildcats patiently, methodically, worked their offense, hitting a remarkable 13 of 18 shots in the opening half.

The result? At halftime Villanova led 29–28.

Still, the Hoyas were a team that played with a relentlessness that usually broke the other club down. But Villanova not only withstood that Georgetown mystique, it played with poise and cunning. As the clock wound down on the second half, the crowd of 23,124 fans in Rupp Arena began to pull for the underdog, even as a David Wingate jump shot put Georgetown ahead 54–53 with 4:50 remaining.

But that's when Villanova took charge of the game. Wildcats reserve Harold Jensen hit a jump shot to put Villanova ahead. 'Nova's 6'9½" center Ed Pinckney stripped the ball under the Hoyas' basket, was fouled and converted both his free throws. And before you could say Hoya Destroya, Villanova had a 59–54 lead with 1:24 remaining on the clock.

The Hoyas tried, but couldn't catch Villanova, which won 66–64 by shooting a tournament record 79% from the field. The Wildcats made 22

of 28 shots in all, including an incredible nine of 10 in the second half. What's more, they made 22 of 27 free throws. Seeded No. 8 in the Southeast region, Villanova became the lowest seeded team ever to win the national championship, beating three teams seeded 1 or 2 to get there.

"Needless to say, this is probably the greatest moment in Villanova basketball history," said Massimino. One of the greatest in college basketball, too; the Georgetown team stayed for the awards ceremony and applauded one of the worthiest and most unlikely victors in NCAA tournament history.

Villanova 66, Georgetown 64

Villanova	fg	fga	ft	fta	r	a	pf	pts
Pressley	4	6	3	4	4	1	1	11
McClain	5	7	7	8	1	3	3	17
Pinckney	5	7	6	7	6	5	3	16
Wilbur	0	0	0	0	0	1	0	0
McLain	3	3	2	2	2	2	2	3
Jensen	5	5	4	5	1	2	2	14
Plansky	0	0	0	1	0	0	1	0
Everson	0	0	0	0	0	0	0	0
Team Rebounds					3			
Total	22	28	22	27	17	14	12	66

Georgetown	fg	fga	ft	fta	r	a	pf	pts
Martin	4	6	2	2	5	1	2	10
Williams	5	9	0	2	4	2	2	10
Ewing	7	13	0	0	5	2	4	14
Jackson	4	7	0	0	0	9	4	8
Wingate	8	14	0	0	2	2	4	16
McDonald	0	1	0	0	0	0	0	0
Broadnax	1	2	2	2	1	2	4	4
Dalton	0	1	2	2	0	0	1	2
Team Rebounds					0			
Total	29	53	6	8	17	18	22	64

Villanova	29	37—66	
Georgetown	28	36—64	

" ... the greatest moment in Villanova basketball history."
—Rollie Massimino

left: Rollie Massimino is carried off the court by jubilant fans and players.

right: Dwayne McClain jams over Georgetown center and later Knick Patrick Ewing.

THE AMATEUR

Francis Ouimet grew up across the street from The Country Club in Brookline, Mass., where he'd occasionally caddied as a boy. Still an avid golfer, 20-year-old Ouimet was working as a salesman at a sporting goods store when the U.S. Open was scheduled to be played at The Country Club in September 1913. Hoping for a big field, a USGA member saw him play golf and urged him to enter, which Ouimet did, albeit reluctantly; he'd just taken some time off from the store for another tournament and thought his boss would be angry.

In 1955 the USGA awarded Ouimet the first Bob Jones Award for distinguished sportsmanship in golf.

And so Ouimet, who hadn't even intended to play, found himself among a record field of 165 golfers who turned out for the U.S. Open that year. The two biggest names in the bunch were highly-regarded pros, Harry Vardon and Edward Ray, both of whom were from Great Britain. Vardon, Ray and another Englishman, Wilfred Reid, were the only golfers really given a chance to win, as golf was still regarded here (and in England) as England's game. Vardon had won the British Open five times and, along with Reid and Ray, had gone into the tournament as 2-to-1 favorites to win at Brookline.

But during the final round, there was a surprise. A tall, lean American dogged their heels, matching them stroke for stroke. Francis Ouimet, the complete unknown, was playing their game. On the 17th hole, he hit a 15-foot putt to tie, despite the constant honking of a car trying to pass through a road behind the green, now blocked by viewers wondering if this boy could beat the giants of the game. Over the last six holes, Ouimet shot two under par and forced a playoff against Vardon and Ray.

Even though he had gone up against the giants and equaled them, the experts continued to regard Ouimet as a fluke, in over his head against the Brits. Wagers were laid at 5-to-1 that one of the two Englishmen would defeat the American in the playoff. Those odds did not deter Ouimet. On Sept. 20, 1913, as the three men fought for the U.S. Open title on a day of heavy mist and dripping grass, Ouimet played brilliantly. As *The New York Times* would report: "All through the crucial journey around the 18-hole course, Ouimet never faltered. In fact his play might be termed mechanical, so perfect was it under the trying weather and course conditions."

Huge galleries followed the golfers through the course, as the bad weather and crowds pounded the greens into

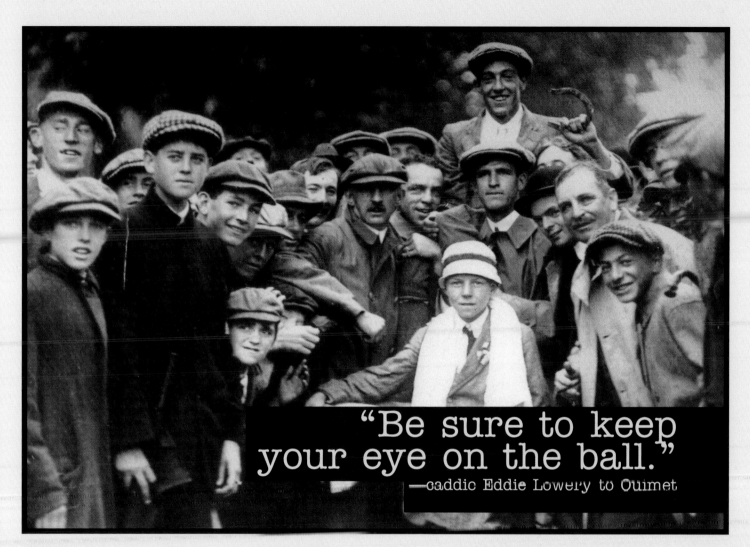

"Be sure to keep your eye on the ball."
—caddie Eddie Lowery to Ouimet

The gallery carries Ouimet off in triumph, led by 10-year-old caddie Eddie Lowery, who insisted on hauling Ouimet's clubs for an exhausting fourth day.

muck. With a little 10-year-old caddie named Eddie Lowery lugging his clubs, Ouimet finished his 18 holes with a two-under-par 72—five strokes better than Vardon, six strokes better than Ray.

The jubilant fans, proud of the cool manner with which their countryman had handled Vardon and Ray, hoisted him onto their shoulders, the women in the mob throwing flowers at him, the men reaching out to touch golf's miracle man—the first amateur to win the Open. Even more important, though, Ouimet made Americans believe they could beat the British at golf. The rest is, really, the history of American golf.

U.S. Open Playoffs

Cards of the Players
Ouimet

Out	5	4	4	4	5	4	4	3	5-38
In	3	4	4	4	5	4	3	3	4-34-72

Vardon

Out	5	4	4	4	5	3	4	4	5-38
In	4	4	5	3	5	4	3	5	6-39-77

Ray

Out	5	4	5	4	5	4	3	3	5-38
In	4	4	5	4	5	6	4	5	3-40-78

U.S. Open Totals
Francis Ouimet 77- 74- 74- 79= 304
Harry Vardon 75- 72- 78- 79= 304
Edward Ray 79- 70- 76- 79= 304

1983 NCAA Championship
North Carolina State vs. Houston

April 4, 1983

KEEP THE DREAM ALIVE

North Carolina State had not been expected to be a force in this 1983 NCAA tournament, with its deep field of 52 college basketball teams. They'd gone 26–10 in the regular season, including a stretch where they'd lost six out of eight games, and finished 8–6 in the ACC, tied for third.

Yet the Wolfpack kept pulling off improbable victories.

"They're probably tired of hearing me talk about dreamers," said Valvano afterwards.

Colorful and emotional, Queens-born coach Jim Valvano and his team beat Pepperdine in double-overtime after trailing by six points with 24 seconds to play in the first overtime. They beat UNLV by a point. They beat a Virginia team led by Ralph Sampson in the West Regional final, and had, with Valvano playing for the cameras, become media favorites with their mantra, "Keep the dream alive!"

And now here they were in the title game, going hammer-and-tong against a Houston team whose airborne antics had earned it the nickname of Phi Slamma Jamma. This was the Houston team of ozone-defying leapers like Clyde Drexler, Larry Micheaux and a 7-foot sophomore from Lagos, Nigeria, Akeem Olajuwon. This was the Houston team that ran the ball and then jammed it down the throats of the opposition. This was the Houston team that had won 18 straight games and came into the final with a record of 30–2.

But the Wolfpack's Valvano constructed a game plan calculated to demystify the powerful Cougars. Valvano's strategy was to slow the tempo and to defend Houston's high flyers from the rear as a means of limiting their dunks.

The strategy helped, and was aided and abetted, many insisted, by the miscalculation of Houston coach Guy Lewis, who spread the floor with more than 10:04 left and the Cougars up 42–35.

Lewis's decision to milk the clock backfired because, as writer Curry Kirkpatrick noted, "...when Phi Slamma can't jam, they take it on the lam. They don't shoot particularly well from outside and are worse from the foul line."

Whatever. The Cougars' lead began to shrink. Valvano's team had been outscored by 17–2 at the time that Lewis ordered the delay game. From then on, three Houston turnovers enabled N.C. State to cut the lead to 44–42 with 6:26 left to play.

When Wolfpack guard Dereck Whittenberg hit a jumper from 24 feet he tied the game at 52 with 1:59 to play.

At the other end of the court, Alvin Franklin, Houston's freshman guard, missed a foul shot in a one-and-one situation with 1:05 to play.

As the game came down to the wire, Whittenberg found himself with the ball 35 feet from the basket and with the clock showing three ticks left.

Whittenberg threw up a heave, just hoping to get the ball near the basket.

The ball fell short of the hoop, but Lorenzo Charles, a 6'7" Wolfpack sophomore, was the right man in the right place. The ball landed in his hands, as Olajuwon for some reason did not jump for the rebound. Charles went up and dunked it for the 54–52 victory and the NCAA title.

Valvano—beside himself with joy—ran through the mob that descended onto the floor, arms outspread, looking to hug one of his Wolfpack upstarts who had capped a Cinderella season with the most timely dunk ever, against the masters of the jam.

"That's the way we designed it on the blackboard," Whittenberg later said, smiling.

North Carolina State 54, Houston 52

North Carolina State	fg	fga	ft	fta	r	a	pf	pts
Bailey	7	16	1	2	5	0	1	15
Charles	2	7	0	0	7	0	2	4
McQueen	1	5	2	2	12	1	4	4
Whittenberg	6	17	2	2	5	1	3	14
Lowe	4	9	0	1	0	8	2	8
Battle	0	1	2	2	1	1	1	2
Gannon	3	4	1	2	1	2	3	7
Myers	0	0	0	0	1	0	0	0
Total	23	59	8	11	34	13	16	54

Houston	fg	fga	ft	fta	r	a	pf	pts
Drexler	1	5	2	2	2	0	4	4
Micheaux	2	6	0	0	6	0	1	4
Olajuwon	7	15	6	7	18	1	1	20
Franklin	2	6	0	1	0	3	0	4
Young	3	10	0	4	8	1	0	6
Anders	4	9	2	5	2	1	2	10
Gettys	2	2	0	0	2	2	3	4
Rose	0	1	0	0	1	0	2	0
Williams	0	1	0	0	4	1	3	0
Total	21	55	10	19	44	9	16	52

North Carolina	33	21—54
Houston	25	27—52

The Wolfpack shot only 39% but they hit them when it counted.

1,000 TO 1 SHOT

When Billy Mills was in the eighth grade at the Haskell Institute in Lawrence, Kans., he took up running to get in shape for boxing.

Two fights—and a pair of black eyes later—he decided to stick to running.

At the University of Kansas, Mills, who was part Sioux Indian, was a two-mile and cross country-champion.

But by October 1964, when 26-year-old Marine Lieutenant Billy Mills turned up in the gold medal 10,000-meter race at the Tokyo Olympics, he was viewed as nothing more than an also-ran.

This was not exactly a shock. Mills's experience at the distance—a little more than six miles—was limited to five races, of which he'd won only one ... and that was in an interservice event against nondescript competition.

What's more, his personal best of 29:10.0 was a far cry from the Olympic record of 28:32.2 seconds set in 1960 by Petr Bolotnikov of the Soviet Union and the world record of 28:32.6 set by Australian Ron Clarke. Even on the U.S. team, Mills was rated behind 18-year-old Gerry Lindgren.

The Associated Press described Mills's chances of winning the race as "a 1,000 to 1 shot."

Lastly, no American had ever won the race.

Yet somehow as that gold medal race wound down, and the field of 38 thinned out to four runners, Mills was up there with the leaders, fighting it out with Clarke, the Ethiopian Mamo Wolde who would win the marathon at the next Olympic Games in Mexico City, and a Tunisian, Mohamed Gammoudi, who, like Wolde, would win gold in 1968, in the 5,000 meters.

By the last of the 25 laps around the National Stadium's 400-meter track, Wolde had fallen back. Into the backstretch, Mills and Clarke ran step for step alongside one another, only to be bumped aside as Gammoudi nudged his way between them. Mills and Clarke were knocked off stride, but Mills later said, "Being knocked farther out on the track helped me; it was less chewed up out there."

At the head of the stretch Clarke had caught up with the Tunisian, and Mills trailed by 10 yards.

But down the stretch it was Mills's finishing kick that was golden. He beat Gammoudi and Clarke to the finish line in an Olympic-record time of 28:24.4.

Claiming that he had trained well, Mills always believed victory was possible.

Men's 10,000 Meters

1	Billy Mills	USA	28:24.4
2	Mohamed Gammoudi	TUN	28:24.8
3	Ronald Clarke	AUS	28:25.8
4	Mamo Wolde	ETH	28:31.8
5	Leonid Ivanov	SOV	28:53.2
6	Kokichi Tsuburaya	JPN	28:59.4
7	Murray Halberg	NZE	29:10.8
8	Anthony Cook	AUS	29:15.8

"I felt the spark and spring coming back to my legs."

—Billy Mills

JACK FLECK UPSETS HOGAN

Nobody knew Jack Fleck. Yet here was the 32-year-old unheralded professional from Davenport, Iowa, going head-to-head with the great Ben Hogan in the final round of the 1955 U.S. Open.

Hogan, who had won the Open four times and was bidding for a record-breaking fifth title, had finished with a par-equaling fourth-round of 70, giving him a total of 287 strokes. In the clubhouse, Hogan sat back and waited with friends to accept his trophy and check.

Still out on the course was Fleck, a golfer who had never won a major tournament and, ironically, was playing the Olympic Country Club course with the Hogan line of clubs. While Hogan spent most of year playing golf, Fleck ran two municipal golf courses in Davenport. He'd once been a caddie and he'd worked in a golf shop after high school. But World War II sent him onto the beaches of Normandy as part of D Day. He came home in one piece, and went to work as a pro. Fleck was hardly golf royalty, but his game on this day was: He had shot a one-under-par 34 on the front nine and, with four holes to go, was still one under.

With word of Fleck's progress, Hogan kept at bay the reporters who were trying to coax "winner's" quotes from him. What might have once seemed like a done deal was now very much in question. This young fella Fleck still had a shot.

And on the 18th hole, Fleck proved Hogan a prophet when he birdied the hole to finish with a 67 and a total of 287, the same as Hogan.

A playoff the next day—June 19, 1955—would determine the winnner.

The experts figured Fleck, good-looking in a solid, American way that would seem at home in a Frank Capra film, would be exposed as some sort of imposter in that spotlit playoff. But Fleck proved he was for real, at least for this one tournament.

Through the first nine holes, he shot a two-under-par 33, two strokes better than Hogan. The gallery swelled, as the spectators tried to see the upstart Fleck, and play had to be stopped at the 11th hole until the crowd quieted.

But Hogan—champion that he was—got to within one stroke after 17 holes. On the crucial 18th hole, Hogan, shooting for a do-or-die birdie 3, slipped on a sandy spot on the tee. The ball sailed into foot-high rough that sealed Hogan's fate.

Fleck beat Hogan 69–72. Afterward, the great Hogan announced his retirement from serious competition.

"Of course, I've dreamed of becoming a champion," said Fleck later. "But actually I hoped to finish only among the first 10 so I wouldn't have to qualify again next year."

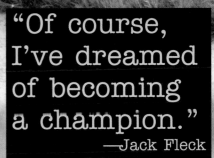

"Of course,
I've dreamed
of becoming
a champion."
—Jack Fleck

top: Fleck blasts out of a bunker on the
6th hole during his playoff with Hogan.

U.S. Open

Out									
Par	5	4	3	4	4	4	4	3	4-35
Hogan	5	4	3	4	5	4	4	2	4-35
Fleck	5	4	3	4	4	4	4	2	3-33
In									
Par	4	4	4	3	4	3	5	4	4-35-70
Hogan	4	4	5	3	3	3	5	4	6-37-72
Fleck	3	5	4	3	4	3	5	5	4-36-69

left: Mrs. Jack Fleck said of her husband, "He's the
best-looking champion the Open has ever had."

BUSTER'S SHINING MOMENT

In February 1990, it was widely accepted that Mike Tyson was, as Tyson himself liked to say, "the *baaaadest* man on the planet," a heavyweight champion who put the fear of God into opponents. The soft-spoken, lisping native of Brooklyn's rough Brownsville neighborhood was not just tough: He was dangerous in every sense of the word.

Tyson was undefeated and was not counting on having that record disturbed by his next challenger, the enigmatic James (Buster) Douglas.

Buster's reign was short. He surrendered the heavyweight belt eight months later when Evander Holyfield knocked him out.

Douglas was a fighter who on some nights flashed skills that made boxing observers take note. In June 1988, on the undercard the night of the Tyson—Michael Spinks fight, Douglas had wowed the experts by knocking down powerfully-built Michael Williams twice ... with jabs!

Yet Douglas had a history of lackluster performances in crucial matches and even in bouts against ordinary opponents. He'd lost to legitimate contenders like David Bey and routine foes like Mike (the Giant) White and Jesse Ferguson. And for every loss, there was always a story that went with it. With Buster, there was never a shortage of reasons why a fight had gone south.

The one time he had previously fought for a title, against Tony Tucker for the IBF heavyweight crown on May 30, 1987, Douglas had appeared to be on the way to victory when he faded badly and was stopped in the 10th round.

That bout, added to his checkered past, had left serious questions about Douglas's dedication to the fight game and his moxie in the ring. Many boxing observers felt Douglas had "quit" against Tucker and rumors were that the critics even included members of Douglas's own camp.

So it was no shock that even those few book makers willing to take a bet on the fight put Buster a 42-to-1 underdog when he stepped into the ring with Tyson, in Tokyo on Feb. 10, 1990.

But the Douglas who fought Tyson—whether inspired, as some claimed, by the death of his mother, or just covetous of this last chance at big-time glory—was not the muddled combatant who'd disappointed his followers so many times before.

This Douglas was a fighter with plenty going for him— that jab for starters. Douglas's jab confounded Tyson's aggressive mentality. Douglas's tactical sense was unerring as he jarred Tyson with combinations and then moved laterally out of range.

Tyson did, finally, connect, in the eighth round and floored Douglas—a knockdown that Tyson's promoter, Don King, would call a long count and try, unsuccessfully, to use in overturning the final result. But neither Tyson's knockdown, nor King's postfight theatrics about it, would forestall the obvious. On this night, Douglas was the better man.

"This was the dream."
—Buster Douglas

The challenger did not wilt under pressure. He gathered his senses and lasted out the eighth round. Then he resumed the work he'd been doing. With a sharp jab, deft movement and lots of attitude, Buster Douglas beat up Mike Tyson, knocking him down and leaving him groping for his dislodged mouthpiece as the so-called baaaadest man on the planet was counted out in the 10th round.

The 42-to-1 underdog had paid off.

Heavyweight Championship

The judges' cards when Buster Douglas knocked out Mike Tyson in the tenth round.

Larry Rozadilla	7-1-1	Douglas
Ken Morita	3-3-3	Draw
Masakazu Uchida	4-3-2	Douglas

OLD MAN
NICKLAUS

Nobody as old as Jack Nicklaus had ever won the Masters. Coming into the 1986 tournament, Nicklaus wasn't even an afterthought. He was the "Olden Bear" now; everyone loved him, but his terrible outings so far that season—160th on the money list, with three cuts missed—had people recommending that he retire from the Tour.

But there he was, 46 years old and shooting up a storm on that final Sunday in Augusta. Beefed up to 190, which made him drive better than he had at the svelte 170 he'd been for a while, Nicklaus again had the plumpness that helped make him so likable throughout his career, but his short game was thought to be gone, offered up to the requirements of his troubled business, Golden Bear, Inc.

That was the indictment on Nicklaus, but out there on the course on this April day, Nicklaus the elder was playing like the golden boy of old—the golfer who had dominated back in the 1960s and '70s.

Down the back nine, Nicklaus dueled with Greg Norman, Tom Kite and Sevie Ballesteros. Kite finished his round first, missing an eight-foot birdie putt on the final hole by one inch for a 68.

Meanwhile, Nicklaus was burning it up. At number 13, he nearly put the ball into the woods and almost gave his son Jackie, who was caddying for him, a heart attack. He birdied the hole, sneaking to two back of Ballesteros. An eagle by the Spaniard, though, put Nicklaus four back almost as quick. At the 500-yard 15th, Nicklaus hit a massive four-iron second shot that left him pin high 12 feet from the hole. He sank the putt for an eagle 3, then birdied the par-3 16th. Ballesteros fell back.

With each hole the crowd swelled, roaring its approval for the old man.

"Walking up the fairways on the last few holes, I had tears in my eyes four or five times. I just welled up," Nicklaus later said. "But then I told myself, 'Hey, you've got golf to play.'"

And Nicklaus did play. At number 17, he went one shot up on Kite and the Great White Shark—Australian Greg Norman—and two up on Ballesteros. Norman came back to tie Nicklaus on the 17th. Nicklaus went into the clubhouse with a 30 on the back nine to finish with a 7-under-par 65, a remarkable nine holes under any circumstances, let alone by a 46-year old, supposedly washed-up golfer against the greatest competitors the game could offer. The score left him one stroke better than Kite and, it would turn out, one stroke better than Norman, who bogeyed the 18th.

Nicklaus had confounded Father Time and the tricky Augusta course, and won his sixth—and sweetest—Masters, his 20th major tournament victory.

Nicklaus's birdie on 17 put him in the lead.

Jack Nicklaus at the Masters

Holes	1	2	3	4	5	6	7	8	9	out	10	11	12	13	14	15	16	17	18	in	totals
Yards	400	550	360	205	435	180	360	535	435	3465	485	455	155	465	405	500	170	400	405	3440	6905
Par	4	5	4	3	4	3	4	5	4	36	4	4	3	5	4	5	3	4	4	36	72
Play	5	4	3	3	3	2	4	4	4	33	3	3	2	4	4	5	2	4	4	30	63

"Just occasionally I want to be as good as I once was."

—Jack Nicklaus

This win came in Nicklaus's 28th appearance at the Masters.

Chapter 6
CONTROVERSIES

Winning is not always as easy as coming in first. Races have photo finishes that can take minutes, and sometimes even years, to settle. Athletes do whatever they have to in order to win, even if it means stretching the rules as the Cubs did when they went into the crowd at the Polo Grounds to find the ball during the Merkle's Boner game. Referees sway the balance to one side or the other with decisions that may or may not be correct. The Fat Lady usually sings to scenes of good sportsmanship, but harmony doesn't prevail when two teams each believe they're the winner, or two runners are each positive they broke the tape first. Sports fans still debate the outcomes of the ten finishes in this chapter.

THE LONG COUNT

From the time the elusive Gene Tunney had lifted his title in September 1926, a beaten Jack Dempsey had spoiled for the chance to get back at the "Fighting Marine." And most of America was spoiling for the same thing. By the end of the '20s, Dempsey, once regarded a near-bestial bad guy, had come to represent an older, rougher America that the Roaring '20s had made obsolete. Dempsey was the favorite of the little guys and workers who'd been run over by the swells. On the other hand, Tunney, a man who quoted Shakespeare and considered fighting declassé, found his fans among the millionaires who now packed the ringside at Chicago's Soldier Field on Sept. 22, 1927, the night Dempsey finally got his rematch.

Though he lost the fight, Dempsey came away with the reputation of a winner who'd been robbed.

More than 145,000 fans gathered there on the shore of Lake Michigan, the largest crowd ever to see a prize fight, and millions more listened at home on radio sets, many for the first time. As Westbrook Pegler would write in the *Chicago Tribune*: "The crowd stretched away ... so far that sitting in the heat and glare of the cone lights just under the ring you couldn't see the last rows of customers. You could only sense that they were there from the combers of sound that came booming down the slope of the stadium out of the darkness."

That sound largely consisted of encouragement for Dempsey. As the newly-appointed sports editor of *The Washington Post*, 22-year-old Shirley Povich, recalled: "It was a Dempsey crowd, and everything he did brought a roar."

It wasn't until the seventh round, though, that the Manassa Mauler, as Dempsey was called, gave the crowd a legitimate reason to get revved. Up until then, Tunney had outboxed Dempsey, as he had a year before, his slicing, scientific approach to boxing and younger legs outpacing the raw power of the aging Dempsey.

But in that fateful seventh round, Tunney finally miscalculated, and walked into a short, jolting left. Dempsey's hook landed on the champion's jaw. Tunney's knees buckled. He began to sink along the ropes. Dempsey helped his demise with a left hook and a hard right.

At ringside, radio announcer Graham McNamee told the nation: "Tunney is down from a barrage of lefts and rights to the face!"

What happened in the moments following the knockdown led to an historic controversy. The Illinois athletic commission's rules mandated that a boxer scoring a knockdown had to retreat to a neutral corner. Dempsey missed the fact that the referee, Dave Barry, was pointing him toward a neutral corner. By the time that Dempsey finally retreated to the designated spot, the timekeeper's count had reached five.

"Tunney is down ..."
—Graham McNamee

In the fateful seventh round referee Dave Barry counts nine as Tunney struggles to his feet.

But only now was Barry prepared to begin his count. Tunney did not get to his feet until the referee's count reached nine. Then he did what fighters in trouble are told to do. Move away from danger. Tunney survived the round, won the fight and left Dempsey's millions of fans bemoaning the long count that, they insisted, had enabled him to beat their Jack. Years later, Tunney continued to contend that he would have beaten the count, long or short.

All was lost for Dempsey, though. As Povich would note: "The loser, Dempsey, emerged from the fight as the hero—gypped out of a legitimate comeback for the title." In his later years he held court at his own restaurant in New York City, a popular fixture always remembered for the long count that marked the end of an era.

Heavyweight Championship

Round 1	Round 2	Round 3	Round 4	Round 5	Round 6
Even	Tunney	Tunney	Tunney	Tunney	Dempsey

Round 7	Round 8	Round 9	Round10
Dempsey	Tunney	Tunney	Tunney

(according to the *Chicago Tribune* and the *New York Herald Tribune*)

MERKLE'S BONER

In the midst of a hotly-contested pennant race, the margin for error narrows, and when mistakes are made, their impact becomes even greater. Ask Fred Merkle.

As the race between the New York Giants and the Chicago Cubs ran down to the wire, the outcome of their head-to-head confrontation on Sept. 23, 1908, at New York's Polo Grounds, became crucial. With only a few weeks left in the season, every game mattered, and it looked as if the Giants had gained some ground when, with Moose McCormick on third and Fred Merkle on first in the bottom of the ninth inning and the score tied 1–1, shortstop Al Bridwell rapped what appeared to be a game-winning single to center. McCormick came around to score and Giants fans ran onto the field to celebrate the clutch victory.

But as McCormick scored from third, Cubs player-manager Frank Chance, of Tinker-to-Evers-to-Chance fame, noticed that Merkle had never bothered to advance to second base, instead taking off directly for the clubhouse when Bridwell's hit occurred. Merkle erroneously assumed that McCormick's run was automatic once McCormick crossed the plate. But Chance knew that the run would be nullified if the Cubs got the ball and tagged second base for a force-out on Merkle.

The rule covering such a point reads: "One run shall be scored every time a base runner, after having legally touched the first three bases, shall legally touch the home base before three men are put out, provided, however, that if he reach home on or during a play in which the third man be forced out or be put out before reaching first base a run shall not count. A force-out can be only made when a base runner legally loses the right to the base he occupies and is thereby obliged to advance as the result of a fair ball not caught on the fly."

The crowd at the Polo Grounds swarmed onto the field, further confusing an already strange situation.

As the mistake became apparent from Chance's protests, New York pitcher Joe McGinnity got the ball. Johnny Evers and Joe Tinker wrestled him for it, but McGinnity gained control and threw the ball into the stands, where a fan caught it. As the Giants tried to get Merkle out of the dugout, members of the Cubs accosted the fan, took the ball and threw it back onto the field where Evers waited to make the force play.

Umpire Hank O'Day nullified the run, and the chaos and coming darkness forced the umpires to declare the game, which should have been a Giants' victory, a 1–1 tie. At the season's end, the two teams were tied for first place, so the game was replayed and the Cubs won, a victory which gave them the National League pennant. Merkle's mental error, which a Giants pennant would have obscured, was now christened Merkle's Boner. The Cubs went on to win the World Series four games to one, over the Detroit Tigers, while the owner of the Giants, John T. Brush, had medals made for each member of his team which said, THE REAL CHAMPIONS, 1908. Nine years later, Fred Merkle was traded to the Cubs, and led them to the 1918 pennant.

> ## "I wish I'd never gotten that hit."
> —Al Bridwell

Chicago Cubs 1, New York Giants 1

Chicago	AB	R	H	RBI	New York	AB	R	H	RBI
Hayden, rf	4	0	0	0	Herzog, 2b	8	1	1	0
Evers, 2b	4	0	1	0	Bresnahan, c	3	0	0	0
Schulte, lf	4	0	0	0	Donlin, rf	4	0	1	1
Chance, 1b	4	0	1	0	Seymour, cf	4	0	1	0
Steinfeldt, 3b	2	0	0	0	Devlin, 3b	4	0	2	0
Hofman, cf	3	0	1	0	McCormick, lf	3	0	0	0
Tinker, ss	3	1	1	1	Merkle, 1b	3	0	1	0
Kling, c	3	0	1	0	Bridwell, ss	4	0	1	0
Pfeister, p	3	0	0	0	Mathewson, p	3	0	0	0
Total	30	1	5	1	Total	31	1	7	1

Chicago	0	0	0	0	1	0	0	0	0—1
New York	0	0	0	0	0	1	0	0	0—1

In his 16 seasons, Fred Merkle batted .273, with 733 RBIs.

THE HEIDI GAME

At 7 p.m., New York time, on Nov. 17, 1968, when NBC abandoned its coverage of the New York Jets–Oakland Raiders game to begin a two-hour movie, *Heidi*, the Jets and quarterback Joe Namath appeared to have the game wrapped up. With 65 seconds left, New York placekicker Jim Turner had booted a 26-yard field goal to give the Jets a 32–29 lead which seemed to seal a very hard-fought game between these two intense rivals.

The next thing millions of viewers knew, the plug was pulled on the game and the film about the diminutive Swiss orphan girl flashed on TV screens.

That was enough to send thousands of enraged football fans to their telephones to strenuously object to NBC about its abrupt blackout of the game. The load of calls was sufficient to cause the NBC switchboard to break down and, even more dramatic, many annoyed fans called the N.Y.P.D. and tied up the emergency police number.

The network's embarrassment would only be compounded once that angry horde of fans discovered how the game had ultimately unfolded.

After Turner's field goal, Oakland mounted a blitzkrieg scoring drive—two passes from Raiders quarterback Daryle Lamonica to Charlie Smith, the second one for the touchdown. When George Blanda added the extra point, Oakland led 36–32.

But the Jets still had 42 seconds left to rally.

Their last chance was short-circuited, though, when Jets return man, Earl Christie, fumbled the ensuing kickoff, the loose ball being scooped up by Preston Ridlehuber, a reserve back, who ran the ball into the end zone.

Final: Oakland 43, New York 32.

It was 22 minutes into *Heidi* when NBC tried to atone by running a crawl at the bottom of the screen giving the final score.

A lot of good that did. Rather than pacify

Heidi starred Sir Michael Redgrave as Grandfather and Jennifer Edwards as Heidi.

"NBC made a mistake.
It regrets it deeply."
—an NBC spokesman

Oakland's Preston Ridlehuber (37) finishes off the Jets with a two-yard touchdown after a New York fumble.

the football crowd, it ignited another barrage of angry calls.

NBC would insist that its intention had been to televise the game to completion and that a miscommunication had caused the cutoff. In the network's defense, earlier that day, NBC had cut away from the San Diego–Buffalo game in favor of the Raiders-Jets game, and the latter had been unusually slow, with 19 penalties in a rough, albeit slow, game.

Seven years later, a Raiders-Redskins game broadcast on NBC went into overtime, right as *Willy Wonka and the Chocolate Factory* was about to begin. This time, NBC stuck with football.

Oakland Raiders 43, New York Jets 32

New York	6	6	7	13—32
Oakland	7	7	8	21—43

New York	FG, Turner, 18
Oakland	Wells, 9, pass from Lamonica (Blanda, kick)
Oakland	Cannon, 48, pass from Lamonica (Blanda, kick)
New York	Namath, 1, run (pass failed)
New York	Mathis, 4, run (Turner, kick)
Oakland	Smith, 3, run (Dixon, pass from Lamonica)
New York	Maynard, 50, pass from Namath (Turner, kick)
New York	FG, Turner, 12
Oakland	Biletnikoff, 22, pass from Lamonica (Blanda, kick)
New York	FG, Turner, 26
Oakland	Smith, 42, pass from Lamonica (Blanda, kick)
Oakland	Ridlehuber, 4, fumble recovery (Blanda, kick)

Statistics of the Game

	Raiders	Jets
First Downs	21	18
Rushing Yardage	146	68
Passing Yardage	291	345
Return Yardage	69	46
Passes	21-34	19-37
Interceptions By	0	2
Punts	5-43	7-39
Fumbles Lost	2	1
Yards Penalized	93	145

DEAD EVEN AT THE HAMBLETONIAN

The margin between victory and defeat can sometimes be paper-thin.

Such was the case with the 1989 Hambletonian, the most prestigious event in harness racing.

The battle at the Meadowlands track in East Rutherford, N.J., that Aug. 5 was expected to have been between a colt named Valley Victory and a filly named Peace Corps.

But Valley Victory was scratched with a viral infection and Peace Corps, in her first confrontation against colts, did not measure up.

No, in the day's first two heats the trotters that emerged were Probe, driven by Bill Fahy (winner of the first heat) and Park Avenue Joe, driven by Ron Waples (winner of the second heat).

By the Hambletonian's rules, an entrant had to win two heats to be declared the winner. That meant a two-horse race-off would now be run between Probe and Park Avenue Joe.

The race-off would turn out to be a most unusual one, as Moira Fanning, publicity director of the Hambletonian Society, recalled: "The race-off was a yawner till the final quarter when both trotters raced side by side, each frantic to hit the wire ahead of the other."

Indeed, the final quarter-mile of the race was run in :26³/₅, the fastest finishing quarter in the 64-year history of the Hambletonian.

And how did the trotters finish?

"The finish," said Fanning, "was too close to call. So close that it took a five-minute delay and two photo-finish prints to determine that the two horses had reached the finish line together. It was one of the most exciting finishes, and certainly the most chaotic and crowded winner's circle ever."

It was the first-ever race-off dead heat at the Hambletonian.

"In harness racing," said Fanning, "a dead heat means both winners share the purse and the title. But in the Hambletonian conditions, still raced by a placing system, Park Avenue Joe was declared the winner, since his combined two-heat finish [2-1-1] was better than Probe's combined two-heat finish [1-9-1]."

The difference in the finish was a costly one. As winner, Park Avenue Joe won $565,000 for Rose Guida's Park Avenue Stables. Probe received $282,750.

"Well, the owners of Probe didn't see it that way and sued," said Fanning. "Two years after the race was contested, an administrative law judge ruled that the two horses would share the title of Hambletonian Winner, but Park Avenue Joe received the greater share of the purse, as stated in the conditions."

The 1989 Hambletonian was the first dead heat in the history of the race.

"The name of the game was to get home."
—Bill Fahy

DEAD HEAT

WIN

A.T.C. PHOTO FINISH

The Hambletonian

First Heat	1/4	1/2	3/4	Mile
Probe	:27.6	:56	1:26.2	1:54.6
Park Avenue Joe				
Egyptian Gentleman				
Second Heat				
Park Avenue Joe	:28	:56.8	1:27.2	1:55.6
Peace Corps				
Shogun Lobell				
Race Off (Dead Heat)				
Park Avenue Joe	:29.8	1:01.6	1:33.8	2:00.4
Probe				

Drivers: Park Avenue Joe/Ron Waples; Probe/Bill Fahy; Peace Corps/John Campbell; Shogun Lobell/Howard Beissinger; Egyptian Gentleman/W. O'Donnell.

Ron Waples and Park Avenue Joe were on the inside, and Bill Fahy and Probe were on the outside.

OLYMPIC HOOPS
ROBBERY

While the corruption involved in the selection of cities like Seoul, Salt Lake City and Melbourne as Olympic Games sites became big news in 1999, it did not surprise anybody with a grasp of the Games' history.

Questionable decisions had pervaded the competitions, going back more than 50 years ago when Olympic honcho Avery Brundage became a willing accomplice of the Nazis in their staging of the 1936 Berlin Olympics.

But for sheer baldfaced meddling with an Olympic event, you could do no worse than to reexamine the gold medal basketball game between the United States and the Soviet Union, at the 1972 Munich Olympics.

Going into these games, the U.S. had won every gold medal since basketball became part of the Olympic program in 1936. Through 36 years of Olympic competition, American teams had never lost in more than 60 games.

But in '72, the U.S. squad would be hard-pressed to beat the U.S.S.R.'s disciplined team. In a game that began at 11:45 p.m. in Munich—the better to accommodate American television—the Soviets led through all but the final three seconds of play. That was when future NBA star, coach and announcer, Doug Collins, having intercepted a pass, was fouled intentionally.

Collins, who had played his college ball at Illinois State, calmly sank both his free throws to give the U.S. its first lead, 50-49.

The Russians inbounded the ball but the pass was deflected at midcourt. The Americans in the crowd streamed onto the court to celebrate, only to be advised that one second remained on the game clock.

The plot thickened when the Soviet coach, Vladimir Kondrashkin, protested that he had called a timeout after Collins's first foul shot. Indeed the timeout horn had gone off just as Collins released his second free throw.

The Soviet basketball team celebrates their controversial victory. The U.S.A. refused to accept its silver medal.

At this point, the head referee Renato Righetto of Brazil and the timekeeper Andre Chopard asserted that one second remained in the game. But they were overruled by Great Britain's R. William Jones, the secretary general of the International Amateur Basketball Federation (F.I.B.A.), who insisted the clock be set back to three seconds. Technically, no rules provided for the autocratic Jones to intercede, but he strong-armed the referee and timekeeper into accepting his decision. On the sideline, U.S.A. coach Hank Iba, legendary coach of Oklahoma State for 36 years but recently retired, stood confused and seemingly unable to stop the railroading his team was taking.

As the U.S.'s Tom McMillen, the 6'11" player from the University of Maryland, hounded the inbounds pass, he was ordered by the referee to back away from the baseline. When he did, the U.S.S.R.'s Ivan Yedeshko threw a length-of-the-floor pass to the Soviets' big man, Aleksander Belov. As the ball soared through the air, Belov bumped off-balance the two American defenders who were vying with him for the ball. And like that, Belov had the ball and a clear path to a layup. When he scored, America's defeat was snatched from the jaws of victory, 51–50, and the golden Olympic ideals were left more than a little tarnished.

Basketball Finals

		W	L	PF	PA
1.	SOV	9	0	757	590
2.	USA	8	1	660	401
3.	CUB	7	2	687	577
4.	ITA	5	4	650	605
5.	YUG	7	2	734	617
6.	PUR	6	3	743	683
7.	BRA	3	5	625	642
8.	CZE	4	5	625	642

"They have to learn how to lose once."
—R. William Jones, Head of FIBA

The Soviets' Alshou Sharmukhamedov (7) drives past Ed Ratleff (15) of the U.S.A.

MELDRICK AND THE STEELE CURTAIN

I t was a classic matchup—Meldrick Taylor, the 1984 feather-weight Olympic gold medalist vs. Julio César Chávez—two great champions of contrasting styles, both undefeated, in a 12-round title showdown.

The winner, it was widely conceded, would earn the bragging rights as the best pound-for-pound fighter in 1990.

On March 17 of that year, in Las Vegas, these junior welterweight titleholders—Chávez the WBC champ, Taylor the IBF king—went at one another, each in his own distinctive fashion.

Although Taylor had, to most spectators, dominated the fight, referee Richard Steele stopped the fight when Taylor did not respond verbally after the knockdown.

Chávez, as always, ripped his trademark left hook to the body—a punch that usually took the starch out of his opponents and left them ready for the kill.

Not against Taylor. Through 11 rounds, he took Chávez's best shots and then would answer back with three-punch combinations that had Chávez swaying like a heavy bag. Taylor was quick on his feet and able to beat the Mexican to the punch time and again.

But what punches Chávez managed to land—though fewer in quantity—put a hurt on the Philadelphian. As the fighters answered the bell for the 12th and final round, it was Taylor who looked the worse for battle. His eyes were swollen nearly shut and his mouth had bled from early in the match.

Yet to most of the crowd and, more important, to two of the three judges, Taylor had a convincing lead. He had boxed beautifully, ripping blurring combinations that evoked the flash of a Sugar Ray Robinson, while standing his ground against the heavy-handed Julio.

As the 12th round ticked down to a finish, Taylor—battered though he was—appeared to be on his way to a grueling but masterly-fought victory.

But with 20 seconds left in the bout, Chávez suddenly staggered Taylor with a right that sent the IBF champion lurching towards a corner of the ring. Another right by Chávez sent Taylor to the canvas.

Steadying himself by grabbing the ropes, Taylor got to his feet as the referee, Richard Steele, wiped his gloves and asked him if he were prepared to continue. By now, the red light on the ring post was on, signifying there were fewer than ten seconds remaining in the match. Taylor's eyes swung to his right, the direc-

"I saw a beaten fighter."
—Richard Steele

In a 1994 rematch, Chávez once again beat Taylor, this time with a TKO in the eighth round.

tion from which trainer Lou Duva had materialized on the ring apron.

With but four seconds to go in the match, Steele asked again if Taylor was ready to continue and then, only two seconds later, waved an end to the fight, indicating that Taylor had failed to respond.

The decision by Steele loosed a controversy, many fans insisting the referee erred in not realizing that only seconds remained in the bout and not taking into account Taylor's being distracted by Duva. "I saw a beaten fighter," said Steele afterward.

But none of that mattered to Taylor. On this night the breaks of the game had gone against the gallant Philadelphian.

Junior Welterweight Championship

The cards at the point of Chávez's knockout of Taylor:

Chuck Giampa	105–104	Chávez
Jerry Roth	108–101	Taylor
Dave Moretti	107–102	Taylor

A MILE-LONG SQUABBLE

On Jan. 28, 1950, Don Gehrmann, a University of Wisconsin senior, and Fred Wilt, an FBI man, were hooked up at Madison Square Garden before 15,000 spectators for the Wanamaker Mile, the major event at the premiere indoor track meet of the time, the Milrose Games.

With a lap to go, J. Edgar Hoover's man Wilt led by two yards and appeared on the way to victory. But as the two men came down the back stretch, Gehrmann turned on the afterburners. With every stride he cut into Wilt's lead. And as both men drove to the tape, they appeared to arrive there simultaneously, both timed in 4:09.3.

Who won?

Well, that would be the subject of much discussion by the tuxedoed track officials.

See, the officials assigned to call win, place and show came up with conflicting responses to the finish. Some saw Wilt as the winner, others declared for Gehrmann.

And what about the Bulova Photo-Timer which was used to sort out close finishes? The officials at the finish line blocked the camera; although Gehrmann's lead foot appeared just ahead of Wilt's, the most important things—the runners' chests—were not visible behind the tuxedoes of the men in charge.

Given those circumstances it was left to Asa Bushnell, the Eastern College Athletic Conference commissioner who was serving as chief judge, to break the deadlock. He named Gehrmann the winner.

But that would not be the end of this notorious mile race. Soon after Bushnell's decision, the Metropolitan AAU registration committee and the board of managers overrode Bushnell and declared Wilt the winner.

But 314 days after the race had been run, on Dec. 9, 1950, Wilt's victory was snatched from him at the National Amateur Athletic Union's annual convention. It was announced that the group's board of governors had voted 314 to 108 to endorse the report of a special committee convened to investigate the decision. That report said Gehrmann was owed the victory.

And so it came to pass that nearly a year after he had run the race, Gehrmann had his victory and the $750 Wanamaker Cup.

Wanamaker Mile

1. Don Gehrmann	4:09.3
2. Fred Wilt	4:09.3
3. John Joe Barry	4:10.2
4. John Twomey	4:11.5
5. George Wade	4:13.4

"Silly and disgraceful."
—committee chairman Charlie Ornstein regarding the yearlong battle

Fifteen minutes passed before Gehrmann was announced as the winner at Madison Square Garden.

JAFFEE BY DECISION

So there he was, skating at a breakneck pace through the first heat of the 10,000-meters speed skating event at the 1928 Winter Olympics in Saint Moritz, Switzerland.

As Irving Jaffee of New York raced Bernt Evensen of Norway to the finish line, he knew his time would be a good one.

And indeed it was: the 18:36.5 was .1 of a second ahead of the crack Norwegian.

Jaffe's time looked good enough to withstand the best efforts of the competition.

But that afternoon, things took a curious turn when, after seven of the 10 contestants had completed their heats, the competition was called off by an official of the International Skating Federation. That meant the day's times would be canceled and the races rescheduled.

The reason for the cancellation?

A sudden surge in the temperature, which altered the condition of the ice for the remaining competitors, a situation that would have forced them to skate on a soggy surface completely different, and more difficult than the one the earlier skaters had.

But to void Jaffe's run seemed terribly unfair to him. His time seemed to most observers unassailable by the rest of the field. So Augustus T. Kirby, the official representative of the United States, did not stand idly by.

Kirby and representatives from Canada and Norway protested the decision, Kirby noted that a day earlier Eddie Murphy of Chicago had been obliged to skate his heat of the 500-meter event in a blinding snowstorm.

When the International Skating Federation rejected Kirby's protest, the American took his case to the International Committee.

"We don't want to raise a row," said Kirby. "We prefer to win the race on the ice, not in committees, but this action does not seem fair to us."

And so it came to pass, after a day of bickering, that Irving Jaffee was officially recognized as the 10,000-meter champion by the Executive Commission of the International Olympic Committee.

Four years later, in Lake Placid, N.Y., Jaffee won the gold medal again. No paper champion, Irving.

Officially the 1928 10,000-meters race did not take place.

"We don't want to raise a row."
—Augustus T. Kirby, USOC

10,000 Meters

1. Irving Jaffee	USA	18:36.5
2. Bernt Evensen	NOR	18:36.6
3. Otto Polacsek	AUT	20:00.9
4. Rudolf Riedl	AUT	20:21.5
5. Keistutis Bulota	LIT	20:22.2
6. Armand Carlsen	NOR	20:56.1
7. Valentine Bialas	USA	21:05.4

THE ORIGINAL HAIL MARY

Desperate times call for desperate measures, and for the Dallas Cowboys on this cold and gloomy day—Dec. 28, 1975—it was an absolute crisis.

In this first round of the NFL playoffs, here were the Cowboys with fourth-and-16 at their own 25, stuck deep in their own territory against a Minnesota Vikings defense anchored by a ferocious front line nicknamed the Purple People Eaters, featuring Alan Page, Carl Eller and Jim Marshall. The biting cold wind of the Minnesota winter whipped through Bloomington Stadium, the forbidding home of the pre–Hubert H. Humphrey Metrodome Vikes and their scrambling Hall of Fame quarterback Fran Tarkenton.

Staubach's superb passing had kept Dallas in control most of the game.

For the Dallas quarterback, Hall of Famer Roger Staubach, the choices were limited. With 44 seconds to go and the Cowboys trailing 14–10, a field goal would not do. It would take a touchdown to beat the Vikings and advance to the National Conference championship game against the Los Angeles Rams.

Earlier on the drive Staubach had asked his wide receiver, six-foot Drew Pearson, whether he had Minnesota cornerback Nate Wright set up for a deep pass. The first couple of times Staubach posed the question, Pearson told him, "Not yet."

Now Pearson told him it was time.

That was, surely, something of an understatement.

As Staubach took the snap from center and Pearson raced downfield, the Dallas quarterback let it fly.

From Pearson's point of view, here's how the play unfolded: "I came off the line 15 or 16 yards, took a step inside and then broke outside. The ball was underthrown and I tried to get back inside."

What happened next was subject to varying interpretations.

The Vikings insisted that while the ball was in the air, Pearson shoved Wright and that pass interference should have been called on him.

"From our side of the field there was no question Nate was pushed," said Vikings coach Bud Grant.

Pearson said, "They were saying I pushed him. He pushed me and I might have put my hands on him."

NFL commissioner Pete Rozelle, after looking at the replay, admitted: "... I couldn't see clearly what happened."

The officials saw no breach of football etiquette. And when Pearson caught the ball at the five and walked into the end zone while Wright lay flat on his back, it was a touchdown.

"The ball hit my hands and then something hit my arm," said Pearson. "The ball slid down and stuck between my elbow and my hip. That's all there was to it. It was a lucky catch."

Not so lucky was 54-year-old field judge Armen Terzian. Enraged by the lack of the pass interference call, with 14 seconds left in the game, an unidentified Vikings fan threw a whiskey bottle from the stands and hit the official on the forehead, causing a bloody gash. Terzian left the field after the unfortunate incident.

Staubach, who is Roman Catholic, later called the pass a Hail Mary, the name which has stuck to desperate, last-second throws towards the end zone.

Dallas Cowboys 17
Minnesota Vikings 14

Dallas	0	0	7	10—17
Minnesota	0	7	0	7—14

Minn.	Foreman 1 run (Cox kick)
Dallas	Dennison 4 run (Fritsch kick)
Dallas	FG Fritsch 24
Minn.	McClanahan 1 run (Cox kick)
Dallas	D. Pearson 50 pass from Staubach (Fritsch kick)

Statistics of Game

	Cowboys	Vikings
First downs	19	12
Rushes-yards	42-131	27-115
Passing yards	225	100
Return yards	18	5
Passes	17-29-0	12-26-1
Punts	6-38	7-40
Fumbles-lost	4-1	2-1
Penalties-yards	4-30	7-60

"I guess it's a Hail Mary pass. You throw it up and pray he catches it."

—Roger Staubach

THE TWO WILLIES

The horse of choice for the 1957 Kentucky Derby was General Duke of the powerful Calumet Farm, the New York Yankees of horse racing at that time.

At least General Duke was the favorite until its trainer, Jimmy Jones, determined that the horse had an internal stone bruise in an area about halfway up the wall of the hoof in his left forefoot. The injury was serious enough for Jones to scratch General Duke 16 minutes before the betting at Churchill Downs opened at 9:30 on a raw and windy morning.

Young Willie Shoemaker was signed on to ride Gallant Man when the horse's regular jockey Johnny Choquete received a 10-day suspension.

That left the 83rd running of the Kentucky Derby wide open to horses like Iron Liege, ridden by Willie Hartack, Gallant Man, ridden by Willie Shoemaker; Bold Ruler, ridden by Eddie Arcaro; and Calumet Farm's other entry. These two great jockeys would amass a combined 13,612 wins between them, yet this would be one of their most memorable, and strangest, meetings.

By the head of the stretch, Arcaro had given up on Bold Ruler and for the last furlong the race turned into a two-horse competition, as Hartack and Shoemaker drove their horses to the finish.

As Whitney Tower would report in *Sports Illustrated*, it looked like this:

> *Iron Liege on the inside, with Hartack whipping left handed and driving to the line, and Gallant Man gaining on him foot by foot. They stormed down this way to the 16th pole, moving almost as one. Gallant Man never seemed actually to be in front but they were head and head.*

At that moment, at the 16th pole, Shoemaker aboard Gallant Man did a most curious thing. He rose in his irons for a fraction of a second, acting as if the race was over.

It wasn't. Willie Shoemaker rode 8,833 horses to victory in his 41 year career. He didn't make a lot of mistakes. But this time the Shoe had misjudged the finish line. In an instant he lowered down and got his horse back into drive.

But it was too late.

Hartack's colt, Iron Liege—Calumet Farm's fortuitous Plan B—had won in a photo finish.

Gallant Man's trainer, Johnny Nerud, blamed his jockey's error on the fact that the poles along the rail were painted the same color, making it easy to confuse the pole indicating

> # "It was just one of those awful things you have nightmares about."
> —Willie Shoemaker

Many race observers felt Iron Liege would have won the race even without Shoemaker's gaffe.

the last sixteenth of a mile before the finish with the pole designating the finish line.

Maybe. But the stewards at Churchill Downs didn't buy that explanation, suspending Shoemaker for 15 days.

Meanwhile, a joyous Hartack was telling reporters: "I'll admit I wasn't sure Iron Liege could do it after seeing some of his races this spring. Today Iron Liege, though, ran gamer than I've ever seen him. When Gallant Man ran to me in the stretch, Iron Liege just gave another spurt, put out his neck and just kept digging on. I'm glad he made a liar out of me."

Kentucky Derby

Starters	Jockeys	P.P.	Time	Value
Iron Liege	Hartack	6	2:02.2	$107,950
Gallant Man	Shoemaker	4		
Round Table	Neves	3		
Bold Ruler	Arcaro	7		
Federal Hill	Carstens	2		
Indian Creek	Tahigueal	5		
Mister Jive	Woodhouse	1		
Better Bee	J. Adams	9		
Shan Pac	J.R. Adams	8		

Chapter 7
MARATHON FINISHES

While the word *marathon* refers, strictly speaking, to a long distance footrace of some 26 miles and 385 yards, this chapter takes the broad definition. The Fat Lady moments here take place over a long period of time. Baseball has its extra innings, basketball has overtime, and hockey and pro football have sudden death; other sports add holes and tiebreakers. Some sports are marathons by their very nature—The America's Cup is won only after thousands of miles of sailing and months on the open ocean. The length of an event often makes an event special, but in our list we've added the ingredient of the Fat Lady … something out of the ordinary.

NO MORE WAITING FOR PABLO

He knew the agony of defeat. Knew it close up and personal. Swimmer Pablo Morales had taken aim on a gold medal at the 1984 Los Angeles Olympics.

At the time he was considered the best butterfly swimmer in the world, and was the favorite to win the 100-meter event. But in a closely-contested finish, he had looked up at the scoreboard and discovered that in the last 10 meters he had blown his lead and lost the race to West Germany's Michael Gross.

Back he came in 1988, but this time his disappointment ran deeper. Morales finished third in the butterfly at the Olympic trials, which, since only the first two finishers qualified for the U.S. squad, left him off the team and out in the cold for the Seoul Olympics.

Morales couldn't even bring himself to watch the butterfly race when it was beamed back to the States on TV: too disturbing.

It was all too much for Morales, who retired from the sport and for three years attended law school at Cornell. But then in 1991, after his mother, Blanca, had died of cancer, he thought of the times that they had watched Bud Greenspan's films of Olympic glory together, and been warmed by the stories of obstacles overcome, of hard-won triumphs.

Morales decided to try a comeback seven months before the 1992 Olympic trials in Indianapolis. It was a long shot at best, but Morales not only managed to make the team but was voted its captain.

That path led him, at the relatively old age of 27, to the

His integrity and commitment made Morales a perfect choice for captain of the U.S. swim team.

> "I haven't cried this much since the day my mother died."
> —Pablo Morales

Morales went through an intensive training campaign to come back after years of rarely swimming.

Bernat Picornell swimming pool in Barcelona, for another shot at the gold. And once again, as he raced to the finish, he was in virtual lock-stroke with another athlete, Rafal Szukala of Poland.

As he reached for the contact pad at the end of the pool, Morales nervously held on to the side of the pool for a few seconds before he turned to the scoreboard to discover his fate.

"There was a moment of silence, eerily reminscent of the silence at the '84 Games," Morales said. "I wasn't going to look too quickly. Then I searched for my name, looked for my number."

His name was in the gold medal slot. Pablo Morales had beaten Szukala by .03 of a second with a time of 53.32 seconds.

He had persevered and, in so doing, become the oldest American gold medalist in swiming since Duke Kahanamoku, who won the 100-meter freestyle in 1920 at the age of 30.

Men's 100-Meter Butterfly

1	Pablo Morales	Santa Clara, Calif.	53.32 seconds
2	Rafal Szukala	Poland	53.35
3	Anthony Nesty	Surinam	53.41
4	Pavel Khnykine	Unified Team	53.81
5	Mel Stewart	Charlotte, N.C.	54.04
6	Marcel Gery	Canada	54.18
7	Martin Lopez-Zubero	Spain	54.19
8	Vladisiav Koulikov	Unified Team	54.26

Wimbledon—Men's Final
Bjorn Borg vs. John McEnroe

July 5, 1980

A BJORN WINNER

American bad boy John McEnroe strutted confidently onto Centre Court at the All England Lawn Tennis Club, amid an eruption of boos, to challenge defending champion Bjorn Borg for the 1980 Wimbledon title. Having been nearly eliminated in the second round by 112th ranked Terry Rocavert, a struggling McEnroe had finally let his notorious temper get the better of him in the semifinal match against Jimmy Connors. Overreacting to a relatively insignificant line call, McEnroe barked repeatedly at the umpire and earned the first public warning ever issued at Wimbledon, reaping the ill will of the British tennis-watching public.

In stark contrast to McEnroe, Borg, the invariably composed and diplomatic Swede, had the overwhelming support of the day's spectators. Moreover, having breezed through his six preliminary matches, losing only two of 20 sets, the reigning champion was strongly favored to claim a record fifth straight Wimbledon victory.

Not to be underestimated, McEnroe opened the match in excellent form, controlling the pace throughout the first set. Borg, somewhat weak on his opening volleys, gave up his first and third service games. Unable to break the lefthanded McEnroe's strong second serve, the Wimbledon champion yielded the set, 6–1. McEnroe continued to regulate the tempo into the second set, bringing Borg to break point four times in two games. This time, however, McEnroe failed to follow through, and, serving to Borg, down 6–5, the match suddenly changed. Fighting from 15–all to 15–30, and then 15–40, Borg finally broke McEnroe's service with a well-placed backhand return, to even the match at one set apiece.

Immediately the momentum changed; Borg got his usual brisk stride back and McEnroe, his rhythm thrown off by the quicker pace, lost his first service in the next set. By the time he returned to form, McEnroe had dropped the third set and faced possible defeat.

John McEnroe's emotional style of play earned him as many detractors as it did fans.

"I was never sure until I won the last point."
—Bjorn Borg

Borg dominated men's tennis during the '70s, with six French Open titles to go with his five Wimbledons. He retired in 1981.

The two contestants battled evenly through the first eight games of the fourth set, until Borg returned a beautiful serve with a perfect crosscourt backhand, breaking McEnroe to go up 5–4. Borg needed only to hold his service to ensure his place in the record books. Three points later, down 40–15, McEnroe stared down the barrel of double-match point. Finding the courage that champions seem to possess in moments of great adversity, McEnroe fought his way to deuce and broke Borg for a third time.

With the set even at 6–6, the contestants began a tiebreaker that would test the mettle of both players. In the staggering 22 minutes it took to complete the game, Borg had five championship points and McEnroe had seven set points.

When, after 32 points at a dead heat, the tiebreaker fell to McEnroe, it seemed only right that this epic duel would be decided by a fifth and final set. Battle recommenced and the world of tennis held its breath as the two combatants fought their way yet again to a 6–6 tie. Then, after three hours and 53 minutes on Centre Court, leading McEnroe 7–6, having let a total of 14 championship points slip by, Borg finally landed a crosscourt backhand that brought both players to their knees and the audience to its feet.

Wimbledon Men's Final

John McEnroe	USA	6	5	3	7	6
Bjorn Borg	SWE	1	7	6	6	8

LITTLE BIG MAN

When he first came into the NBA during the 1950–51 season, 6'2", 180-pound Bob Cousy wasn't the purists' idea of a guard.

Too small, too much razzle-dazzle, too little defense, they said. But with his sloping shoulders and long arms, Cousy could improvise in a way that was startling for those times.

If Cousy was a question mark when he came into the pro game, he proved his competitive fire once and for all at the end of the 1952–53 season, in a playoff game against the Syracuse Nationals led by Dolph Schayes and George King. Up to that time, the Celtics had never won a single round in the play-offs. That's why they were encouraged when they beat Syracuse 87–81 in the first game of a three game series.

But with less than a minute to play in the second game, on March 21,

Cousy led the NBA in assists eight straight seasons, and finished his career with a total of 6,955.

1953, in Boston, the situation was not nearly as promising. When Cousy lost control of the ball with Boston trailing by a point, Syracuse only had to keep possesion for the final seconds to win, even though their star, Schayes, had been thrown out for fighting in the second quarter.

Easier said than done. The Celtics stole the ball. This time Cousy drove to the basket, was fouled, and hit the free throw to send the game into overtime.

In that overtime, Boston again trailed by one in the final seconds. And again, Cousy went to the foul line with the outcome depending on him. The Cooz sank the shot to send the game into a second overtime. As the final seconds of the second OT ticked off, it was Cousy again with the bucket that tied the game and sent it into a third overtime. And guess who it was who hit a long push shot to tie the game 99–99 at the buzzer ending that third overtime? Right. Bob Cousy.

The pressure was tremendous by this point, so great in fact that Boston publicity director Howie McHugh fainted during the fourth overtime. By then, however, Boston had the lead and went on to win 111–105.

Boston's little big man had taken charge. Cousy had scored 25 points in the four overtimes and 50 points in all, setting an NBA playoff record that would stand, until Wilt Chamberlain scored 56 against Syracuse in a 1962 playoff game.

> ## "He could lead an team without saying a word."
> —Red Auerbach

Boston Celtics 111, Syracuse Nationals, 105

Syracuse	G	F	Pts	Boston	G	F	Pts
Schayes, lf	2	4	8	Donham	1	0	2
Gabor, rf	3	3	9	Harris, lf	4	6	14
Lockmuler	1	1	3	Cooper, rf	2	5	9
Osterkorn	1	0	2	Brannum	3	0	6
Lloyd	4	5	13	Mahnken	0	1	1
Rocha, c	5	9	19	Macauley, c	4	10	18
Jorgenson	2	4	8	Mahoney	0	0	0
King, lg	4	8	16	Cousy, lg	10	30	50
Cern	0	9	9	Sharman, rg	3	3	9
Seymour, rg	5	8	18	Rollins	0	2	2
Total	27	51	105	**Total**	27	57	111

University of Kansas Jayhawks vs. UNC Tar Heels

March 23, 1957

TRIPLE *OT*

Basketball big men in 1957 simply were not as quick or nimble as Kansas's Wilt Chamberlain. They tended to be wide-beamed fellas who moved in slo-mo, or spindly uncoordinated sorts. Chamberlain was the sleek state-of-the-art pivotman, a quantum leap in basketball's evolution.

The 1957 NCAA championship game would pit Wilt & Co. against a North Carolina team undefeated in 31 games. North Carolina coach Frank McGuire had assembled a team of savvy players like Pete Brennan, Joel Quigg, Tommy Kearns and the Tar Heels' leading scorer, Lenny Rosenbluth, and indeed in the finals against Kansas, UNC showed the Jayhawks that Chamberlain, by himself, would not throw the Tar Heels off kilter. The Tar Heels ran out to a quick 19–7 lead and kept it through the half, but the score was deadlocked at 46 after regulation. For the first time in the history of the NCAA tournament, a championship game would go into overtime.

Three overtimes, to be exact. Two wrestling incidents, one involving Chamberlain and Brennan, and the other between Kearns and Gene Elstrum of Kansas, ratcheted up the intensity. Both teams continued to play with uncommon caution. Before the shot clock, teams could stall as long as they

UNC had to win a three-overtime semifinal over Michigan State to reach this three-overtime final.

"We're a chilly club."
—Tommy Kearns

wanted and stall they did, scoring only two points each in the first overtime and then going scoreless in the second.

In the third overtime, with 20 seconds left, Kansas inched ahead 53–52 on a free throw by Elstrum. They at the other end of the court, Kearns, the Tar Heels' 5'10" guard, had his shot blocked by Chamberlain. Quigg recovered the ball for Carolina and was fouled by big Wilt as he went for the score.

It came down to two shots from the line. Quigg hit both to give UNC a 54–53 lead with six seconds left, and then blocked a pass to Chamberlain to squelch the Jayhawks' last shot.

North Carolina 54, Kansas 53

N. Carolina	fgm	fga	ftm	fta	r	pf	pts
Rosenbluth	8	15	4	4	5	5	20
Cunningham	0	3	0	1	5	4	0
Brennan	4	8	3	7	11	3	11
Kearns	4	8	3	7	1	4	11
Quigg	4	10	2	3	9	4	10
Lotz	0	0	0	0	2	0	0
Young	1	1	0	0	3	1	2
Total	21	45	12	22	42	21	54

Kansas	fgm	fga	ftm	fta	r	pf	pts
Chamberlain	6	13	11	16	14	3	23
King	3	12	5	6	4	4	11
Elstun	4	12	3	6	4	2	11
Parker	2	4	0	0	0	0	4
Loneski	0	5	2	3	3	2	2
L. Johnson	0	1	2	2	0	1	2
Billings	0	0	0	0	0	2	0
Total	15	47	23	33	28	14	53

Regulation:	Tied 46-46
First Overtime:	Tied 48-48
Second Overtime:	Tied 48-48

A RUNNER STAGGERS AND FALLS

At the 18 mile mark, the 1908 Olympic marathon appeared to be a two-man race between Charles Hefferon of South Africa and Dorando Pietri of Italy.

As they ran over the London course that would take them from Windsor Castle to the Olympic Stadium in Shepherd's Bush, it was Hefferon who appeared in control. After 20 miles, he boasted a comfortable lead of 3 minutes, 52 seconds.

But on this muggy day in July, Hefferon began to wilt as Pietri closed on him. Looking for a quick pick-me-up, Hefferon accepted a drink that turned out to be champagne. The South African developed cramps and became dizzy over the next mile, but nonetheless raced on.

A half mile from the stadium, he was passed by Pietri, who himself was falling apart from having committed to too rapid a pace. When the Italian entered the stadium, he had only to run the final 385 yards to the finish tape and he would be the winner.

But the moment Pietri appeared in the stadium, first among the field of 58, it was obvious that he was in bad shape. In fact, as Pietri came onto the track, he turned in the wrong direction and righted himself only after officials pointed out his error.

But that wasn't going to help poor Pietri on this day. As the British Queen, Alexandra, and the other spectators watched, Pietri struggled to finish. *The New York Times* would describe Pietri's tormented final steps in this fashion: "Staggering like a drunken man, he slowly totttered down the home stretch. Three times he fell, struggled to his feet and each time, aided by track officials, he fought his way toward the tape."

This assistance by the officials of course put him out of the race, but his struggles were so pitiful that they continued to aid him until he was pushed across the line.

With Pietri disqualified for being assisted, the crowd's eyes now turned to the next runner entering the stadium. He was an American, John Hayes, a 22-year-old clerk at Bloomingdale's department store in New York City.

By the time Hayes crossed the finish line, race officials had run up the Italian flag to signify that Pietri had won. But an American protest resulted in Hayes being declared the winner.

While Pietri would receive a special gold cup from the Queen and come to be regarded as a celebrity, Hayes came away with the precious gold medal ... not to mention a promotion from Mr. Bloomingdale himself to manager of the sporting goods department.

But Hayes gave up his Bloomingdale's job when the controversy over the race provided both Pietri and him a lucrative opportunity to race professionally, including a couple of showdowns against each other. Pietri won both times.

Mr. Bloomingdale built a cinder track on top of the department store for Hayes to train on during breaks.

Hayes's biggest victory prior to the Olympics was the 1907 Yonkers Marathon.

"I believe I could have finished unaided."
—Dorando Pietri

Marathon

1. John Hayes	USA	2:55:18.4	OR
2. Charles Hefferon	SAF	2:56:06.0	
3. Joseph Forshaw	USA	2:57:10.4	
4. Alton Welton	USA	2:59:44.4	
5. William Wood	CAN	3:01:44.0	
6. Frederick Simpson	CAN	3:04:28.2	
7. Harry Lawson	CAN	3:06:47.2	
8. John Svanberg	SWE	3:07:50.8	
DISQ: Dorando Pietri (ITA) 2:54:46.4			

A RIOTOUS GARDEN PARTY

O vertime games are no anomaly in the NBA. But when the Boston Celtics and the Phoenix Suns went at it on June 4, 1976, in the fifth game of the NBA Finals, overtime begat overtime—three OTs in all—with the emotional ante being raised moment by moment on the parquet floor of the old Boston Garden. For all the raucous games played in this loud, small and overheated arena, this was the most amazing.

In the early stages, few would have suspected the tumult that lay ahead. At first it looked like an old-fashioned blowout, as Boston jumped off to a 36–18 first-quarter lead. At the half it was still Boston with a commanding margin, 61–45.

But the Suns' defense stiffened in the second half, forcing the Celtics to shoot from distant zip codes. Phoenix came from behind to tie the game 95–95 at the end of regulation time.

As one writer, Barry McDermott, put it: "The first overtime merely caused television sets to smoke, ending at 101–101. The second overtime was the thriller."

Indeed it was. Boston led by three points, with 15 seconds left in that second OT, circumstances favorable enough to the Celtics for their fans to begin chanting, "We're Number 1!" But then the Suns' Dick Van Arsdale scored and Paul Westphal, later coach of the Suns and the SuperSonics, stole the ball from Havlicek, which led to a Curtis Perry jumper that put Phoenix ahead 110–109.

At the Celtics' end of the court, Havlicek answered back with a running jump shot that sent Boston back into the lead, 111–110. Hundreds of Celtics fans raced onto the court, assuming the game was over. Their celebrating turned nasty, with fights developing on the Garden floor. One fan even grabbed referee Richie Powers, and had to be dragged away by arena security. Suns' players had to shove their way off the court through the mob.

And amidst all the tumult, Powers was signaling that the game was not over—there was still one second to play.

On the sideline, with Celtics' fans hovering by Phoenix's huddle and shouting insults, the Suns' Westphal improvised a bit of strategy that coach John McLeod agreed to. Rather than inbound the ball from the end line 90-odd feet from the basket, Westphal suggested calling a timeout, which was illegal since Phoenix had no timeouts left. But the result would

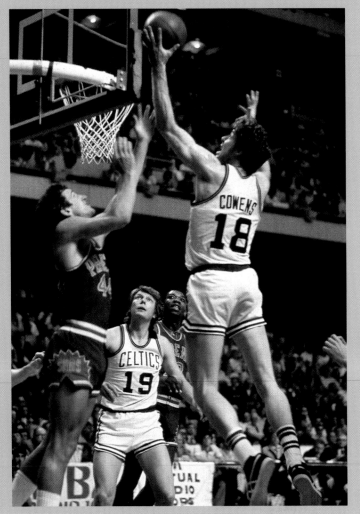

Boston's Dave Cowens and Paul Silas dominated the boards, with 19 and 14 rebounds respectively.

GUEST 110 0:04 HOME 109 PERIOD 4

"I'm surprised nobody was seriously hurt."
—Suns coach John MacLeod

John Havlicek drives past Ricky Sobers at the end of the second OT.

be a technical foul, followed by Phoenix taking possession of the ball at half-court.

Jo Jo White hit the technical to give Boston a 112–110 lead. And then the incredible happened. The Suns inbounded to Garfield Heard, a well-travelled player who averaged 11 points per game that season. Heard threw up a high-arcing bomb from behind the key that swished through the net. Since the three-point shot hadn't yet been introduced to the NBA, Heard's prayer only tied the game and sent it into a third OT.

The tumultuous atmosphere continued, with fans in the upper balconies raining cups, waste paper and rubber balls onto the floor, and police at courtside breaking up near-altercations between the agitated fans and the Phoenix players. The third OT made signs of being another miracle finish, as the Suns scored two baskets in the last 12 seconds, but the Celtics finally put the game away, 128–126, and sealed the title by winning Game 6, 87–80.

Boston Celtics 128, Phoenix Suns 126

Boston	min	fgm	fga	ftm	fta	reb	a	pf	pts
Havlicek	58	8	19	6	7	9	8	2	22
Silas	44	8	11	1	1	14	4	6	17
Cowens	55	9	23	8	11	19	4	6	26
White	60	15	29	3	3	6	9	2	33
Scott	33	3	14	0	0	4	3	5	6
MacDonald	13	3	5	2	2	1	3	2	8
Ard	16	3	6	2	2	2	1	1	8
Kuberski	13	2	5	0	0	3	0	1	4
Stacom	3	0	0	0	0	0	0	0	0
Nelson	20	1	4	2	2	4	1	1	4
Total	315	52	116	24	29	62	33	26	128

Phoenix	min	fgm	fga	ftm	fta	reb	a	pf	pts
Perry	52	10	20	3	4	15	6	5	23
Adams	37	9	16	2	2	9	5	6	20
Westphal	42	11	20	3	3	2	2	4	25
Van Arsdale	35	1	5	3	4	4	1	1	5
Erickson	4	0	2	0	0	0	1	0	0
Avtrex	23	2	3	3	3	4	0	6	7
Lumpkin	12	0	2	0	0	1	4	0	0
Newthorne	8	1	3	2	2	4	0	3	4
Total	315	53	112	20	24	53	29	28	126

Phoenix	18	27	27	23	6	11	14—126
Boston	36	25	16	18	6	11	16—128

Attendance 15,320

SWEET REDEMPTION

In 1984 he had come within .16 of a second of earning a bronze medal in the 500-meter speed skating event at the Sarajevo Olympics. And though he left Yugoslavia disappointed, Dan Jansen of Milwaukee was 18 and optimistic. There would be other chances.

But fate had some ornery twists and turns in store for the skater.

Take the 1988 Calgary Olympics. Jansen arrived there as one of the favorites to win the 500-meter race, his best event. But on the morning of the race, he got word that his older sister Jane had died of leukemia. The hurt of losing Jane would be compounded when Jansen slipped and fell during his race.

Nor was that the sum of Jansen's Olympic misfortune in Calgary either. Four days later—another mishap. During the 1,000-meter race, he tumbled to the ice again, blowing any chance of a medal in Calgary.

He tried again at the 1992 Albertville Olympics—a cofavorite in the 500 meters—but he botched a turn and finished fourth. The result appeared to undermine his psyche. He finished 26th in the 1,000 meters.

By the time he turned up at the 1994 Lillehammer Olympics, Jansen was 28, married and the father of a nine-month-old daughter, Jane, named after his beloved sister. His past Olympic failures had troubled him enough to seek counseling from a sports psychologist, who came to the Games as part of Jansen's support group.

But once again, the skater seemed snakebitten when, in the 500-meter race, on Valentine's Day, he slipped and finished eighth. With the 500 meters—his specialty—over, a mood of deep gloom fell over the skater, who felt he had let down his supporters. He sought out Dale Hoffman of his hometown paper, the *Milwaukee Journal Sentinel* and told him, Sorry, Milwaukee.

But Jansen had one more shot at Olympic gold—the 1,000-meter race. And after 10 agonizing years in pursuit of Olympic glory, finally it appeared he might seize the moment. He skated through the first 200 meters in a brisk 16.71. His 600-meter split time was on world-record pace, bringing a roar from the crowd of 12,000 in Hamar's Vikingskipet skating hall.

Jansen reacts as the news of his world record flashes on the scoreboard of the Vikingskipet Olympic Hall in Hamar, Norway.

"The saga ended today."

—Dan Jansen's wife, Robin

Though the 1,000 meters was not his favorite distance, Jansen had won five of the eight races he'd skated at that distance in the season leading up to the Olympics.

But then ... on the second-to-last turn, Jansen slipped, his left hand brushing the ice and bringing him to within an inch of stepping on a lane marker and falling. But somehow he managed to right himself and drive hard to the finish.

The scoreboard lit up with the news: 1:12.43— a world record and sweet redemption for Dan Jansen, an Olympic gold medalist at last.

Men's 1,000 Meter

1. Daniel Jansen	USA	1:12.43	WR
2. Igor Zhelezovsky	BLR	1:12.72	
3. Sergei Klevchenya	RUS	1:12.85	
4. Liu Hingbo	CHN	1:13.47	
5. Sylvain Bouchard	CAN	1:13.56	
6. Patrick Kelly	CAN	1:13.67	
7. Roger Strom	NOR	1:13.74	
8. Junichi Inoue	JPN	1:13.75	

AUSTRALIA'S CUP

By the end of the fourth race of the 1983 America's Cup, the Australian press was already mourning the loss of another opportunity to claim the world's most coveted sailing title. American skipper Dennis Connor had captained the *Liberty* to a 3–1 margin over the Aussies in the best-of-seven regatta and after taking a commanding 37-second lead at the start of the fifth race, the future seemed grim indeed for the Australian team.

Then, four minutes into the first leg, *Liberty*'s jumper strut snapped and had to be jury-rigged to the mast using only sail-ties and duct tape. A 20-knot wind and heavy seas forced Connor to exercise unusual caution on port tack and Aussie captain John Bertrand was able to parlay his advantage into a heavy-handed 1:47 victory over the crippled American vessel. Elated Australian broadcasters woke their countrymen to the news that *Australia II* had captured a second victory against the Americans, more than any Australian team in history had achieved before.

In the sixth race, despite beating Bertrand to the start, Connor, guessing the shifting winds wrong, again lost the lead in the first leg. The winds continued to favor the Australian team who established a staggering 2:29 lead as they completed the first leg. As *Liberty* neared the fourth mark on the second windward leg, some three minutes behind the

Australia II *crosses the finish line 41 seconds ahead of Liberty, as the cannon marks the race's end.*

Australians, Connor made a last-ditch attempt to use his right-of-way to force contact and disqualify the approaching *Australia II*. But Bertrand anticipated the desperation play and maneuvered out of harm's way, cruising on to an impressive 3:25 win.

In the 132-year history of the America's Cup, the U.S. team had bested each and every rival to vie for the title. Never before had a challenger claimed as many as three wins and threatened to seize the Cup from the long-reigning American team. Taking a lay day to savor the historic moment and heighten the drama of the approaching showdown, the Australians pushed the seventh race back to Monday, when the forecast for gentle seas favored the lighter *Australia II*. On the morning of Sept. 26, Conner skippered a more agile *Liberty* out of Newport Harbor, having jettisoned 1,000 pounds of ballast in preparation for the day's sailing conditions. The American captain was steeled to defend the 132-year legacy that had been entrusted to him.

At 1:05, with an eight-knot southwesterly wind, the race of the century was begun, and yet again Conner won the start, beating Bertrand to the mark by eight seconds. But the lead was short-lived. By the first crossing *Australia II* was several lengths ahead.

Australia II maintained the lead after the second crossing, but the American skipper's bag of tricks was not yet empty. Showing Bertrand a fake tack, Connor managed to buy the American team an open run as the Australians fell for the ruse, maneuvering to starboard. When *Liberty*'s bow slid across the first windward mark she was again in the lead, with *Australia II* 29 seconds astern. Rounding the fourth mark, 15 miles into the course, *Liberty* had widened her lead to 57 seconds. The race seemed all but won for the American team. But then, in a baffling move, Connor jibed to port, leaving the lighter, faster *Australia II* uncovered on the starboard side. Seemingly in recognition of Connor's error, the wind gods

> ## "It's the race of the century, of the millenium."
> — Rob Mundel, Australian broadcaster

The crew of Australia II *celebrates their commanding victory in the sixth race.*

smiled upon the Australian ship and by the next crossing, Bertrand had made up *Liberty*'s tremendous lead and edged into the front position.

Australia II began the final upwind leg of the course with the American team 21 seconds in tow. Having learned from Connor's mistake, Bertrand kept the American vessel tightly covered throughout the homestretch, despite *Liberty*'s last minute maneuvers to try and shake the Australians loose.

When the 1983 America's Cup was finally over, for the first time in 132 years the United States team admitted defeat. After a celebration perhaps as exhausting as the race itself, Bertrand and the crew of *Australia II* carried the long-awaited trophy back to an exultant Australian nation. Four years later, sailing the *Stars & Stripes*, Connor returned the Cup to America.

1983 America's Cup Final

Boat		1st Mark	2nd Mark	3rd Mark	4th Mark	5th Mark	Finish
Liberty Skipper: Dennis Conner	USA	by 0:29	by 0:45	by 0:23	by 0:57		
Australia II Skipper: John Bertrand	AUS					by 0:21	by 0:41

FIFTEEN ROUNDS
OF FOOTBALL

It was wild and woolly NFL football. No playoff game had generated the volume of scoring, or the cockeyed twists and turns of San Diego versus Miami on Jan. 2, 1982, and no game ever had seen a one-man display of talent and courage to equal that of the Chargers tight end Kellen Winslow.

It had started as a rout, San Diego scoring 24 first-quarter points while putting the Dolphins' offense under house arrest. So outplayed was Miami that the partisan Orange Bowl crowd of 74,735 booed the home team. So desperate was Dolphins coach Don Shula that, with 12:05 to play in the second quarter, he benched his starting quarterback, 23-year-old David Woodley (two completions in five passes for 20 yards, with one interception) for his 31-year-old backup, Don Strock.

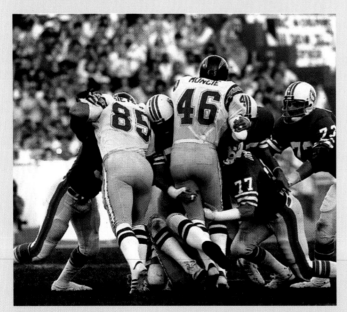

Chuck Muncie of San Diego balanced Dan Fouts's aerial attack with 120 yards on the ground.

There's a reason Shula is in the Hall of Fame: The quarterback change turned the game around. With Strock at the helm, the Dolphins came alive. Uwe von Schamann kicked a 34-yard field goal. Strock hit Joe Rose with a one-yard scoring pass. Then, when Strock completed a 15-yard pass to wideout Duriel Harris, Harris lateraled to trailing running back Tony Nathan, who ran the ball 25 yards for a touchdown. The flashy play electrified the crowd and the millions watching on television at home. It wasn't just that the Dolphins were coming back, they were coming back with style. By halftime the Dolphins had rallied to within a touchdown of the Chargers, 24–17.

Strock kept the Dolphins airborne. His 15-yard touchdown pass to Rose tied the game 24–24, and his 50-yard pass to Bruce Hardy tied the game again at 31–31 at 13:32 of the third quarter. Meanwhile, Chargers Hall of Fame quarterback Dan Fouts, maybe the greatest quarterback never to win an NFL title, was matching Strock for aerial pyrotechnics. In all, he would complete 33 of 53 passes for 433 yards and four touchdowns, including a nine yard strike to James Brooks in the final minute of regulation play. It tied the game 38–38 at the very moment that Miami—having made a 24-point comeback—appeared on the verge of an improbable victory.

But wait a minute. With only 58 seconds left here came the Dolphins again, Strock taking his team to the San Diego 25 in less than a minute. With four seconds left, in came von Schamann to try a 43-yard field goal. Four times before in this season von Schamann had booted game-winners. But this time, after a high snap, von Schamann hit a low liner of a kick that San Diego's workhorse tight end, 6'5" Kellen Winslow jumped up and deflected, sending the game into overtime.

Winslow seemed to be everywhere throughout the game. Along with his game-saving field goal block, the tight end caught 13 passes, then a playoff record, for 166 yards, another record. As the game pushed into overtime, Winslow often had to be helped back to the sidelines by teammates, as he made big catches, threw blocks, did whatever had to be done to get the Chargers into the AFC Championship Game.

"When you get a little desperate, you find something extra."

—Dan Fouts

In overtime, von Schamann would get a second chance. Alas, it would not be his day. Eleven minutes and 27 seconds into overtime, his 34-yard field goal was blocked by defensive end Leroy Jones. Meanwhile, the Chargers kicker, Rolf Benirschke, who'd blown an overtime field goal, too, got a second chance 13:52 seconds into overtime. Benirschke, kicked the game winner to give San Diego a 41–38 victory in a game that took over four hours to play.

After the final whistle, Winslow had to be carried off the field, battered and exhausted. He was the last man to arrive at the postgame celebration, but he did make it to the party, and into NFL history as the hero of one of the sport's greatest games.

San Diego Chargers 41
Miami Dolphins 38

San Diego	24	0	7	7	3—41
Miami	0	17	14	7	0—38

S.D.   Benirschke 37 FG
S.D.   Chandler 56 punt return (Benirschke, kick)
S.D.   Muncie 1 run (Benirschke, kick)
S.D.   Brooks 8 pass from Fouts (Benirschke, kick)
Miami   von Schamann 34 FG
Miami   Rose 1 pass from Strock (von Schamann, kick)
Miami   Nathan 25 lateral from Harris (von Schamann, kick)
Miami   Rose 15 pass from Strock (von Schamann, kick)
S.D.   Winslow 25 pass from Fouts (Benirschke, kick)
Miami   Hardy 50 pass from Strock (von Schamann, kick)
Miami   Nathan 12 run (von Schamann, kick)
S.D.   Brooks 9 pass from Fouts (Benirschke, kick)
S.D.   Benirschke 29 FG

Statistics of the Game

	San Diego	Miami
First downs	33	25
Rushes-yards	29-149	28-78
Passing-yards	415	388
Return yards	99	42
Passes	33-54-1	30-47-2
Sacks by	3-29	2-18
Punts	4-40	5-42
Fumbles lost	3-3	2-1
Penalties-yards	8-45	7-44
Time of Possession	37:44	36:08

WATSON HANGS TOUGH

It couldn't have been staged more dramatically.

The old master, the Golden Bear, 37-year-old Jack Nicklaus, went up against the young turk, a 27-year-old psychology major out of Stanford named Tom Watson. The two of them had been hot as pistols throughout this 1977 British Open at Scotland's Turnberry, a windswept, old-fashioned course always in sight of the sea.

As Nicklaus and Watson teed off for the final 18 holes on July 9, 1977, they were dead even. In fact, their scores for the first three rounds had been identical: 63, 70, 65. Not only that, the two of them—pretournament co favorites—were paired together for this final round, making their mano a mano a spotlit spectacle. Turnberry cooperated with a rare calm day, eliminating wind, the course's major hazard and setting the stage for a display of pure skill.

As Barry Lorge, writing in *The Washington Post*, would put it: "It all came down to man against man, with the madding crowd pressed around them, and the rest of the field over some distant fairway, and far out of sight. Seldom has medal play seemed so much like match play."

For Watson, who'd won that year's Masters and was the Tour's leading money winner going into the British Open, the day began as an exasperating game of catch-up. After four holes, he was down three strokes

When he rallied with birdies on the 7th and 8th holes to pull even, Nicklaus shot ahead by two strokes after 12.

But then Watson nailed a 12-foot birdie putt on the 13th hole and a 60-footer from 10 feet off the green on the 15th. As that shot was rolling to the hole, Watson was doing a little jig to encourage it. When it dropped, he and Nicklaus were dead even again.

Three holes left.

They both made par on the 16th.

On the 500-yard par-5 17th, nicknamed Lang Whang, Watson hit a three-iron onto the green that left him 20 feet from the cup, in excellent position to nail a birdie. He got his

Watson broke the British Open record by eight strokes with his 268.

Watson's victory marked a changing of the guard in the world of golf.

birdie, but Nicklaus, missing a critical four-foot putt, did not. Watson now led the tournament.

But Nicklaus didn't make it easy for Watson. He birdied the final hole with a 32-foot putt, which meant that Watson could not afford to blow his two-footer or the match once again would be even. No chance. Watson tapped in the winner.

For Watson, who shot 65 and a record 72-hole total of 268, a day of head-to-head catch-up had crowned him, after beating the greatest golfer ever, the master of the world of golf.

British Open

Tom Watson	63	70	65	65-268 $17,000
Jack Nicklaus	63	70	65	66-269 13,000
Hubert Green	72	66	74	67-279 10,200
Lee Trevino	68	70	72	70-280 8,500
Ben Crenshaw	71	69	66	75-281 7,225
George Burns	70	70	72	69-281 7,225
Arnold Palmer	73	73	67	69-282 6,375
Raymond Floyd	70	73	68	72-283 5,930
Johnny Miller	69	74	67	74-284 4,985
Tommy Horton	70	74	65	75-284 4,985
Mark Hayes	76	63	72	73-284 4,985
John Schroeder	66	74	73	71-284 4,985
Peter Thomson	74	72	67	73-286 3,740
Howard Clark	72	68	72	74-286 3,740
Jerry Pate	74	70	70	73-287 2,295

Chapter 8

FLUKE FINISHES

My first contact with the word fluke was from my grandmother—we had fish every Monday night whether we wanted it or not, and on occasion, we had fluke. In the world of sports, a fluke generally refers to a strange or bizarre play, so-called Lady Luck. Could that lady be our Fat Lady in disguise? Luck, according to one of my professors in college, could be defined as "preparation meeting opportunity," but this explanation would never hold up in our 10 Fluke Finishes. How can such a definition explain Mickey Owen's dropped third strike in the 1941 World Series, or Tony Leswick's strange goal in the 1954 Stanley Cup finals? At times there's even—apologies to my grandmother—something fishy about the fluke finish; just ask anyone who saw how the Oakland Raiders won the Holy Roller game. Whether it is good luck or bad, mental mistake or crafty plan, the Fat Lady's presence is always there when odd things happen.

THE DEADLY TIMEOUT

Dean Smith's University of North Carolina team had gone on an 11-2 tear at just the right time against Michigan.

With that run, the Tarheels led the 1993 NCAA championship game at the Superdome in New Orleans 72–67 with 1:01 remaining on the clock.

Coach Steve Fisher tried to calm down his rattled Michigan team.

But the Wolverines still had plenty of fight left in them. One of the most highly touted—and youngest—squads in college basketball history, the Fab Five of Michigan featured an amazing lineup, including forward Juwan Howard, guard Jalen Rose and the team leader, sophomore Chris Webber. As deep in attitude as they were in talent, the Fab Five were still smarting from their loss in the previous year's title game against Duke. Michigan had a lot to prove.

First Ray Jackson hit a jump shot from the right side with 47 seconds to go.

Michigan took a timeout, then forced UNC's Brian Reese to step across the right sideline in the backcourt with 45 seconds to go.

Then Webber scored off a Rose misfire to bring Michigan to within a point of the lead, 72–71, with 36 seconds left. That gave Webber 23 points, and 14 of them had come in the hotly-contested second half.

And it would be Webber who would snare the rebound as the Tarheels' Pat Sullivan, who had hit his first free throw, missed his second.

At that moment, with 20 seconds left in the game, the score stood 73–71, in UNC's favor, and Michigan's crucial last chance was in the balance.

As Webber brought down the rebound, he appeared to drag his pivot foot before dribbling. *Sports Illustrated's* Alexander Wolff would write: "Every last Tarheel player, coach and team manager leaped high in protest when no whistle sounded. None could have known that Webber would soon make amends for the referee's oversight."

Hounded by Tarheels' Derrick Phelps and George Lynch, Webber dribbled up the sideline. With the clock showing 11 seconds, he came to a halt and with his hands fashioned a "T" to indicate to the officials he was requesting a timeout.

A bad mistake.

Michigan had used up its quota of timeouts. By calling a timeout the Wolverines didn't have, Webber obliged the officials to call a technical foul.

Webber's costly error allowed UNC's Donald Williams to make a pair of free throws for the technical foul, and then two more with eight seconds remaining when Williams was fouled as the Tarheels inbounded the ball.

The final score was 77–71. Dean Smith won his second national title at UNC. But the headlines the next day would be about Chris Webber's misfortune, and the fall of the Fab Five.

"I cost our team the game."
—Chris Webber

Chris Webber went hardship after this game and entered the NBA draft, where he was drafted by the Orlando Magic.

North Carolina 77, Michigan 71

N. Carolina	Min.	fgm	fta	ftm	fta	r	a	pf	pts
Reese	27	2	7	4	4	5	3	1	8
Lynch	28	6	12	0	0	10	1	3	12
Montross	31	5	11	6	9	5	0	2	16
Phelps	36	4	6	1	2	3	6	0	9
Williams	31	8	12	4	4	1	1	1	25
Sullivan	14	1	2	1	2	1	1	2	3
Salvadori	12	0	0	2	2	4	1	1	2
Rodi	11	1	4	0	0	0	0	0	2
Calabria	1	0	0	0	0	0	0	0	0
Wenstrom	2	0	1	0	0	0	0	0	0
Cherry	1	0	0	0	0	0	0	0	0
Totals	200	27	55	18	23	27	13	10	77

Michigan	Min.	fgm	fta	ftm	fta	r	a	pf	pts
Webber	33	11	18	1	2	11	1	2	23
Jackson	30	2	3	2	2	1	1	5	6
Howard	34	3	8	1	1	7	3	3	7
Rose	40	5	12	0	0	1	4	3	12
King	34	6	13	2	2	6	4	2	15
Riley	14	1	3	0	0	3	1	1	2
Pelinka	17	2	4	0	0	2	1	1	6
Telley	8	0	0	0	0	0	0	1	0
Voskuil	4	0	1	0	0	0	1	0	0
Totals	200	20	62	6	7	31	17	18	71

North Carolina	42	35—77	
Miohigan	36	35—71	

AN AWFUL
MISTAKE

She had just captured the 1957 United States Golf Association's Women's Open in Mamaroneck, N.Y., and now the winner, jovial 235-pound Jacqueline Pung beamed as the crowd applauded before she moved on to the interview tent where reporters pushing deadlines peppered her with questions.

Pung, a 35-year-old Hawaii-born player, had clinched the tournament with a final round 72 and a total of 298 strokes. That was one stroke better than Betsy Rawls of Spartanburg, S.C.

Or was it?

As Pung sat talking to the press at the Winged Foot Golf Club, Joseph C. Dey Jr., executive director of the USGA, stepped forward with a disturbing announcement.

Pung and her playing partner, Betty Jameson, had both been disqualified for turning in incorrect scores. While Pung had written in her final-round total of 72 correctly, she and Jameson had erred by incorrectly marking down 5s instead of 6s for the par-5 4th hole.

In almost every other sport such an inadvertent mistake, seemingly so irrelevant to the action of the game, would certainly receive a penalty of some sort, but one appropriate to the crime. Too many men on the ice in hockey? A two minute penalty. Your basketball jersey comes untucked? Technical foul. Golfers, though, pride themselves on their honor, and believe very much that it remains a sport of ladies and gentleman. Playing balls where they lay, taking strokes, ball placements: It is so easy to cheat an inch or two here or there, or dust aside a particularly annoying rock in the way of your ball, that professional golfers rely on each other to be unfailingly honest in how they play the game and how they interpret the rules.

Sadly for Mrs. Pung, the rules were unforgiving on this count. A player turning in a score for any hole lower than it was played shall be disqualified.

The announcement brought tears from Mrs. Pung, who was accompanied by her 15-year-old daughter.

"It was an awful mistake and it is due a great deal to the excitement," Pung said.

Betsy Rawls won four tournaments that year. She was inducted into the USGA Hall of Fame in 1960.

"Both Betty and I knew we had 6s and concentrated on our score. I knew I had a 72, including that 6. My mistake and Betty's was in not repeating to each other what we had at that hole and seeing it was on the card.

"Of course, I'm heartbroken. I thought I won this tournament. It means a lot to me and my family. I would have won $1,800 besides a bonus from the manufacturing company I represent. Now I have absolutely nothing for play here this week."

In sympathy for the blow the fates had delivered Pung, the reporters covering the tournament started a collection which ended up amounting to some $2,367.

It took some but certainly not all of the sting out of the cruel twist victory had taken.

USGA Women's Open

Betsy Rawls	74	74	75	76-299
Patty Berg	80	77	73	75-305
Betty Hicks	75	77	76	80-308
Louise Suggs	76	81	75	76-308
Betty Dodd	74	78	76	82-310
Jo Anne Prentice	75	78	84	74-311
Alice Bauer	72	73	87	79-311
Mrs. Marlene Bauer Hagge	72	81	81	77-311
Fay Crocker	78	81	75	78-312
Beverly Hanson	78	76	79	79-312
Wiffi Smith	81	71	79	77-313
*Barbara McIntire	78	77	82	76-313
Mary Lena Faluk	76	79	83	75-313
*Mrs. J. Douglas Streit	79	79	75	82-315
Judy Frank	80	79	81	76-316
Jacqueline Pung disqualified				
*Denotes amateur				

"I'm heartbroken."
—Jacqueline Pung

Many felt that the USGA had acted by the letter of their rules, but not the spirit since they were not required to disqualify Pung.

DOUBLE KNOCKDOWN

Strange things happen in boxing—fixed fights, bogus decisions, odd and, well, suspect moments. Take the Ad Wolgast–Mexican Joe Rivers fight ... please.

The bout was fought on July 4, 1912 in Vernon, Calif. for the lightweight title. Wolgast, known as the "Michigan Wildcat," was the champion at the time. He'd won his title in 1910 against Battling Nelson, in a fight that ended in the 40th round with Wolgast's hand raised. He was known as a fighter of questionable tactics. Indeed, in a later title defense, against one Willie Ritchie, he would lose his title on being disqualified.

So it came to pass, 13 rounds into a hotly-contested bout against Rivers, that Wolgast hit Rivers with a punch that landed below the belt. But the impact of Wolgast's punch—formidable as it was—would be matched by the blow that Rivers uncorked at the same moment: a legitimate hook that caught the champ flush on his jaw. Both fighters hit the canvas.

By the rules of boxing, the referee is obliged to begin counting over both men in a double knockdown. First man up before the count of 10 would be declared the winner. Of course, with one punch a foul, the offending fighter should have been penalized, but Jack Welsh the referee, had his own notion of what to do.

With the crowd screaming in indignation at Wolgast's foul, Welsh got to the count of four over both fighters as if there'd been no foul and then reached down with his left hand to help the miscreant Wolgast to his feet. He did that without missing a beat on his count over the fallen Rivers until the bell ending the round sounded before he got to 10.

As both fighters headed towards their corners, Welsh approached Wolgast, raised his arm and declared him the winner. Was the fight fixed? Was Welch simply confused? Welsh claimed Wolgast tripped over Rivers's feet.

As *The Ring* magazine later would note: "You'd be hard-pressed to find a more bizarre ending in ring history. And for that we are thankful."

Lightweight Championship

Round 1 Rivers	Round 2 Rivers	Round 3 Even	Round 4 Rivers	Round 5 Even	Round 6 Rivers
Round 7 Rivers	Round 8 Wolgast	Round 9 Wolgast	Round 10 Wolgast	Round 11 Even	Round 12 Rivers

Round 13
Wolgast, Winner by KO

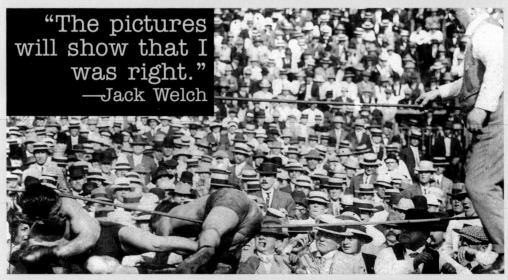

"The pictures will show that I was right."
—Jack Welch

Welch claimed that Rivers did not land a blow to Wolgast (left); rather, he believed the champion tripped over Rivers's feet.

LONG SHOT

LEW

Y ou couldn't blame Chandler Harper for thinking he had the 1953 world professional golf tournament at Tam-O'-Shanter in Chicago wrapped up after his final round 70 gave him a 72-hole score of 279, nine under par.

You couldn't have blamed him for thinking how he would spend the winner's $25,000 that constituted golf's richest prize at the time. He'd played well, and only Lew Worsham had any sort of shot at catching him. But was it a realistic shot? Worsham would have to get birdies on the final two holes in order to tie. While that was possible, it constituted a long shot by any realist's definition. Also, Worsham hadn't had a great history at this course: the year before he'd taken the lead into the final nine and lost. Still, he was the 1947 U.S. Open champion.

Two birdies to tie. Worsham got his first birdie on the 17th hole with a seven-foot putt. Now came the 410-yard final hole. Worsham's drive sailed far down the fairway, drawing an oooh from the crowd that surged around him.

The ball lay 140 yards from the cup of the par-4 hole.

Worsham picked out his wedge and laid into the ball. It flew toward the green, and as the crowd drew in a collective breath, the ball covered some 30 feet on three bounces ... before, shockingly, it rolled into the cup. Forget the tie.

Worsham's eagle on the final hole at Tam-O'-Shanter had usurped Harper's moment. Victory belonged to Worsham with a 68 for the round and 278, 10 under par, for the tournament. Of that 140-yard shot, the Associated Press would note: "Old-timers agreed that Worsham's wedge shot must rank with the greatest of tournament finishes."

Said Worsham, "It was the luckiest shot I ever had in my life. I'm sorry I had to do it to my friend Harper."

Men's Pro				
Lew Worsham	65	72	73	68-278
Chandler Harper	69	69	71	70-279
Al Besselink	69	70	70	72-281
Cary Middlecoff	70	70	73	69-282
Jim Ferrier	72	70	70	70-282
Freddie Haas	68	71	72	71-282
Lloyd Mangrum	72	71	70	70-283
Dave Douglas	72	65	72	74-283
Jimmy Demaret	70	70	72	72-284
Doug Ford	70	72	67	75-284

> "The son of a bitch holed it."
> —Jimmy Demaret, on national television

Lew Worsham (second from left) accepts his prize, along with (from left) Frank Stranahan, men's amateur winner; Patty Berg, women's pro; and Wiffi Smith, women's amateur champion.

THE PASSED BALL

By 1941, the Brooklyn Dodgers had been the symbol of ineptitude on the baseball diamond for more than 20 years. The last time the Dodgers had won a pennant was in 1920, a quick taste of success followed by a record of unmitigated failure—two seventh-place finishes in the eight-team National League; and 10 sixth places, including five in succession from 1925 through 1929.

No wonder over the years a Brooklyn fan known as Abie the Truck Driver would abuse the players by shouting "youse bums" as the team bumbled its way through still another loss. Pretty soon "Dem Bums" became a sort of affectionate tag for the hapless Dodgers, who seemed to do their best to live up to their image.

But by '41, with the war coming closer, the Dodgers' creative front office man, Larry MacPhail, had assembled a ball club that made die-hard Brooklyn fans glow. The offense was sparked by powerfully-built first baseman Dolph Camilli, who led the league in home runs with 34 and in RBIs with 120, and by outfielder Pete Reiser, who led the league in batting (.343), doubles (39) and triples (17). The pitching staff was led by Whitlow Wyatt and Kirby Higbe, both 22-game winners, and ably handled by catcher Mickey Owen, who made only three errors all season. These Dodgers could play. In a season that saw Joe DiMaggio hit safely in 56 straight games and Ted Williams lead the American League in batting with a .406 average, a Brooklyn team at last had emerged that could do battle. The Dodgers won the NL pennant, then rumbled with the Yankees in the World Series.

By Game 4, at Ebbets Field, the Dodgers were on the verge of tying the series at two games apiece. The Bums led 4–3 going into the ninth. When Brooklyn's ace reliever, Hugh Casey, retired Johnny Sturm and Red Rolfe on infielder grounders, Dodgers fans got ready to celebrate as the Yankees' Tommy Henrich—the potential final out—came to bat.

Casey worked the count on Henrich to 3 and 2. Owen called for a curve. Casey had a great curve and Heinrich had trouble hitting the curve, period. The pitch broke in sharply, exactly as it was supposed to. Henrich—nicknamed "Old Reliable"—tried but failed to check his swing. Strike three. Ball game. "Old Reliable" finally missed one, right?

Not quite. The curve was so good that even though Owen knew the curve was coming, the ball bounced off the tip of his catcher's mitt and rolled toward the the first base line. Henrich reached first base safely on the passed ball. The delicate balance of momentum tumbled to the

New York Yankees 7, Brooklyn Dodgers 4

New York	AB	R	H	RBI	Brooklyn	AB	R	H	RBI
Sturm, 1b	5	0	2	2	Reese, ss	5	0	0	0
Rolfe, 3b	5	1	2	0	Walker, rf	5	1	2	0
Henrich, rf	4	1	0	0	Reiser, cf	5	1	2	2
DiMaggio, cf	4	1	2	0	Camilli, 1b	4	0	2	0
Keller, lf	5	1	4	3	Riggs, 3b	3	0	0	0
Dickey, c	2	2	0	0	Medwick, lf	2	0	0	0
Gordon, 2b	5	1	2	2	Allen, p	0	0	0	0
Rizzuto, ss	4	0	0	0	Casey, p	2	0	1	0
Donald, p	2	0	0	0	Owen, c	2	1	0	0
Breuer, p	1	0	0	0	Coscarart, 2b	3	1	0	0
a Selkirk	1	0	0	0	Higbe, p	1	0	1	0
Murphy, p	1	0	0	0	French, p	0	0	0	0
Total	39	7	12	7	Wasdell, lf	3	0	1	2
					Total	35	4	9	4

a Batted for Breuer in eighth.

New York Yankees	1	0	0	2	0	0	0	0	4	—7
Brooklyn Dodgers	0	0	0	2	2	0	0	0	0	—4

"I should have had the ball."

—Mickey Owen

Tommy Henrich sprints to first as Owen chases after the passed ball.

Yankees' side. Before you could say "Dem Bums", DiMaggio singled and Charlie (King Kong) Keller doubled both runners in and sure-fire victory for Brooklyn turned to a most bitter defeat. Instead of the series being tied, the Yankees led it three games to one. The Bronx Bombers wrapped up the series the next day, winning 3-1 behind pitcher Ernie Bonham.

Wrote sports columnist Red Smith: "Nowhere else in this broad, untidy universe, not in Bedlam nor in Babel nor in the remotest psychopathic ward ... only in the ancestral home of the Dodgers ... could a man win a World Series game by striking out."

And so began the Brooklyn Dodgers' bittersweet run into the heart of baseball history; always one game, one run, one pitch away from glory.

Owen went on to play for the Cubs and the Red Sox, after four more seasons in Brooklyn.

Connie Carpenter

BIG WHEELS
TURNING

It would be the first time women had competed in an Olympic cycling event.

The race for the gold on this hot July day in 1984 would be 79.2 kilometers (49.2 miles) of spinning wheels over a hilly and tortuous Mission Viejo, Calif., road course.

The two favorites were American women—Rebecca Twigg, a 21-year-old biology student at the University of Washington, and Connie Carpenter, a 27-year-old former Olympic speed skater who had competed at the 1972 Winter Games and then given up skating to become a competitive cyclist.

The transition had been virtually seamless. By the time the '84 Games arrived, Carpenter—who was married to Davis Phinney, an Olympic cyclist too—had won a record 12 national cycling championships. She came to these Los Angeles Games, vowing that this would be her last race.

While the press had made it seem as if Carpenter and Twigg were enemies, both women claimed that that was merely tabloid fiction. They were competitive rivals and nothing more than that.

But that was enough, to generate excitement in the women's race: two Americans going for gold. Along the course, the locals had set up folding chairs and raised up signs saying "Pedal 4 a Medal" and "Go for the Gold."

The race evolved into a six-woman pack that included the

"I threw my bike at the end."
—Connie Carpenter

two Americans, along with Sandra Schumacher of West Germany, Unni Larsen of Norway, Maria Canins of Italy and Jeannie Longo of France.

But when the race came down to the final 200 meters, it was Carpenter in pursuit of Twigg, and closing fast. Still, at 100 meters Twigg held the lead. Carpenter kept coming.

As they raced to the finish line, Carpenter threw her bike, in a manner reminiscent of children playfully shooting over a curb.

"In a close sprint, you can push your bike with your body, move it a foot forward" explained Carpenter. "It's like leaning into the tape for a runner, a calculated move. It was a shot I could only take one time."

Her shot paid off. Carpenter had nipped Twigg at the wire and won the gold medal.

"Everything I have done this last year was cool and calculated for this race, to ride the best race of my life," said Carpenter. "This is it, the last bike race of my life."

The last ... and the best. A solid-gold performance.

Carpenter's gold medal was America's first cycling medal since 1912.

Connie Carpenter tucked her head down and drove to the finish to beat fellow American Rebecca Twigg.

Women's Cycling Road Race

1	Connie Carpenter-Phinney	USA	2:11:14.0
2	Rebecca Twigg	USA	2:11:14.0
3	Sandra Schumacher	GER	2:11:14.0
4	Unni Larsen	NOR	2:11:14.0
5	Maria Canins	ITA	2:11:14.0
6	Jeannie Longo	FRA	2:12:35.0
7	Helle Sörenson	DEN	2:13:28.0
8	Ute Enzenauer	GER	2:13:28.0

ICING A GAME IN SUDDEN DEATH

The partisan Red Wings' crowd of 15,791 that was jammed into the Olympia in Detroit had been waiting half the night, it seemed, for the local team to bust out.

Down 1–0 and despite a lineup boasting Gordie Howe, considered by some to be the greatest hockey player ever, the Red Wings could not dent the net through most of the first two periods of this crucial Game 7 of the 1954 Stanley Cup finals against the defending champion Montreal Canadiens, powered by greats Bernie (Boom Boom) Geoffrion and Maurice Richard.

That changed when, with 1:17 left in the second period and Montreal's Paul Masnick off for hooking, Howe's line-mate, rough and tumble Ted Lindsay, found Detroit defenseman Red Kelly alone to the left of the Montreal goal. Kelly took the pass and fired a low 15-footer past Montreal goalie Gerry McNeil to tie the game at 1.

From that moment on, both teams fought furiously to get the go-ahead goal.

Montreal had a great opportunity on a Gaye Stewart breakaway. But Detroit's formidable Hall of Fame goalie, Terry Sawchuck, stopped that shot, and several others.

The third period wound down, the tension mounting as both McNeil and Sawchuck proved inpenetrable despite the strenuous efforts of both teams to get the puck past them.

At the 16-minute mark of the third period, Richard threw a scare into the crowd when he put the puck past Sawchuck. But referee Bill Chadwick disallowed the goal, claiming that Richard had picked up the loose puck and thrown it into the net—a rules infraction.

That was as close as either team came in regulation play. The game would go to overtime.

Four minutes and 29 seconds into that overtime, Tony Leswick, who generally restricted himself to checking high-scoring opponents, saw a standard play turn into victory. Montreal defenseman Doug Harvey tried to clear the puck from behind

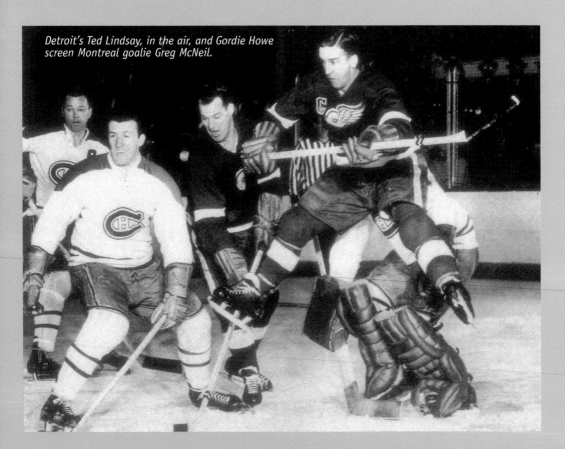

Detroit's Ted Lindsay, in the air, and Gordie Howe screen Montreal goalie Greg McNeil.

the Montreal net, but the shot hit off Detroit's Glen Skov and landed in front of Leswick 40 feet out. Leswick waited until Skov skated out front of goalie McNeil, screening the shot Leswick now lifted casually towards the net. As Leswick turned to change lines, never thinking the shot had a chance, the puck deflected off Doug Harvey's glove, then over McNeil's shoulder and into the net for a goal.

The home crowd erupted but the Canadiens left the ice, ignoring the traditional series-ending handshake. Only former Red Wing Gaye Stewart stayed behind to congratulate the Wings. The Stanley Cup was going back to Detroit for the sixth time in the team's history.

Doug Harvey made the NHL first All-Star team 10 times in his long career.

> ## "It's like the end of the world."
> —Gerry McNeil

Detroit Red Wings 2
Montreal Canadiens 1

Montreal	1	0	0	0—1
Detroit	0	1	0	1—2

First Period: 1) MTL Curry 4 (Masnick) 9:17
Penalties- Harvey MTL (holding) 14:20; Skov DET (hooking) 17:11

Second Period: 2) DET Kelly 5 (Lindsay, Delvecchio) PPG 1:17
Penalties- Masnick MTL (hooking) :20

Third Period: No Scoring
Penalties- None

First Overtime Period: 3) DET Leswick 3 (Skov) 4:29
Penalties- None

Goalies: Montreal-McNeil; Detroit-Sawchuk

IT'S A FAKE

N o American had won the Olympic marathon since 1908.

And though 24-year-old Frank Shorter was considered a strong candidate to break the marathon hex at the '72 Games in Munich, the Yale graduate had more on his mind than this 26 mile, 385 yard race.

In the days preceding the marathon competition, Arab terrorists had murdered Israeli athletes, creating an atmosphere of fear and paranoia. Shorter was not without his own concerns.

He had told teammate Kenny Moore, "Do you realize how easily we could get shot out there?"

But come start time for the marathon, the Munich-born Shorter was front and center, ready to run for the U.S. team. More ready, it turned out, than the rest of the field.

Where rivals like Karel Lismont of Belgium and the 1968 marathon winner, Mamo Wolde of Ethiopia, seemed satisfied to accept the slow pace of the race, Shorter was not. He was determined not to let the pace drag, for a slower pace would favor runners with a stronger finishing kick than his, such as Wolde.

So at the 10-mile mark Shorter accelerated the pace. The strategy worked. He began to distance himself from the rest of the pack. Steadily, he held to that quickened pace, leaving his competition more than two minutes behind him as he entered the stadium in Munich, hellbent on the finish line and fully expecting to hear the approving roar of the crowd.

But no ... what he heard instead were boos and whistles, raucous disapproval. Shorter looked nervously around, wondering what was happening.

Viewers at home knew the answer. While all reports had

Shorter leading the race, another person, a man wearing the number 72, came running into the Olympic stadium posing as the race leader. Those watching ABC's coverage heard announcer Erich Segal, Shorter's friend and author of *Love Story*, yell over and over, "It's a fake! It's a fake!"

The imposter was on the backstretch when Shorter entered the stadium to the boos and whistles. Once the fake was hustled out of the stadium by security men, a puzzled Shorter finally began to hear the cheers—cheers for his gold medal time of 2:12:19.8.

Marathon

1. Frank Shorter	USA	2:12:19.8
2. Karel Lismont	BEL	2:14:31.8
3. Mamo Wolde	ETH	2:15:08.4
4. Kenneth Moore	USA	2:15:39.8
5. Kenji Kimihara	JPN	2:16:27.0
6. Ronald Hill	GBR	2:16:30.6
7. Donald Macgregor	GBR	2:16:34.4
8. Jack Foster	NZE	2:16:56.2

In the wake of the horrors of the Munich Olympics, Shorter was concerned to hear boos as he entered the stadium.

Shorter maintained a healthy lead through much of the race.

"I'm scared."
—Frank Shorter

THE
HOLY ROLLER

In the final seconds of the game—the San Diego Chargers versus the Oakland Raiders on Sept. 10, 1978—on a play that started from the San Diego 14, Raiders quarterback Ken (Snake) Stabler found himself under pressure from the Chargers' defense. Unable to spot an open receiver, and caught in the grasp of San Diego's Woody Lowe, he intentionally fumbled the ball forward.

At least he later said it was intentional.

An Associated Press report of the play said it was "knocked loose and bounced towards the end zone, with players from both sides scrambling to pick it up."

By NFL rules, an intentional forward fumble is to be treated as a forward pass. In other words, that forward fumble ought to have been ruled an incomplete pass since it hit the ground without being caught.

But no call was made by the officials.

Instead, Raiders running back Pete Banaszak tried to scoop up the ball and, failing to find a handle, propelled the ball towards the goal line.

The ball struck the foot of Oakland's tight end Dave Casper and bounced into the end zone. Casper dove on the ball to give the Raiders the touchdown as time expired. Errol Mann then kicked the extra point to give Oakland the victory, 21–20.

And that's how the outcome went into the record books.

But ... it was a touchdown that, on review, never should have happened.

To begin with, when Stabler intentionally fumbled forward, the ball should have been declared dead. Banaszak later said that, seeing his chance of advancing the ball was hopeless because of the wave of Chargers defenders coming at him, he deliberately batted it towards the goal line. What Banaszak did was—according to NFL Rule 12, Section 2, Article 17, subsection a: "A player may not bat or punch a loose ball [in the field of play] towards the opponent's goal line"—illegal.

As for Casper, he admitted that he nudged the ball into the end zone with his foot. This revelation prompted the NFL competition committee which met after the '78 season to reiterate that an intentional fumble must be treated like a forward pass and to add a supplemental note under Rule 8, Section 4, Article 2: "After the two-minute warning, on any fumble that occurs during a down (including a PAT), the fumbled ball may only be advanced by the offensive player who fumbled the ball, or by any member of the defensive team."

The regulation became known, appropriately, as the Raiders' fumble rule, but this unlikely Oakland victory still stands.

Oakland Raiders 21
San Diego Chargers 20

Oakland	0	7	0	14—21
San Diego	0	13	0	7—20

SD	Curran 14 pass from Fouts (Benirschke kick)
Oak	Casper 6 pass from Stabler (Mann kick)
SD	Bauer 1 run (kick failed)
SD	Bauer 2 run (Benirschke kick)
Oak	Bradshaw 44 pass from Stabler (Mann kick)
Oak	Casper recovered fumble in end zone (Mann kick)

Attendance 51,653

Statistics of the Game

	Raiders	Chargers
First downs	17	24
Rushes yards	18-84	53-197
Passing yards	270	175
Return yards	107	156
Passes	15-35-3	17-29-0
Punts	7-44	9-37
Fumbles lost	3-1	0-0
Penalties yards	4-36	6-55

1 Raiders quarterback Ken Stabler has fumbled the ball forward and tight end Dave Casper (87) veers towards the loose ball.

2 Casper scoops the ball up, then shoves it into the end zone.

3 Casper then falls on top of the ball in the end zone for the tying touchdown.

"I fumbled it on purpose. Yes, I was trying to fumble."
—Ken Stabler

AND THE BAND PLAYED ON

Stanford University had battled back from a 10–0 halftime deficit against the University of California at Berkeley on Nov. 20, 1982 to take the lead at 14–10 on two touchdown passes by future Denver Bronco's great John Elway. Like all Stanford-Cal games, the taste to win went deeper than usual this afternoon. These two Bay Area schools looked forward to the game for the Axe, their annual football meeting, all year long. This season, the two rivals would not let the game end.

California regained the lead in the third quarter, so the Stanford Cardinals had to rally again, late in the fourth. That's when Mark Harmon booted a 35-yard field goal with a scant four seconds left to give Stanford a 20–19 lead.

When Stanford drew a 15-yard unsportsmanlike conduct penalty on the go-ahead score, it was obliged to kick off from its own 25.

That set up one of the strangest finishes in college football.

As Harmon's squib kick rolled downfield, the Stanford marching band began to edge onto the field. It should be noted that the Stanford band has been known historically as something of a behavior problem. Unlike other big schools' marching bands, happy to play medleys of showtunes as they form shapes, the Stanford marching band expresses the unique Bay Area combination of individuality and smarts with an offbeat and at times controversial selection of music. If a marching band was ever going to get into the action, it was Stanford's.

Meanwhile, Kevin (Moon Dog) Moen fielded the ball at his 43 and took off running. Confronted by a Cardinal tackler, he lateraled the football to Richard Rodgers who lateraled to Dwight Garner at the Stanford 44.

Garner was hit by three tacklers but as he went down he managed to lateral the ball again, this time back to Rodgers at the Stanford 48. Rodgers proceeded to lateral the ball to Mariet Ford at the Cardinal 46 yard line..

Ford raced downfield but, trapped at the 25, flipped the ball over his shoulder on the chance that a nearby teammate might grab it.

As luck would have it, Moen materialized and caught the random toss. By now, though, the Stanford band had tramped onto the field, creating an obstacle course for Moon Dog.

But the Dog was up to it. He navigated past saxophones and tubas, into the end zone, where he mowed down a slow-moving trombone player. A perfect finish to a screwball sequence that gave Cal coach Joe Kapp a 25–20 victory and the coveted Axe.

Stanford did not go down quietly though. Most players believed that Dwight Garner, the third Cal player to field the ball, was actually taken down at midfield. Said Gordy Ceresino, Stanford's T.V. announcer, 'The question wasn't really so much whether his knee touched, although it looked like it did, but his lack of momentum. There were five guys pushing him back. He was stopped."

In fact, Stanford band manager John Howard claimed that the reason the band went out onto the field was that many had seen Garner's knee touch the ground.

Still, Stanford lost their bid to a Bowl game, John Elway despite setting NCAA records for pass attempts in a career and Pac-ten single season marks for passing yards, completions and pass attempts, was especially bitter afterwards. "It's something I'll have to live with the rest of my life" he said. Two Super Bowls later, the sting may be gone but John Elway has surely not forgotten the Game.

Confusion reigned as Cal players react with joy amid the Stanford band that had drifted onto the field during this amazing play.

> "This was an insult to college football. They ruined my last game as a college football player."
>
> —John Elway

California 25, Stanford 20

Stanford	0	0	14	6—20
California	0	10	0	15—25

CAL   Cooper FG 30
CAL   Ford 29 pass from Gilbert (Cooper kick)
S   White 2 pass from Elway (Harmon kick)
S   White 43 pass from Elway (Harmon kick)
CAL   Cooper FG 35
CAL   Howell 32 pass from Gilbert (pass failed)
S   Harmon FG 22
S   Harmon FG 35
CAL   Moen 57 kickoff return (no PAT attempt)

Statistics of the Game

	Cal	Stanford
First Downs	19	21
Rushing (TCB/Net Yds.)	42-163	34-95
Passing (PA/PC/HI)	31-17-0	39-25-0
Passing Yards	289	330
Total Offensive Plays	73	73
Total Offensive Yards	452	425
Punts/Average	8-44.8	9-39.0
Penalties/Yards	7-60	8-60
Fumbles/Lost	2-0	1-1

Courage is basic to sports; it takes guts to perform in front of thousands of people and millions of viewers, to get hit by tacklers or a pair of gloved fists, to stand in against a 98-mph fastball, to dive from a 10-meter platform. Add injury or adversity and you've got the makings for a Fat Lady moment. When Greg Louganis slams his head into a diving board, then comes back the next night to nail a gold medal—that's more than just courage, that's Fat Lady courage. When Willis Reed limps onto the court for Game 7 of the NBA Finals with an injured knee, or Ben Crenshaw fights his fear to win the Masters, or Tenley Albright skates in the Olympics with stitches in her ankle, the Fat Lady knows better than to count them out.

Chapter 9
COURAGEOUS FINISHES

LOUGANIS'S COMEBACK

He was the master diver, who had won 19 consecutive international springboard competitions between 1982 and 1987.

Nobody dominated men's diving like Greg Louganis did.

While he was expected to be challenged at the 1988 Seoul Olympics by China's Tan Liangde—who had studied tapes of Louganis for six years—Louganis was regarded as one of the U.S.'s surest gold-medal bets.

So it was a shocking moment when, on his ninth dive in the preliminary round— a reverse two and a half somersaults in the pike position—Louganis did the unthinkable. He blew his dive by hitting his head on the board and falling awkwardly into the water.

It was, as *Sports Illustrated* writer Craig Neff wrote, "... as if

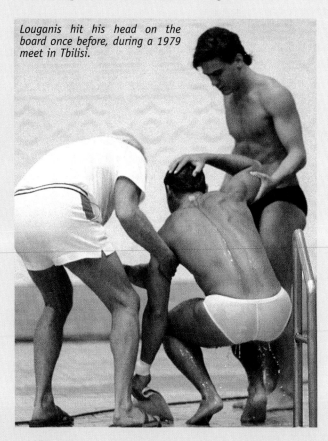

Louganis hit his head on the board once before, during a 1979 meet in Tbilisi.

Baryshnikov had fallen off the stage or Rodin had slipped with his chisel and *The Thinker*'s chin had plopped into his lap."

Louganis emerged from the pool with a gash on his head that would require four temporary sutures, which were later replaced with five stitches covered by a waterproof patch.

Worse, however, was the obstacle his misstep now presented to the athlete's psyche. Could Louganis rebound from the unfortunate mistake, or would it shoot his confidence to smithereens? Also Louganis was HIV positive at the time. He knew, but no one else did. He had additional concerns about bleeding in the pool.

Two dives later Louganis had managed to qualify for the finals. And while those dives helped bolster him, it was no guarantee that the bloody miscalculation would not somehow linger in his mind, creating pressure that would undermine him the next day in the men's diving finals at Chamshil Indoor Swimming Pool.

By Olympic regulations, the qualifying scores have no bearing on the finals. The divers all start anew.

On the day of the finals, while Louganis would concede that his pride hurt more than his head, it did not trouble his performance. He led Tan by almost 20 points when it came time for that same reverse two and a half in Round 9.

The crowd tensed as Louganis stepped onto the board. This time he made sure to spring away from the board, and the dive was good enough to generate scores between 8.0 and 9.0 and to bring a roar from the crowd.

In the end, the gold was his. He had shaken off the doubts that could have stolen his confidence, and had performed.

"We must all learn from Louganis's grit and determination," said Chinese coach Xu Yiming. "In adversity he was able to rise up and win the championship. We must emulate this kind of spirit. I am personally humbled."

Greg Louganis as he hit his head during a reverse two and a half somersault. In 1983 Sergei Shalibashvili of the Soviet Union died after hitting his head during a platrform dive, and Nathan Meade of Australia did the same in 1987.

"I think my pride was hurt more than anything."

—Greg Louganis

Springboard Diving

1.Greg Louganis	USA	730.80
2.Tan Liangde	CHN	704.88
3.Li Deliang	CHN	665.28
4.Albin Killat	GER	661.47
5.Mark Bradshaw	USA	642.99
6.Jorge Mondragon	MEX	616.02
7.Jesús Mena	MEX	598.77
8.Edwin Jongejans	HOL	588.33

DEVERS' ROAD TO GOLD

In 1988 she had been a rising star among American sprinters, long jumpers and hurdlers, good enough to make the Olympic team as a hurdler. And though she did not qualify for the finals in Seoul, tripping on the last hurdle and stumbling just before the finish line in her heat, her best years as an athlete appeared to be ahead of her.

Then Gail Devers' world came apart.

Suddenly her health deteriorated.

"I lost weight, strength and memory," Devers said. "I had terrible migraine headaches. I had involuntary shakes. Convulsions. And I lost a lot of blood."

Over the next two and a half years, one doctor after another—13 in all—would examine her and fail to find the source of her failing health.

But then her physical therapist noticed her eyes were bulging and wondered whether the cause of her problem

Gail Devers had set the American record in 1988 for the 100-meter hurdles, before she was diagnosed with Graves disease.

might be Graves' disease, the hyperthyroid condition that can be controlled with medication.

The problem for Devers was that the medication, a beta blocker, was banned for Olympic athletes. So Devers chose to undergo radiation treatments instead ... with disastrous effect.

"My feet were swollen and oozing yellow fluid," Devers recalled. "I had little holes all over my skin."

Her condition worsened to the point where her parents moved in with her so they could carry her to the bathroom. In March 1991, one doctor warned that if she continued walking on her plagued feet, they might have to be amputated.

Then, suddenly—the light at the end of the tunnel. A diagnosis that the radiation was the problem proved correct. Within a month, Devers had changed therapies and was back on the UCLA track, slowly working her way into shape for the 1992 Barcelona Olympics.

Her long road back would lead her to the starting blocks of the 100-meter finals.

At the starter's gun, Devers and Irina Privalova of Russia had the early jump. But as they pounded down the straightaway, the field came together—Devers, Privalova, Juliet Cuthbert and Merlene Ottey of Jamaica and Gwen Torrence of the U.S.A.—all driving hard for the finish line.

As the five women crossed that line, it was impossible for the naked eye to distinguish a winner—that was how close they were. Indeed, it was the closest women's 100 meters since automatic timing was introduced in 1972. The first five runners had finished within .06 of a second of one another, and now they stood, staring up at the stadium scoreboard to see which of them the electric eye would determine had finished first.

Suddenly, the photograhers were rushing to Devers and the officials were saying yes, yes, yes.

A little more than a year after nearly having her feet amputated, Gail Devers had won the gold in Barcelona.

From the top, Devers, Cuthbert, Ottey, Torrence, Privalova

"The last two years of my life have definitely been a miracle."
—Gail Devers

Women's 100 Meters

1	Gail Devers	Palmdale, Calif.	10.82
2	Juliet Cuthbert	Jamaica	10.83
3	Irina Privalova	Unified Team	10.84
4	Gwen Torrence	Decatur, Ga.	10.86
5	Merlene Ottey	Jamaica	10.88
6	Anelia Dultcheva Nuneva	Bulgaria	11.10
7	Mary Onyali	Nigeria	11.15
8	Liliana Allen Doll	Cuba	11.19

THE GIPPER WINS ONE

Knute Rockne's Notre Dame team was undefeated and being touted as the best college squad in the nation when it traveled to Indianapolis to play Indiana on Nov. 13, 1920.

For most fans crowding into Washington Park that day, the main attraction was the Irish's halfback, George Gipp.

Gipp was a triple threat as a swivel-hipped runner, a deadly-accurate passer and a strong-legged drop kicker. He was also a bit of a rebel, given to drinking and gambling. In fact, for the Indiana game, Gipp had placed a $100 bet on Notre Dame with a bookie.

Gipp was a good enough player, however, to be accorded the respect of the elite eastern football writers. Walter Camp listed him among a group of elite players while the New York Herald said that Gipp was the best back in the land.

Gipp's wager looked very shaky through three quarters as Chick Mathys and the rest of Indiana's upstart team shocked the Irish by dominating them while taking a 10-0 lead. The Hoosiers also beat up on Gipp, driving him from the game in the first quarter with a separated shoulder and a bloody nose and mouth.

It seemed as if Notre Dame's dream of a championship season was crashing to the ground.

If you're looking for the moment when the legend of Notre Dame football began, this is it. Knute Rockne's rough and inspiring coaching—the dreaded Four Horsemen on the offensive line, the line of greats that continued through Joe Montana and Touchdown Jesus across from the stadium in South Bend—this is the first of all those echoes that wakes when the fight song plays.

The Irish fought back. Behind substitute Johnny Mohardt, Notre Dame made it to the one-yard line in the final quarter, then the drive stalled. Rockne called on the injured Gipp. With his shoulder heavily taped, the Gipper crashed into the line for no gain. On the fourth down, he tried it again and slammed into the end zone. Gipp then kicked the extra point. Notre Dame trailed 10-7. Gipp kicked off and reinjured his shoulder when he was in on the tackle, forcing him out of the game once again. But in the final minutes, Gipp re-entered the game and hit Hunk Anderson with a pass at the one. Then, with Gipp acting as a decoy, Joe Brandy kept the ball and went in for the score. Gipp missed the conversion, but his courageous play had inspired an Irish comeback, 13-10.

Four weeks later, George Gipp died after contracting a bad cold during the Northwestern game. Legend has it that before he passed away he told Rockne that someday when the Irish had their back against the wall, he should ask them "to win one for the Gipper," a legend that found immortality as part of the film *Knute Rockne—All-American*. George Gipp, the gambling, boozing hero of the Irish, is played, of course, by future president Ronald Reagan.

Notre Dame 13, Indiana 10

Notre Dame	0	0	0	13—13
Indiana	0	3	7	0—10

Notre Dame		Indiana
Kiley	L.E.	Bell
Coughlin	L.T.	Risley
H. Anderson	L.G.	McGaw
Larson	C.	Pierce
Smith	R.G.	Muriby
Shaw	R.T.	Leonard
E. Anderson	R.E.	Haney
Brandy	O.B.	Mathys
Gipp	L.H.B.	Thomas
Mohardt	R.H.B.	Minton
Wynne	F.B.	Kyle

Touchdowns: Notre Dame, Gipp, Brandy; Indiana, Haney.
Goals from touchdowns: Notre Dame, Gipp; Indiana, Risley.
Field goal: Risley

"Win one for the Gipper."
—George Gipp

Despite the colorful and less than exemplary reality of George Gipp's life, he has come to represent the Notre Dame ideal.

In 13 years at Notre Dame, Knute Rockne coached the Fighting Irish to 105 victories and three national championships.

1970 NBA Finals—Game Seven
New York Knicks vs. Los Angeles Lakers

May 8, 1970

THE GREATEST
REBOUND EVER

When the New York Knicks' Willis Reed fell to the floor, trying to drive past Wilt Chamberlain at 3:56 of the first quarter of Game 5 of the 1970 NBA Finals, New York's chances of winning its first-ever pro basketball title appeared to be shot.

Reed celebrates after winning the NBA title. He would later become the general manager of the New Jersey Nets.

For without the Cap'n, as his teammates called the 6'10", 235-pound Reed, the Knicks would be hard-pressed to challenge a Los Angeles Lakers team loaded with stars like Chamberlain, Jerry West and Elgin Baylor. And as Reed winced in pain while being helped from the court, he appeared to be finished for the season. In a city that liked to believe the city game was its property, the disappointment hit hard.

When the Knicks lost Reed that night—he had severely strained muscles in his thigh—they were obliged to improvise a game plan against a now physically-superior Lakers team in a series that was tied at two games apiece.

At halftime, New York's Bill Bradley, Princeton graduate and later senator from New Jersey, suggested to coach Red Holzman a 1-3-1 offense that college teams used against zones. The virtue of the 1-3-1 was that its back man, designated as the "rover," would force Chamberlain away from the basket. Should Chamberlain choose not to go outside, he left the rover, Dave DeBusschere, with an open shot. The rest of the game plan featured intensified, double-teaming defense.

The plan worked. Trailing 53–40 at the half, New York rallied, urged on by a frenzied Madison Square Garden crowd. The building shook as the Knicks won 107–100 to take a 3-2 series lead.

But back in Los Angeles, the Lakers won the next game 135-113 as the Knicks struggled without Reed.

The teams returned to New York for the final game. For Knicks fans, the crucial question was whether Reed's injury would respond to hours of whirlpool, hot packs, massages and ultrasound and be able to play.

The answer came as the teams warmed up. No sign of Reed during the layup drills. Then suddenly the crowd stirred as the Cap'n—freshly injected with a shot of cortisone, an anti-inflammatory agent, and a shot of Carbocaine, a painkiller—made his way to the court. The crowd roared as he limped onto the floor, even the Lakers paused in their warmups to watch Reed hoist up a few practice shots.

When a gimpy Reed hit the first basket of the game, from behind the key, and another jumper from 20 feet on the right side, the crowd went crazy. The Cap'n had delivered an electric jolt of inspiration. Reed came out after a few minutes and his teammates took it from there. The Knicks dominated the Lakers 113–99 in a championship victory that would forever be remembered for Reed's courage.

Though Chamberlain was the superior center, Reed brought a kind of leadership and intensity to the Knicks that took them all the way.

New York Knicks 113, L.A. Lakers 99

New York	min	fgm	fga	ftm	fta	r	a	pf	pts
Barnett	42	9	20	3	3	0	2	4	21
Bowman	21	3	5	0	1	5	0	5	6
Bradley	42	8	18	1	1	4	5	3	17
DeBusschere	37	8	15	2	2	17	1	1	18
Frazier	44	12	17	12	12	7	19	3	36
Reed	27	2	5	0	0	3	1	4	4
Riordan	10	2	3	1	2	2	1	2	5
Russell	6	1	4	0	0	3	0	0	2
Stallworth	11	1	5	2	2	2	1	3	4
Total	240	46	92	21	23	43	30	25	113

Los Angeles	min	fgm	fga	ftm	fta	r	a	pf	pts
Baylor	36	9	17	1	2	5	1	2	19
Chamberlain	48	10	16	1	11	24	4	1	21
Egan	11	0	2	0	0	0	0	2	0
Erickson	36	5	10	4	6	6	6	3	14
Garrett	34	3	10	2	2	4	1	4	8
Hairston	15	2	5	2	2	2	0	1	6
Iresvant	12	0	4	3	3	2	0	2	3
West	48	9	19	10	12	6	5	4	28
Total	240	38	83	23	38	49	17	19	99

Knicks	38	31	25	19—	113
Los Angeles	24	18	27	30—	99

"He ain't hurt."
—Walt Frazier

A STITCH IN TIME

As the 11-year-old daughter of a Newton Center, Mass., surgeon, Tenley Albright had been stricken by a mild strain of polio which weakened her muscles but did not cause paralysis.

Until then Tenley had skated every winter on a backyard rink that her father, Hollis, created by flooding the area, and done so with a rather casual attitude. But when doctors recommended that she use the backyard rink to rebuild her muscles, something about figure skating clicked for Tenley and she began to practice in earnest.

Albright waves as silver medalist Carol Heiss of the U.S. (left), and Austrian Ingrid Wendl, the bronze medalist look on.

Junior and national titles followed. And at the 1952 Winter Olympics in Oslo, at the age of 16, she won a silver medal, finishing behind Jeanette Altwegg of Great Britain.

Four years later, when Albright—by then a premed student at Radcliff College and twice a world champion—

geared up for the Cortina d' Ampezzo Olympics, she and another American, a 16-year-old rising star named Carol Heiss, were the class of the field. With Heiss in the competition, Albright knew she would have to be in top form.

But the challenge would intensify when, two weeks before the Olympics, Albright stumbled over a rut in the ice during a practice session. Her left skate slashed into her right ankle, cutting to the bone. The damage incurred would severely limit her in her practice sessions as it stubbornly refused to heal. Her father, now a surgeon in Boston, came to Italy to tend to her injury.

"I'm not letting her do any jumps yet," he said before the finals, "And of course with all that tape on her ankle she doesn't have the flexibility she needs."

When it came time for the figure skating event at Cortina d' Ampezzo, Tenley proved that toughness bolstered her charming exterior. On her double loop jump, Albright appeared to flinch when she landed but, after an instant's hesitation, she resumed her routine and dazzled the crowd at the Olympic ice stadium, whose wooden bleachers were packed when she appeared.

Dressed in a dark-rose wool sweater, with red flowers in her straight blonde hair, she skated flawlessly. As Fred Tupper would write in *The New York Times*: "The tempo quickened and Tenley was all out, flying into a double toe loop and a cross-foot spin. She spun up, whirling to the finish, and the spectators let out a long roar."

The judges turned out to be just as enthusiastic. By the final count, Albright had 169.67 points, beating out Heiss's total of 168.02.

Bad ankle or not, Tenley Albright was good as gold, thanks to the careful attention of her father and her own courage. Albright retired from skating the next year to complete her studies and became an esteemed surgeon, just like her father.

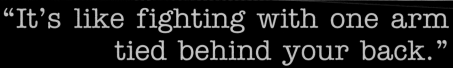

"It's like fighting with one arm
tied behind your back."
—Tenley Albright

Women's Figure Skating

Pl.	Pts.	Judging Pts.
1-Tenley Albright, Newton Center, Mass	13	169.6
2-Carol Heiss, Ozone Park, N.Y.	20	168.1
3-Ingrid Wendl, Austria	40	159.3
4-Yvonne Sugden, Gt. Britain	52½	158.9
5-Hanna Eigl, Austria	51	157.1
6-Carole Pachl, Canada	70	154.7
7-Hannerl Walter, Austria	85½	153.9
8-Catherine Mahado, Los Angeles	97	153.5
9-Ann Johnston, Canada	94	152.6
10-Rose Pettinger, Germany	104	152

Albright practices despite the bandage on her right ankle.

CHANG AGAINST THE WORLD

Ivan Lendl, the frosty Czech, was at the top of his game in 1989. Ranked No. 1, he looked every bit of that in the 1989 French Open when he took on a 17-year-old American, Michael Chang, in the fourth round.

Cool and seemingly mechanical, Lendl won three French and U.S. Opens, appearing in the finals of the U.S. eight times. He retired in 1994.

The 29-year-old Lendl won the first two sets 6–4, 6–4, and appeared to be a sure bet to move on to the quarterfinals. But the 5'8", 135-pound Chang refused to give in to Lendl. Suddenly he was drawing Lendl into extended volleys from the baseline and outmanuevering him, while showing a mental toughness players that young rarely possess.

As television analyst and former tennis star Tony Trabert said, "Chang is a little bit different from other young players. Too many of them aren't patient and willing to play long points. I think it should be a personal point of pride to be a well-rounded player."

Chang, the son of research chemists who'd emigrated from Taiwan, had that pride ... and more. He took the third set 6–3 and then the fourth set by the same score. But by the end of the fourth set and early into the fifth, Chang had another opponent—intense cramping. Nearly doubled over at times, Chang now had to battle cramps so severe that he was consuming bananas during changeovers for the potassium content and at times moved more like a groggy fighter between rounds than a tennis player between points. The low point may have been when Chang, feeling so assailed by cramps, served underhand to Lendl because he was unable to stretch out his body for the standard overhand serve.

Nonetheless, he battled on against Lendl, endearing himself to the crowd at the Roland Garros Stadium, with his tenacity. "I've never seen a player show such courage on a tennis court," said Trabert.

> ## "I've never seen a player show such courage on a tennis court."
> —Tony Trabert

Chang collapsed in pain after Lendl double-faulted to end the match.

At the end, Chang used a bit of gamesmanship. Standing directly behind the service line to receive Lendl's serve, in order to unnerve his opponent, the unconventional tactic worked. Lendl double-faulted on match point. After 4:39, Chang had overcome tennis's top dog 4–6, 4–6, 6–3, 6–3, 6–3.

Chang, who would go on to become the youngest French Open champion by beating Stefan Edberg in the 1989 final, also became the first American to win the tournament since 1955, when Trabert beat Sven Davidson.

French Open
Men's Fourth Round

Michael Chang	USA	4	4	6	6	6
Ivan Lendl	CZE	6	6	3	3	3

CRENSHAW'S MYSTICAL MASTERS

When Ben Crenshaw was a boy of six, he was educated to the game of golf by Harvey Penick. Penick, who late in his life became famous as the author of the bestselling golf instructional *Harvey Penick's Little Red Book*, was for decades the head pro at the Austin (Texas) Country Club. He was Crenshaw's only coach, and the 43-year-old Crenshaw cherished their relationship deeply.

That's why, when Penick died at the age of 90 on April 2, 1995, Crenshaw—who was in Augusta, Ga., preparing for the 60th Masters tournament—didn't hesitate. With another Penick student, fellow pro Tom Kite, he flew to Penick's funeral.

Crenshaw's second green jacket was surely his sweetest.

On Thursday of that week, as the Masters began, Crenshaw—who was often susceptible to mood swings when his game was troubled—played with an equanimity that felt otherworldy to him.

"It was," he would say, "like I felt this hand on my shoulder, guiding me along."

In other words, the spirit of Harvey Penick.

To Crenshaw it was welcome company. Coming into the Masters, he had been playing at a surprisingly sorry level. He had missed the cut in three of his last four starts. He hadn't broken 70 in two months. He was in trouble. People were beginning to whisper that Ben Crenshaw was washed up.

But that week in Augusta, under the mystical influence of Harvey, he was a different Crenshaw, playing his shots expertly and reasserting the magic of his putter.

By Sunday, as the final round of the Masters played out, it had become a three man competition between Crenshaw, Greg Norman and Crenshaw's good friend, Davis Love III.

But then Norman self-destructed on the 17th hole when he three-putted.

That left it to Crenshaw and Love. Playing ahead of Crenshaw, Love birdied the 17th hole and parred the 18th to finish the day with a 66 and the tournament with a 13-under 275.

Now all he could do was sit and wait to see what Crenshaw would do.

It had been a day of sweet fortune for Crenshaw, a day when the Fates treated his shots kindly. On the 2nd hole, when his misdirected drive struck a tree, the ball bounced charitably onto the fairway, prompting Crenshaw's wife, Julie, to say: "Look, there's Harvey."

On the 14th hole, Crenshaw got another Harvey bounce when an eight-iron shot from under a tree caromed off a dirt pile to within 12 feet of the hole.

"I just had this strong feeling the whole week," Crenshaw later said. "I never had a week like this where I really enjoyed playing golf the whole week."

Crenshaw birdied the 16th and 17th holes and bogeyed the 18th for a 68 and a 14-under-par, one-stroke victory.

"He was here with me," said Crenshaw of Penick, tears rolling down his cheek. "I could feel it."

Masters

	RD1	RD2	RD3	RD4	Total	Par
Crenshaw	70	67	69	68	274	-14
Love	69	69	71	66	275	-13
Norman	73	68	68	68	277	-11
Haas	71	64	72	70	277	-11
Frost	66	71	71	71	279	-9
Elkington	73	67	67	72	279	-9
Mickelson	66	71	70	73	280	-8
Hoch	69	67	71	73	280	-8
Strange	72	71	65	73	281	-7

"He was here with me."
—Ben Crenshaw

THE ROCKET REVIVES

Back in the early 1940s, the word on Maurice Richard was that he was too brittle to be an NHL player. His great speed on the ice, which would later give him his nickname the Rocket, wasn't enough to overcome the doubts that injuries can create in a sport that values playing with pain.

That was the conclusion, at least, drawn by Montreal Canadien general manager Tommy Gorman after Richard was the victim of several serious injuries—broken ankle (1940), broken wrist (1941), broken ankle (1942).

Gorman was so sure Richard was damaged goods that he dropped Richard from the Canadiens' reserve list. But Dick Irvin, the astute Montreal coach, suspected that Gorman

was wrong about Richard and persuaded him to restore the Rocket to the Canadiens' list.

It was a shrewd move. For Richard at right wing became an integral member of Montreal's famous Punch Line, which included Elmer Lach at center and Toe Blake, the team's leader, at left wing. In 1944–45 Blake became the first player in NHL history to score 50 goals in a season, a remarkable achievement during the league's six-team era, and one not eclipsed until Bobby Hull scored 54 in 1965–66.

By the 1951–52 season, Richard had put to rest any lingering doubts that he hadn't the toughness necessary to play hockey. But the Rocket went himself one better in the Stanley Cup semifinals—Montreal versus the Boston Bruins led by Milt Schmidt and Woody Dumart—when he scored as gutsy a goal as you'd want to see.

Here's how he did it:

In the seventh and deciding game of the series, with the score tied 1–1 in the second period, Richard was knocked hard to the ice. Bleeding from a head wound, he was taken to the Forum clinic and needed six stitches.

It wasn't until late in the third period that the Rocket made it back onto the ice. He was still a bit woozy from the doctor's ministration. But at 16:19 of the final period of this deadlocked game, Richard took a pass from Butch Bouchard, shot past four Boston skaters, fended off Bill Quackenbush and fired the puck past goalie "Sugar" Jim Henry to give Montreal a 2–1 lead.

The always intense Maurice Richard finished his career with 544 goals.

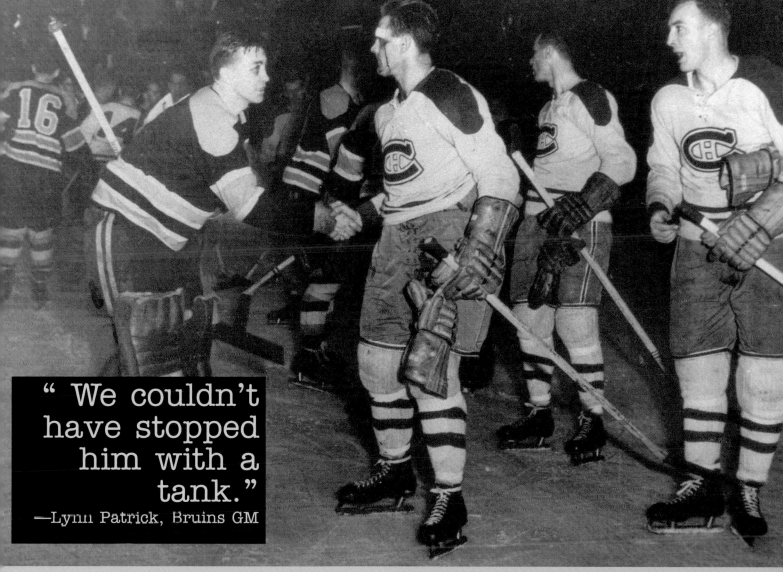

> " We couldn't
> have stopped
> him with a
> tank."
> —Lynn Patrick, Bruins GM

Showing the sportsmanship traditional to hockey, Richard and Bruins goalie Jim Henry shake hands after the game.

The 14,598 fans in Montreal's legendary Forum, usually a reserved cathedral to the sport, erupted at Richard's goal. They threw programs, money, overshoes and hats onto the ice, in celebration of Richard's fourth—and most important—goal of the series.

And why shouldn't they go crazy? For as Elmer Ferguson, sports editor of the *Montreal Herald*, later said: "You know what that guy did? He scored that last goal while he was semiconscious."

With the goal, the Rocket launched his team into the NHL finals, but the Detroit Red Wings brought an end to the magic and swept the Canadiens in four games to win the Stanley Cup.

Montreal Canadiens 3
Boston Bruins 1

| Montreal | 1 | 0 | 2—3 |
| Boston | 1 | 0 | 0—1 |

First Period: 1) MTL, Mazur (unassisted), 4:25; 2) BSN, Sandford (Makell, Quackenbush), 12:25
Penalties-Masnick, 1:38. Chrevefils, 5:58.

Second Period: No Scoring
Penalties-Masnick, 2:12. Laycoe, 7:27.

Third Period: 3) MTL Richard (Bouchard), 16:19; 4) MTL, Reay (Curry, St. Laurent), 19:26.
Penalties-Laycoe and Reay, 13:55.

THE RETURN OF LITTLE BEN HOGAN

They said that Ben Hogan would never shoot another round of competitive golf. Not after what he'd been through. In February 1949, Hogan's broken body was lifted from his car after it collided with a speeding bus. At the time doctors gave Little Ben, as the newspapers called him, no better than a 50-50 chance to survive. And golf? No way. Forget it, they said. Yet here he was at the 1950 U.S. Open in Merion, Pa., fighting through the pain and the fatigue that still plagued him—and would continue to for the rest of his career—to vie with the leaders.

With wife Valerie at his side, Hogan accepts the cup for his surprising, and inspiring, victory.

In spite of an extensive preround ritual that included soaking in a tub of hot water and Epsom salts, generously rubbing liniment onto his body and wrapping his legs in elastic bandages, Hogan still experienced leg cramps and shooting pains through the first two rounds. Yet a first-round two-over-par 72 and a second-round one-under-par 69 left him just two shots behind Open leader Dutch Harrison as the final day's double round loomed.

On his morning round, the pain hit Hogan so severely on the 13th hole that he thought of dropping out. But when he expressed it to his caddie, the lad supposedly to have told him, "No, Mr. Hogan, you can't quit because I don't work for quitters." Whatever drove him, be it the caddie's comment or the fierce intensity that characterized his playing style, Hogan forged on, shooting 72 to keep within two strokes of the lead, now held by Lloyd Mangrum. Harrison was in second place. Johnny Palmer and Cary Middlecoff were tied with Hogan.

Though the pains grew worse, Hogan played through the final 18 holes with a steadiness that at one point brought him a three-shot lead. But all the while he was showing signs of a body under seige, staggering after hitting a tee shot, leaning on others in his fatigue. By the 18th hole, his three-shot lead was gone.

But a stunningly expert second shot on that final hole—a one-iron, Hogan said—brought him within 40 feet of the cup. And when he two-putted, it put him into the next day's playoff against Mangrum and George Fazio. And while Hogan, the wounded warrior, suffered his pains in silence, he outperformed both Mangrum, who shot a 73, and Fazio, 75, carding an impressive 69 to win a U. S. Open that a year earlier seemed an impossible dream. "The 1950 U.S. Open was my biggest win," Hogan said later.

Many consider Ben Hogan's swing to be the perfect golf swing.

U.S. Open

Par. out	4	5	3	5	4	4	4	4	3-36
Hogan. out	4	5	3	5	4	4	3	5	3-36
Mangrum. out	4	4	4	5	4	4	4	4	3-36
Fazio. out	5	4	3	5	4	5	5	3	3-37
Par. in	4	4	4	3	4	4	4	3	4-34-70
Hogan. in	4	4	4	3	4	4	4	2	4-33-69
Mangrum. in	5	3	5	3	5	3	6	3	4-37-73
Fazio. in	4	4	4	3	5	5	5	3	5-38-73

"No, Mr. Hogan, you can't quit."

—Hogan's caddie

AGAINST THE ODDS

The pain struck days before the discus competition at the 1964 Tokyo Olympics.

Said Al Oerter, the four-time world-record holder who had won gold in his event in 1956 and 1960: "I was practicing ... all warmed up, throwing well and then ..."—he snapped his fingers—"It went."

It was Oerter's lower ribs. Hurling the discus involves spinning a few revolutions, then twisting violently as the heavy disk is flung forward. The midsection is where the action is as the body torques around to force speed and power behind the discus, so an injury there would have meant the end of that competition for most athletes.

But not for Oerter. The 6'4", 251-pound discus thrower from West Babylon, N.Y., had torn muscles and cartilage in his midsection, and the pain would force him to use ice packs to stop internal bleeding and then be heavily taped when he appeared for the morning qualifying trials on Oct. 15, 1964. But that wasn't all. He also had a preexisting neck injury and so he wore a neck brace.

In the days before the competition, he flirted with the notion of withdrawing from the competition but ultimately chose not to.

Six days after his injury, Oerter, a 28-year-old computer analyst at the Grumman Aircraft Company on Long Island, made his first practice throw and doubled over in pain.

Again, he entertained the idea of dropping out.

But, as he said, "Then the competition came and the adrenalin started flowing."

With a throw of 198' 7½", Oerter made it into the finals.

There, up against the world-record holder, Ludvik Danek of Czechoslovakia, who had broken Oerter's previous record of 206' 6" with a toss of 211' 9", Oerter somehow transcended his pain. In spite of his first four throws being short, he gathered himself on the fifth of his alloted six throws, hurling the discus an Olympic record throw of 200' 1½".

Despite his injury, Oerter blasted an Olympic-record throw to win the gold.

"I do not like to be mediocre."
—Al Oerter

With his neck in a brace, Al Oerter qualified at the U.S. Track and Field trials at Downing Stadium in New York in July.

The toss edged out Danek whose best throw for the day was 198' 6¾".

In pain, and under pressure, Al Oerter had shown a champion's mettle, as he would four years later, when he won his unmatched fourth Olympic gold medal in the discus, at the 1968 Games in Mexico City. Danek would have to wait until Oerter retired to win his own gold medal, in Munich in 1972. At the age of 40, Oerter tried another amazing comeback in 1980, coming in fourth at the U.S. trials and proving himself to be one of the greatest Olympians of all time.

Discus

1- Al Oerter, West Babylon, N.Y. (Olympic record)	200' 1½ "
2- Ludvik Danek, Czech.,	198' 6¾"
3- Dave Weill, Walnut Creek, Calif.	195' 2"
4- Jay Silvester, Tremonton, Utah	193' 10¼"
5- Jozsef Szecsenyi, Hungary	187' 9"
6- Zenon Begier, Poland	187' 2½"
7- Edmund Piatkowski, Poland	183' 1¼"
8- Vladmir Trusenev, Soviet Union	179' 8½"
9- Kim Bukhantsov, Soviet Union	178' 4¾"
10- Roy Hollingsworth, Great Britain	176' 8¾"
11- Hartmut Losch, Germany	170' 10¼"
12- Victor Kompaneyets, Soviet Union	170' 5¾"

Chapter 10
DRAMATIC
FINISHES

he seconds tick down, the sun is setting; if there was ever a time to make magic happen, this is it. Despite all the quarrels we may have with the state of sports today, the ultimate drama of the bases loaded in the bottom of the ninth, the buzzer beater, the plunge across the goal still makes us love athletics. These finishes are the epitome of Fat Lady grace. When perfection was necessary, Mary Lou Retton was perfect; when Gene Sarazen needed a miracle to win the Masters, he delivered one. Here are ten moments of courage, of inspiration, of wonder at how exciting sports can be.

A SHOWER OF SPARKS

On the afternoon of May 16, 1992 the world of NASCAR prepared itself for a major jolt. At precisely 8:58 that evening, the first ever night superspeedway race would get underway. The Winston Grand National, NASCAR's version of an All-Star race, would be run under the Charlotte Motor Speedway's new $1.7 million, 1.2 billion-watt lighting system. An additional format change designed to make the event more suitable for

In 1993, Davey Allison died at Alabama's Talladega Superspeedway in a helicopter crash.

prime-time viewing separated the race into two 30-lap segments, each paying $50,000 to the winner and determining the starting lineup for a final 10-lap dash worth $200,000 for first place.

A crowd of 100,000 filled the stands to witness the his-

toric event. Taking first in the qualifier, Davey Allison, the '91 Winston Grand National winner, rolled 007, his Ford Thunderbird, into the pole position. Starting second and third were stock car legend Rusty Wallace, in a Pontiac Grand Prix, and Bill Elliott, also driving a Thunderbird. At two minutes to nine, 20 drivers sped off on the first of 30 1½-mile laps. Twenty minutes and 45 miles later Allison cruised past the finish line, well ahead of the pack.

As preparations were made for the second 30-lap run, yet another quirky new Winston rule took effect. Fans in attendance at the Charlotte Motor Speedway, given the option to invert the starting positions in the second race from those used in the first, voted to do just that, sending Allison to the rear of the field. Knowing how crucial starting position would be in the 10-lap sprint, 007 and her driver jockeyed past 13 cars to claim the No. 6 spot for the next and final race of the night. The 10-lap main event threatened to be one of the more risky races run in NASCAR history. The cooling effect of the night air on engine performance and tire traction promised greater speeds from all cars.

Moreover, as this would be a no-points affair, the drivers, without the threat of losing precious points towards the Winston Cup championship from a crash, were less likely to exercise caution in the $200,000 sprint.

True to form, as the 10-lap dash got underway, the action more closely resembled short track stock car racing than a high-velocity superspeedway event. Coming off the ninth lap, Dale Earnhardt was in the lead spot, followed closely by Kyle Petty and Davey Allison. Going into the third turn, Petty, making a move for first, sent Earnhardt's Chevrolet Lumina careening off course. As Petty hesitated to avoid the spinning Chevy, Allison seized his opportunity and moved to the inside on the front straight. With 50 yards of track remaining and Allison and Petty both vying for the

The moment of contact. Kyle Petty in the number 42 Mello Yello Pontiac nudged Allison's Ford number 28 car as he passed on the inside. Allison won by three feet.

same real estate, the cars made contact. Allison spun 180 degrees through the checkered flag, into the wall, and in a brilliant shower of sparks slid 300 yards to a messy halt.

After being cut free from his Thunderbird and evacuated by helicopter to the Carolina Medical Center, Allison woke with a concussion and a bruised lung asking the $200,000 question: "Who won?"

Winston Grand National

	Driver	Car	Laps
1.	Davey Allison	Ford Thunderbird	70
2.	Kyle Petty	Pontiac Grand Prix	70
3.	Ken Schrader	Chevrolet Lumina	70
4.	Ricky Rudd	Chevrolet Lumina	70
5.	Bill Elliott	Ford Thunderbird	70
6.	Rusty Wallace	Pontiac Grand Prix	70
7.	Alan Kulwicki	Ford Thunderbird	70
8.	Ernie Irvan	Chevrolet Lumina	70
9.	Richard Petty	Pontiac Grand Prix	70
10.	Terry Labonte	Oldsmobile Cutlass	70
11.	Darrell Waltrip	Chevrolet Lumina	70
12.	Harry Gant	Oldsmobile Cutlass	70
13.	Geoff Bodine	Ford Thunderbird	70
14.	Dale Earnhardt	Chevrolet Lumina	69
15.	Michael Waltrip	Pontiac Grand Prix	68
16.	Dave Mader III	Ford Thunderbird	66
17.	Mark Martin	Ford Thunderbird	64
18.	Dale Jarrett	Chevrolet Lumina	11
19.	Morgan Shepherd	Ford Thunderbird	4
20.	Hut Stricklin	Chevrolet Lumina	2

THE PERFECT 10

No American woman had ever won an individual Olympic gymnastics gold medal.

But then came the 1984 Games in Los Angeles and a 16-year-old dynamo from Fairmont, W.Va., named Mary Lou Retton.

Retton, who stood 4'9" and had a smile that could have lit up Times Square, came into the final evening of the women's all-around championship leading all 36 women with her score of 39.525 points, based on her performance in the team events.

But as the individual all-around competition moved to the finish, Retton had been passed by Romania's Ecaterina Szabo, a 17-year-old blonde, by .05 of a point going into the vault.

That meant that if Retton scored a commendable 9.95 on the vault, she would only tie Szabo, unless Szabo had a misfortune on her last routine. The margin for error was paper-thin.

Simply put, Retton needed a perfect 10 to win.

As the crowd of 9,023 in Pauley Pavilion tensed, and while Szabo was finishing up on the uneven bars, Retton, wearing an American-flag leotard rich in stars and stripes, eyed the vault apparatus. Then she began her run towards the gold—a layout back somersault with a double twist.

As she descended from all that airborne twisting and turning, she landed upright and rock still.

The crowd roared, and then the judges scored.

Retton had done it: a perfect 10 that made the final score 79.175 points for Retton, and 79.125 points for Szabo, who scored 9.90 on the uneven bars.

"I can't describe how I felt," said Retton. "I had goose-bumps going up and down me. I knew from the takeoff, I knew from the run—I just knew it."

As the scores were beamed to the Pauley Pavilion crowd, and to viewers across the world, Retton's personal coach, Bela Karolyi raced onto the floor and swept up the pixieish Retton in a bearhug.

For him, and for Mary Lou Retton, the moment was golden.

"I just knew it."
—Mary Lou Retton

top: Retton also scored a 10 in her floor exercise.

Women's All-Around Gymnastics Final

			Vault	U. Bars	Beam	Floor	Total Pts.
1	Mary Lou Retton	USA	19.95(1)	19.7(4)	19.6(3)	19.925(1)	79.175
2	Ecaterina Szabó	ROM	19.85(2)	19.5(8)	19.85(1)	19.925(1)	79.125
3	Simona Pauca	ROM	19.625(6)	19.575(6)	19.85(1)	19.625(5)	78.675
4	Julianne McNamara	USA	19.725(3)	19.95(1)	19.075(13)	19.65(4)	78.4
5	Laura Cutina	ROM	19.7(4)	19.725(3)	19.125(11)	19.75(3)	78.3
6	Ma Yanhong	CHN	19.3(15)	19.95(1)	19.55(4)	19.05(13)	77.85
7	Zhou Ping	CHN	19.525(7)	19.4(9)	19.175(10)	19.375(8)	77.775
8	Chen Yongyan	CHN	19.525(7)	19.275(11)	19.5(5)	19.425(7)	77.725

left: Retton's perfect 10 was an emotional highlight of the
1984 Olympics for the American team.

LAST GASP FOR GOLD

Through two days and nine events, the two men, Rafer Johnson of Kingsburg, Calif., and C.K. Yang of Taiwan, had battled one another, attempting to score enough points to make the exhausting final event of the 1960 Olympic decathlon superfluous. Johnson and Yang also happened to be best friends. But only one could win the unofficial title of the World's Greatest All-Around Athlete.

But neither Johnson nor Yang could gain enough of a lead so he would be able to coast through the finale—the 1,500-meter race. While Yang who, like Johnson, had trained for the decathlon under UCLA coach Ducky Drake, had beaten

Johnson's edge in the strength events gave him a lift, but he was unable to set a new world record.

his friend in six of the nine events, Johnson's superiority in the strength events–the shot put, discus throw and javelin throw–generated enough points to make the metric mile they were about to run the event that would decide the gold.

The odds were against the American as the two men joined four other decathletes at the starting line in the chilly night of Rome's Stadio Olimpico. Historically, Yang, had been 10 seconds faster on average than Johnson in the 1,500-meter race. If he could repeat that margin of victory now, he would win the decathlon.

Johnson, however, was determined not to let Yang put that kind of distance between them. As the race began, Johnson settled in behind Yang, a comfortable two steps to the rear. Yang, who had the lean build of a runner, in contrast to Johnson's more muscular torso, tried but could not shake the American.

As the crowd of 50,000 cheered their efforts, Yang and Johnson continued their lonely, frantic race against time, and each other. Johnson ran with his eyes focused on Yang's neck, pushing himself along the track as he never had before.

And so they came down to the last lap, Yang trying desperately to break away from Johnson. But Johnson matched his accelerated pace, refusing to allow Yang to put enough distance between them to yield the points that would give Yang the gold.

As Yang ran down the last straightaway, he looked back, hoping to find Johnson wilting. But Johnson clung to him like a shadow, a mere 1.2 seconds and four yards behind. In running the 1,500 meters six seconds faster than he ever had, Rafer Johnson had outscored Yang to win the gold—an Olympic record of 8,392 points to Yang's 8,334 points.

"I wanted this one real bad," Johnson said afterward. "But I never want to go through that again—never. I'm awfully tired."

Rafer Johnson slumps on the shoulder of his friend C.K. Yang after beating him in the decathlon.

"I knew he would win. He is that way."

—C.K. Yang

Decathalon

		100M	LJ	SP	HJ	400M	110H	DISC	PV	JAV	1500M	Total
1. Johnson	USA	10.9	7.35	15.82	1.85	48.3	15.3	48.49	4.10	69.76	4:49.7	8392
2. Yang	TAI	10.7	7.46	13.33	1.90	48.1	14.6	39.83	4.30	68.22	4:48.5	8334
3. Kuznyetsov	SOV	11.1	6.96	14.46	1.75	50.2	15.0	50.52	3.90	71.20	4:53.8	7809
4. Kutyenko	SOV	11.4	6.93	13.97	1.80	51.1	15.6	45.63	4.20	71.44	4:44.2	7567
5. Kamerbeek	HOL	11.3	7.21	13.76	1.80	51.1	14.9	44.31	3. 80	57.49	4:43.6	7236
6. Sar	ITA	11.4	6.69	13.89	1.80	51.3	14.7	49.58	3.80	55.74	4:49.2	7195

ROPE-A-DOPE

In January 1973, George Foreman had shocked the boxing world when, as the challenger, he had demolished Joe Frazier in two rounds to become heavyweight champion. That night in Kingston, Jamaica, Foreman's punches actually lifted Frazier off the canvas. Over the two rounds, Foreman knocked Frazier to the canvas many times before the fight was stopped, and emerged with an image of the inconquerable destroyer.

It was why when Muhammad Ali deigned to take on

	ALI		FOREMAN
	32	AGE	24
WEIGHT	212 lbs.*		220 lbs.*
HEIGHT	6ft. 3in.		6ft. 3in.
REACH	80 in.		78½ in.
BICEPS	15 in.		16 in.
CHEST (Normal)	43 in.		43 in.
CHEST (Expanded)	45 in.		45½ in.
FOREARM	13½ in.		14 in.
THIGH	26 in.		25 in.
FIST	13in.		12½ in.
CALF	17 in.		17 in.

*Estimated Weights

Foreman (who was undefeated in 40 bouts, with 37 KOs) in Kinshasha, Zaire, Ali's close friends worried that he would be risking permanent damage.

Who could blame them? Even the experts saw Foreman as an unforgiving hammer of malice. As *New York Times* columnist, Dave Anderson would write: "For a few rounds, Ali might be able to escape Foreman's sledgehammer strength, but not for 15 rounds. Sooner or later, the champion will land one of his sledgehammer punches, and for the first time in his career, Muhammad Ali will be counted out."

The buildup to the fight was dramatic, as both men trained under the intense scrutiny of the world press. A cut to Foreman's right eye eight days before the original fight date, September 25, delayed the bout for another month, which only stirred interest more. As tension rose, Ali emerged as the people's favorite, if not the pundits, and Foreman, with his pet German shepherd—to Zairians an unsavory symbol of police domination—at his side, represented to many the hand of power.

When, early in the bout, Ali retreated to the ropes and let Foreman wing away at him, as if resigned to taking a beating, the concerns of Ali's friends and the prophecies of the experts appeared to be well-founded. To give Foreman carte blanche to fire away seemed reckless and a sure-fire way to defeat. Ali's longtime trainer, Angelo Dundee, and the rest of Ali's corner looked on in dismay, shouting for their man to get off the ropes and use the clever movement that was so integral to his earlier successes.

But Ali had a plan. He had improvised a strategy he would later dub the Rope-a-Dope. He had decided that he could not only endure the punches Foreman was throwing but that he could sap Big George's energy in the process.

The Rope-a-Dope worked to perfection. After seven rounds, and with dismay among the crowd turning into

"Now it's my turn."
—Muhammad Ali

expectation, Ali sensed Foreman was tiring. In the ring, Ali told Foreman, "Now it's my turn."

By now, Foreman's punches lacked the explosiveness that had chilled past opponents. His movements in the hot African night were labored, nearly robotic. Ali took advantage. He began pumping the jab into Foreman's puffy face, knocking him off stride. And as Foreman lurched this way and that, Ali caught him with a right to the jaw that sent Foreman tumbling to the canvas.

Foreman struggled to get to his feet, but he failed to beat the count of referee Zack Clayton. At 2:58 of the eighth round, Muhammad Ali was champion again. Zaire exploded into celebration with a triumph that much of black Africa regarded as their own.

Heavyweight Championship					
Round 1	Round 2	Round 3	Round 4	Round 5	Round 6
Foreman	Foreman	Foreman	Foreman	Foreman	Foreman
Round 7	Round 8				
Foreman	Ali	Winner by KO			

left: Though the two fighters matched up well, Foreman's youth and fierce reputation led most to pick him as the going-away favorite.

THE FIGHTING FINISH

The swells were there, as they always are at the Kentucky Derby. The big hats, the mint juleps, the singing of *My Old Kentucky Home*. The scene, as it always is, was gentility incarnate: elegant and consummately Southern. The Derby in 1933, as today, was as much a social event as it was a sporting contest. For the 1933 running, the crowd of 40,000 included Mrs. Woodrow Wilson; James Roosevelt, son of President Franklin Delano Roosevelt; and the governors of Kentucky, Illinois, Ohio, Virginia and West Virginia. The race

The win by Broker's Tip was even more surprising because it was his first ever.

was as much about consuming mint juleps and glad handing as it was about thoroughbreds charging down the Churchill Downs track.

But for this mile and a quarter race, the aristocratic atmos-phere would undergo a radical change once the horses headed for the finish. The key horses down the stretch would be Broker's Tip, owned by E.R. Bradley—a three-time winner at the Derby—and ridden by Don Meade ... and Head Play, owned by Mrs. Silas B. Mason and ridden by H.W. Fisher. But it would take a while for those two horses, and their jockeys, to get it on.

Going past the half-mile mark, Head Play had bolted past Isiah and Good Advice, drawing off to a lead of a length or more. As Workman and Charley O. challenged Head Play, Broker's Tip bided its time in the rear guard of the 13-horse field.

But by the final straightaway, Charley O. was fading as Head Play and the fast-arriving Broker's Tip drew away, with both their jockeys calling for every bit of speed. As *The New York Times*'s Bryan Field would write: "It was whip and heel from outside the furlong pole to the wire."

At close quarters, the horses pounded to the finish line, their jockeys urging them on.

Did Broker's Tip's jockey Meade foul his rival jockey, Fisher? That's what an irate Fisher would insist happened as the two horses crossed the finish line so closely locked that only the placing judges could separate them.

Fisher was so enraged by Meade's tactics—real or imagined—that he rapped Meade with his whip as the race ended and then lodged a claim of foul with the stewards that was disallowed.

To add insult, Broker's Tip, not Head Play, was declared the winner, giving owner Bradley his fourth victory in the Derby and his second in a row, not to mention prize money of $48,925. Peace would again reign in Bluegrass Country, but for a fleeting moment the niceties of Derby time had the back alley's mean spirit.

"I felt certain of winning."
—Don Meade

Despite H.W. Fisher's claim that Don Meade grabbed his saddle cloth during the stretch run, it appears in this photo that the opposite was true.

Kentucky Derby

Starters	Jockeys	P.P.	TIme	Value
Broker's Tip	Meade	11	2:06	$48,925
Head Play	H. Fischer	7		
Charley O.	Corbett	1		
Ladysman	Workman	4		
Pomponius	Bejshak	12		
Spicson	R. Fischer	9		
Kerry Patch	Schaefer	5		
Mr. Khayyam	Walls	13		
Inlander	Bellizz	6		
Strideaway	Beck	8		
Dark Winter	R. Jones	3		
Isiah	McCrossen	10		
Good Advice	Legere	2		

HURRICANE
FORCE

*I*t was to be a coronation for the undefeated Cornhuskers from Nebraska. According to the wire service polls, they were the No. 1 college football team of the 1983 season when they came into the Orange Bowl game against Miami.

Not only was coach Tom Osborne's team 12–0, but it had run roughshod over the opposition, averaging 401.7 rushing yards per game and 52 points. It was no surprise that Nebraska, with a 22 game winning streak, was an 11-point favorite to beat the Hurricanes of coach Howard Schnellenberger.

Not that Miami was regarded as a patsy. After losing its season opener to Florida, in Gainesville, 28–3, Miami had reeled off 10 straight victories.

When Schnellenberger arrived on the Miami campus five years earlier, in 1979, the university had been struggling with the question of whether it wanted a big-time football program or not. Schnellenberger had silenced the debate by quickly building a team that, while underrated by the bookmakers, was convinced it could meet Nebraska head-on.

That became clear soon enough as the Hurricanes, led by freshman quarterback Bernie Kosar, jumped out to a 17–0 first-quarter lead on two touchdown passes by Kosar and a 45-yard field goal by Ed Davis.

Stymied, Nebraska resorted to a trick play in the second quarter to get its offense jump-started—a 19-yard run by the right guard, Dean Steinkuhler, on an intentional fumble. Steinkuhler, pulling left, picked up the ball and ran it in for a touchdown.

A 64-yard drive later in the quarter, ending on a quarterback sneak by Nebraska quarterback Turner Gill, made the score 17–14 at halftime, in favor of Miami.

Miami increased the lead to 31–17 after three quarters, but the Cornhuskers did not crumble, even when the team lost its Heisman Trophy winner, tailback Mike Rozier. Rozier, who left the game with an injured ankle in the third quarter, did not return.

With Jeff Smith replacing Rozier, Nebraska fought back. Smith scored twice in the final period on runs of one and 24 yards. The last touchdown came with 48 seconds left and narrowed Miami's lead to 31–30. Osborne's dilemma now was whether to play for a tie by kicking the extra point, or roll the dice and go for two points.

Another great coach had once faced a similar choice with similar stakes on the line. Fabled Notre Dame coach Ara Parseghian opted for the tie in a late-season game against Michigan State in 1966.

Miami's Eddie Brown led all receivers with six catches.

"I knew they'd go for two. They're champions. They had to."
—Kenny Calhoun

Although the Irish ended the year on top of the polls and were considered the national champions, to many, Notre Dame's otherwise great year was tainted by Parseghian's cautious move. Osborne may well have heard the echoes of Parseghian's critics when he made his call: The Nebraska coach elected to go for two.

Gill took the snap, then rolled to the right and threw to Smith in the end zone. But Miami defensive back Ken Calhoun batted the pass down, much to the joy of the partisan Orange Bowl crowd of 72,549 fans.

Miami had survived to win 31–30. When the dust had settled on the other crucial bowl game—Texas, ranked No. 2, lost to Georgia in the Cotton Bowl—the Hurricanes stood alone as the top college team in the nation, and Tom Osborne suffered for making a brave call.

Miami 31, Nebraska 30

Miami	17	0	14	0—31
Nebraska	0	14	3	13—30

Miami	Dennison 2 pass from Kosar (J. Davis kick)
Miami	FG J. Davis 45
Miami	Dennison 22 pass from Kosar (J. Davis kick)
Nebraska	Steinkuhler 19 run with intentional fumble by QB Gill (Livingston kick)
Nebraska	Gill 1 run (Livingston kick)
Nebraska	FG Livingston 34
Miami	Highsmith 1 run (J. Davis kick)
Miami	Bentley 7 run (J. Davis kick)
Nebraska	J. Smith 1 run (Livingston kick)
Nebraska	J. Smith 24 run (pass failed)
Attendance	72, 549

Statistics of the Game

	Miami	Nebraska
First Downs	22	24
Rushes yards	28-130	56-287
Passing yards	300	172
Return yards	50	40
Passes	19-35-1	16-30-1
Punts	4-42	3-30
Fumbles lost	1-1	6-1
Penalties yards	13-101	4-51
Time of possession	27:53	32:07

THE
MIRACLE STEAL

By the 1964–65 season, the Boston Celtics were the NBA's elite franchise–a dynasty like no other. Between 1956–57 and 1964–65, the Celtics had won seven NBA titles and eight straight Eastern Division championships.

The rivalry between Bill Russell of the Celtics and the Sixers' Wilt Chamberlain existed on the court and off.

And on April 15, 1965 at Boston Garden, the Celtics appeared to have wrapped up another division crown against the archrival Philadelphia 76ers led by larger-than-life center Wilt Chamberlain, the foil to Boston's quietly dominating Bill Russell. In the series' seventh and deciding game, the Celtics led 110–107 when Chamberlain made an uncontested layup with five seconds remaining. Now, with the score 110–109, all Boston had to do was inbound the basketball and kill the clock so they could move on to the championship round against the Los Angeles Lakers.

But when Russell made the throw-in from the baseline, over Chet (Butterbean) Walker's outstretched arms, he hit the guide wire that supported the backboard. Russell screamed at the ref, claiming that Walker was over the line, and the crowd in the Garden went wild. The gravel-voiced Celtics announcer Johnny Most howled over and over, "He hit the wire! He hit the wire! He hit the wire!" Boston lost the ball and now Philadelphia had one more chance to win the game.

The Sixers took a timeout and diagrammed their last shot. Philadelphia guard Hal Greer would inbound the ball to Walker, take the return pass and shoot. In the Celtics huddle, coach Red Auerbach, whose custom of lighting up a victory cigar had been delayed by the tight game and now seemed entirely in peril, looked at his stricken team and said, "So, what do we do now?" Boston guessed the ball would be going to either Chamberlain or Greer.

"Havlicek stole the ball."
—Celtics' announcer Johnny Most

Time in. Greer took his place on the line, but his inbound pass never made it to Walker. The Celtics' brilliant sixth man John (Hondo) Havlicek anticipated the throw and managed to deflect it to Sam Jones, who dribbled away the final seconds of the game. The Celtics held on to their 110–109 lead to win their ninth straight division title.

Upstairs in the radio booth, Johnny Most had a new chant: "Havlicek stole the ball! Havlicek stole the ball!"—a call that for Celtic fans became what Russ Hodges' "The Giants win the pennant" was to New York Giants faithful. The Garden crowd mobbed the court.

And Red Auerbach lit up his victory cigar.

Boston Celtics 110, Philadelphia 76ers 109

Boston	G	F	P	Philadelphia	G	F	P
Heinsohn	1	0-0	2	Walker	10	4-5	24
Sanders	8	2-2	18	Jackson	3	2-4	8
Russell	7	1-2	15	Chamberlain	12	6-13	30
S.Jones	15	7-9	37	Greer	5	2-2	12
K.C. Jones	2	2-3	6	Costello	1	1-1	3
Havlicek	10	6-7	26	Gambee	6	13-14	25
Siegfried	2	2-3	6	Bianchi	3	1-1	7
Total	45	20-26	110	Kerr	0	0-2	0
				Total	40	29-42	109

Boston	35	26	29	20	—110
Philadelphia	26	36	20	27	—109

THE MAD DASH HOME

We admire the grace and natural skills of the great athletes.

Michael Jordan resisting the law of gravity.

Pete Sampras rifling a backhand down the line.

Sandy Koufax throwing smoke.

They are men born to greatness, athletes with God-given skills that we recognize as being a level beyond those possessed by their contemporaries.

But there is another species of athlete worth admiration, too—the individual whose grit and competitiveness make him special.

Such a ballplayer emerged during the 1946 World Series between the St. Louis Cardinals and the Boston Red Sox.

In the crucial and deciding seventh game, Enos (Country) Slaughter, the Cardinals rightfielder, made a snap decision that not only became the pivotal moment of the Series but underscored the competitive fire of this player.

The game was tied 3–3 in the bottom of the eighth inning when Slaughter cracked a single to center. For a while it looked as though Slaughter would die on first as Red Sox relief pitcher Bob Klinger retired the next two batters.

But then Cardinals leftfielder, Harry (the Hat) Walker, smacked a line drive double into centerfield. At the crack of the bat Slaughter took off, running hard.

The hit was not such a shot and it didn't seem that Slaughter, even though he'd taken off with the pitch, would be able to score, but he kept running. Slaughter came around second, then third as the ball was relayed in to the Boston shortstop Johnny Pesky, who was long blamed for holding the ball with his back to the infield as Slaughter kept circling the bases. Pesky, like everyone else, had expected Slaughter to hold at second or maybe third. But packed to the rafters, Fenway Park rocked with noise and Pesky could not hear his teammates calling for him to immediately turn and make the throw. Finally the shortstop spun and threw, but it was too late. The Cardinals had the lead, 4–3.

Pitcher Harry (the Cat) Brecheen would give up singles to Rudy York and Bobby Doerr in the ninth, then set down the next three batters on infield rollers to clinch the Series.

Despite Brecheen's three wins in the Series, it would be the heroics of the incredible running man, Enos Slaughter, that would be reenacted 25 years later, in St. Louis by those who'd taken part the first time around, including both Slaughter and Pesky.

"I would have needed a rifle to nail Slaughter."
—Johnny Pesky

top: Not known for his speed, Slaughter stole all of nine bases in 1946.

left: The Cardinals celebrate after winning the title. Left to right, Whitey Kurowski, Enos Slaughter, Marty Marion and Stan Musial.

St. Louis Cardinals 4, Boston Red Sox 3

Boston	AB	R	H	RBI	St. Louis	AB	R	H	RBI
Moses, rf	4	1	1	0	Schoendienst, 2b	4	0	2	1
Pesky, ss	4	0	1	0	Moore, cf	4	0	1	0
DiMaggio, cf	3	0	1	3	Musial, 1b	3	0	1	0
Culberson, cf	0	0	0	0	Slaughter, rf	3	1	1	0
Williams, lf	4	0	0	0	Kurowski, 3b	4	1	1	0
York, 1b	4	0	1	0	Garagiola, c	3	0	0	0
c Campbell	0	0	0	0	Rice, c	1	0	0	0
Doerr, 2b	4	0	2	0	Walker, lf	3	1	2	2
Higgins, 3b	4	0	0	0	Marion, ss	2	0	0	0
H. Wagner, c	2	0	0	0	Dickson, p	3	1	1	1
a Russell	1	1	1	0	Brecheen, p	1	0	0	0
Partee, c	1	0	0	0	**Total**	**31**	**4**	**9**	**4**
Ferriss, p	2	0	0	0					
Dobson, p	0	0	0	0					
b Metkovich	1	1	1	0					
Klinger, p	0	0	0	0					
Johnson, p	0	0	0	0					
d McBride	1	0	0	0					
Total	**35**	**3**	**8**	**3**					

a Batted for H. Wagner in eighth.
b Batted for Dobson in eighth.
c Ran for York in the ninth.
d Batted for Johnson in ninth.

Boston	1	0	0	0	0	0	0	2	0—3
St. Louis	0	1	0	0	2	0	0	1	x—4

Davis Cup—Interzone Final
Don Budge vs. Baron Gottfried von Cramm

July 20, 1937

BUDGE OUTLASTS VON CRAMM

American Don Budge was already the toast of the tennis world on July 20, 1937, when he took the court at Wimbledon to face Baron Gottfried von Cramm of Germany in the interzone finals of the Davis Cup. Though he had only been playing tennis since he was 15, the 22-year-old

Baron von Cramm (left) was imprisoned by the Gestapo in 1938 for refusing to promote Nazism during his travels, though he later served on the Russian front.

had beaten von Cramm in straight sets at this same stadium for the British championship just weeks earlier. With his powerful serve and aggressive game, Budge was clearly the sport's man to watch and the heavy favorite this afternoon at Wimbledon.

The match opened with von Cramm holding serve. Oddly, Budge did not score a point. Soon enough it was clear that this day Budge would not be the dominator he'd been two weeks ago. The two battled through the first set, but even though he was not himself Budge forced von Cramm as far as he could before the German won the first set 8–6. The second set was more of the same, with every point played hard and evenly. Budge's serve was broken in the eleventh game putting von Cramm ahead 6–5 and he finally took the set 7–5.

Ahead two sets to love, von Cramm had to feel he was on the brink of a big upset and, maybe even sweeter, a large helping of revenge with his own straight-sets win. Tall, blond and magnetic, von Cramm was known for his endurance and his will to win, which makes what happened next all the stranger. Whether von Cramm let down or Budge's competitive fire finally sparked, just when the match looked to be over, Budge came alive. He won the third set handily at 6–4, and then blew von Cramm off the court in the fourth set 6–2, a score which makes the set seem even closer than it was— Budge won the first four games in five minutes.

It looked as if the American at last had the match settled, but there were more turns in store. Now Budge came unglued: von Cramm broke his service in the fourth game to take a 3–1 lead and, holding service, extended his lead to a commanding 4–1 margin. Two more games and the match was von Cramm's.

Up against the wall, Budge changed tactics and began to rush the net. The move worked. The German seemed flustered and Budge won the next three games to tie the set at 4–all. The match went to 6–all when Budge broke von Cramm's service with a love game and it seemed all over (especially when Budge held serve for 7–6). But von Cramm

"Don, this was absolutely the finest match I have ever played in my life."

—Baron Gottfried von Cramm

Between 1937 and '39, Don Budge ran through a winning streak of 92 matches and 14 tournaments, all as an amateur.

had one more great game left. The two struggled through 16 points before Budge slammed a forehand past von Cramm to take the set 8–6 and the match, three sets to two.

Budge went on to win the U.S. Open in 1937 and took the Sullivan Award as the year's top American amateur athlete. As great a year as that was for him, it couldn't match 1938, when he won the grand slam—the Australian, British, French and U.S. men's singles titles—and led the U.S. team to victory in the 1938 Davis Cup. Through these years of triumph, though, this match is Budge's most memorable.

Davis Cup Interzone Final

Don Budge	USA	6	5	6	6	8
Baron Gottfried von Cramm	GER	8	7	4	2	6

THE *SHOT* HEARD 'ROUND THE *WORLD*

Gene Sarazen had blazed through practice at Augusta National the week leading up to the 1935 Masters. His 271 for four rounds stood as the course record for thirty years, and it would take Jack Nicklaus in 1965 to break it. But it was Sarazen's co-favorite, Craig Wood, who appeared to have the second Masters tournament wrapped up late in the final round on Sunday. As Sarazen approached the 15th tee, he was down two strokes to Wood. The 15th is a long, straight hole—a 485-yard par-5. Wood was already on number 18.

Sarazen's drive was strong and deep down the fairway, maybe 230 yards from the pin, and it was likely he could pick up a stroke on Wood, but as he walked towards the ball with Walter Hagen, with whom he was paired, they heard a cheer from 18, where Wood had birdied. Sarazen was now three shots behind. Hagen said, "Well, that's that," conceding to Wood.

But Sarazen had something else in mind. He asked his caddy, a man nicknamed Stovepipe for the hat he wore, "What do I need to win?"

The caddy laughed and said four 3s. Hagen stood on the side, a little impatient now, as Sarazen mulled over the possibility of going for broke. "Hurry up, Gene," he said. "I've got a date tonight."

With most people on the course standing at 18, watching Wood sink what was assumed to be the winning putt, only a handful of spectators saw Sarazen pull out his four-wood and a lucky ring. He rubbed the ring on Stovepipe's head, took his stance and swung. The ball cleared a small pond, hit just before the green and began to roll towards the cup. And kept rolling. The legendary Bobby Jones was watching and thought, My God, he's going to have a chance at a 3.

Jones was close. The ball fell into the

On 12, Sarazen putts as his partner Walter Hagen, in the black sweater, stands by.

"What do I need to win?"

—Gene Sarazen

Since everyone was at 18 watching Wood, there are no photos of Sarazen hitting his famous shot on the 15th. Here he is teeing off earlier in the round.

cup for a 2. In the distance, Sarazen could see people around the green jumping up and down, which told him he'd made a double eagle, tied Wood, and added a phrase to golf history—"the shot heard 'round the world."

Sarazen made par on the last three holes, forcing a playoff with Wood. The next day was rainy and bitter cold, but Sarazen was not deterred by the intemperate weather. From the start he played with the steadiness befitting a former British and American Open champion. His 144 for 36 holes topped Wood by five strokes and gave Sarazen his second Masters title, a title that now seems to pale beside the famous shot that made it possible.

The Masters

PAR									
Out	4	5	4	3	4	3	4	5	4-36
In	4	4	3	5	4	5	3	4	4-36-72
Gene Sarazen									
(morning round)									
Out	5	4	4	3	4	4	3	5	4-36
In	3	4	3	5	4	5	3	4	4-35-71
(afternoon round)									
Out	4	5	4	3	4	3	4	5	4-36
In	4	4	3	5	4	5	3	5	4-37-73-144
Craig Wood									
(morning round)									
Out	4	5	4	3	4	3	4	5	4-36
In	4	5	4	6	4	5	3	4	4-39-75
(afternoon round)									
Out	5	5	5	3	5	3	5	5	4-40
In	4	4	3	4	4	5	2	4	4-34-74-149

Grantland Rice, the legendary American sportswriter, once wrote: "When the One Great Scorer comes to mark against your name, He writes not that you won or lost but how you played the game."

All of us who love sports must wonder whether this noble concept of sportsmanship has vanished from the scene. Driven by our society's total preoccupation with winning, both winning games and winning big contracts, players now have cell phones in the locker room; loyalty by players and to players seems forgotten. Managers and coaches have become celebrities, with their own agents, and television shows. Shoe companies have endorsement agreements with just about everyone, and college football bowl games and sports arenas have added corporate sponsorship to their nomenclature. Quick-what does Aflac do, anyhow? Nokia? At least we know that Poulon makes Weed Eaters because they told us with the rousingly named Poulon Weed Eater Independence Bowl. In the Olympics now it's all about winning gold and making sure you get to be a host city. Both guarantee lots of up-close-and-personal time and money!

Television brings you those up-close-and-personal moments, as well as World Series games that end after everyone goes to bed. It is the dynamic most responsible for the change in sports behavior. Universities offer degrees in sports management. We have pregame and postgame shows, 24-hour sports talk radio, and, of course, ESPN and Fox. Each and every athlete and play is studied under the microscope, as we try to learn everything possible in the world about why, for example, a baseball went through Bill Buckner's legs in the 1986 World Series. Sadly our love of sports and our hunger for more can diminish when sports is everywhere. Steak for dinner every night makes noodles look good by Wednesday.

Growing up in the Bronx in the 1940s and 50s, I idolized the New York Yankees. Once I walked pitcher "Steady" Eddie Lopat back to his apartment after a game. I used to leave self-addressed postcards in the cars of the Yankees ballplayers—they parked right alongside Yankee Stadium and these cards were posted and returned with signed autographed at no charge. I even remember LaSalle basketball player Tom Gola writing me a wonderful note with a photo simply because I showed an interest in him. He would never have imagined, as players must now, that I was just looking for something to collect and sell.

I'm just as guilty as anyone when it comes to winning. It probably began for me as a Little League parent, where we conducted player drafts with the sole intent of finishing first. All kids were to play and learn, but the focus was always on the ballplayer who had game. My worst job was as the Little League's players', agent, responsible for trading unhappy players to other teams for like value. I even taught my own son, Michael, a very good Little League shortstop, to come up with his glove high in the air, helping the umpire to make the correct decision in our favor.

EPILOGUE

As trivial a thing as that was, part of me wishes now that I hadn't done that.

The event that to me most symbolizes the way sports used to be played in this country-or maybe the way we wish they still would be played-was the Nov. 14, 1940 college football game between Ivy League teams, Cornell and Dartmouth, known now as the Fifth Down Game.

Cornell was a football power in 1940—possessing an 18-game victory streak dating back to the 1938 campaign. The 1939 Cornell club had upset the heavily favored Ohio State Buckeyes 23–14 in Columbus. As a result, the Rose Bowl committee tendered a bid for the Ivy League school to play Southern California, but Cornell's president, Edmund Ezra Day, turned down the invitation-academics came first. The 1940 Cornell team again beat Ohio State, this time 21–7, and headed to Dartmouth, which was coached by the great Red Blaik, who subsequently gained national fame at West Point, but at this stage of the season, Dartmouth's record was only 3–4. The Big Red did not figure to have any trouble in this last game of the season with a Dartmouth team listed as a 4-to-1 underdog.

Yet on that day, on a wet slippery field and before a Dartmouth crowd of 10,000 fans, the Indians rose up against Cornell and held this football juggernaut scoreless through three quarters. In the third quarter the Indians had turned back a Cornell drive with an end-zone interception and then had driven into position for placekicker Bob Krieger to boot a fourth-quarter 27-yard field goal that gave Dartmouth a 3–0 lead and visions of a major upset.

But with only 2:30 remaining, Cornell attempted to stave off defeat. The Big Red drove from their own 42 to a first down at the Dartmouth six. Three plays later, Cornell had advanced the ball to the one-yard-line. But an extra timeout penalty brought the ball back to the six.

On the next play Cornell's forward pass was knocked down in the end zone—a defensive stop that should have given Dartmouth the football.

But as The New York Times reported: "Unfortunately for the Green, however, Cornell received another down. It was assumed at the time that both teams had been offside."

Wrong. What occurred was that the official, referee W.H. (Red) Friesell Jr., erred and gave Cornell a fifth down. With less than three seconds to play, Big Red quarterback Walter Scholl passed to Bill Murphy, who leaped high into the air to share the ball that gave Cornell a 7–3 victory.

Or so it seemed as the once-again "unbeaten" Cornell team ran joyously from the field.

The next day, the referee reviewed charts kept by the press and motion pictures taken by both colleges and admitted that he'd been mistaken in giving Cornell a fifth down.

On the Monday following the game, which would be two days later, the Cornell team, led by Captain Walt Matuszoh, was called together by President Day, coincidently a Dartmouth graduate, who advised: "I'll tell you what we should do. We'll do good sports and give it to them. Dartmouth will be better sports. They won't accept it." Cornell's director of athletics, James Lynah, and football coach, Carl Snavely, wired Dartmouth that "Cornell relinquishes claim to the victory and extends congratulations to Dartmouth." But Dartmouth did accept the offer of victory, saluting Cornell as an "honorable and honored opponent."

Such a gesture of sportsmanship as Cornell made seems impossible today. It's too late in the game; things are too far gone. All is not lost, though. Sports still has true hearts and real emotions and dreams and lessons worth learning. All 100 of the sports events in this book prove that, too. Play catch with your kid this weekend if you don't believe me. There's hope for sports yet because if there's one thing you should know by now, it's that It Ain't Over 'Til the Fat Lady Sings!

Acknowledgements

We're grateful to the following for all their help on making this book happen (quickly): Ralph Keyes and Colleen Mohyde of the Doe Coover Agency, Liz Gray, Bill Woodward, Bill Reynolds, The Francis Ouimet Foundation, Elvis Braithwaite, Larry Schwartz, Norman Currie, Michael Eby, Rich Antanasio, Jo Gutierrez, Moira Fanning, John Lewis, Ann Tatum, Tony Terry, Bruce Bennett, Anne-Marie Parron, Angela Triorisi, David Gerhardt, Jim Strong, John Heissler and Bill Bennett.

At HarperCollins, Frank Foschetta and Bill Heulster; and at Barnes & Noble, John Kelly, Ned Lebo and the unflappable Frank Hoffman.

At Balliett & Fitzgerald, copyeditor Tony Scheitinger, proofreader Barbara Erlichman, researcher and writer Alex Blau, editorial assistant Nellie Sunshine Peck and designer and production editor Mike Walters.

Photo Credits

p.VII (top) © Photofile; p.VII (bottom) © AP/Wide World Photo; VIII (top)© Corbis/Bettman-UPI; VIII (bottom) © AP/Wide World Photos; p. IX (top) © Corbis/Bettman-UPI; p. IX (bottom) © Corbis/Bettman-UPI; p.XI © Dick Raphael; p.2 Transcendental Graphics; p.4 © AP/ Wide World Photos; p.5 © Corbis/Bettman-UPI; p.6 © Corbis/Bettman-UPI; p.7 © Corbis/Bettman-UPI; p.8 © Corbis/Bettman-UPI; p.9 © Corbis/Bettman-UPI; p.11 (inset) © Photofile; p.11 © Transcendental Graphics; p.12 © Corbis/Bettman-UPI; p.13 © Corbis/Bettman-UPI; p.14 © John Iacono/Sports Illustrated, Time Inc.; p.15 © Corbis/Bettman-UPI; p.16 © AP/Wide World Photos; p.17 © Boston College; p.18 © Photofile; p.19 © Corbis/Bettman-UPI; p.20 © Pittsburgh Post Gazette; p.21 © Transcendental Graphics; p.22 © Brian Masck/Allsport; p23 © Brian Masck/Sports Illustrated, Time Inc.; p.24 © Corbis/Bettman-UPI; p.26 © Tom Cruze/Chicago Sun-Times; p.27 © Corbis/AFP; p. 28 © AP/Wide World Photos; p.29 © AP/Wide World Photos; p.30 © Dick Raphael; p.31 © Dick Raphael; p.32 © Reuters/Blake Sell/Archive Photos; p. 33 © Tom Cruze/Chicago Sun-Times; p. 34 © Indiana University; p. 35 © Jerry Wachter/Sports Illustrated, Time Inc.; p.36 © Corbis/Bettman-UPI; p. 37 © AP/Wide World Photos; p.38 © AP/Wide World Photos; p.39 © Corbis/Bettman-UPI; p.40 Jonathan Daniel/Allsport; p.41 © Reuters/Steve Falk/Archive Photos; p.42 © UCLA; p.43 © Joe Raymond; p.45 © Providence Journal; p.46 © Corbis/Bettman-UPI; p.48 © Rob Lindquist; p.49 © Rob Lindquist; p.50 © Photofile; p. 52 © B. Bennett/B. Bennett Studios p. 53 © Reuters/Ray Stubblebine/Archive Photos; p.54 © Corbis/Bettman-UPI; p.55 © Transcendental Graphics; p. 56 © Transcendental Graphics; p. 57 © Corbis/Bettman-UPI; p.58 courtesy Howard Peretz; p.59 © B. Bennett Studios; p.60 © Photofile; p.61 © John Iacono/Sports Illustrated, Time Inc.; p.62 © B.Bennett Studios; p.63 © Corbis/Bettman-UPI; p.65 (inset) © Corbis/Bettman-UPI; p.65 © AP/Wide World Photos; p.66 © Photofile; p.67 © Herb Scharfman/Sports Illustrated, Time Inc.; p.68 © AP/Wide World Photos; p.70 courtesy of Billiards Digest; p.71 courtesy of Billiards Digest; p.72 © Richard Mackson/Sports Illustrated, Time Inc.; p.73 © Jerry Wachter/Sports Illustrated, Time Inc.; p.74 © New York Daily News; p.75 AP/Wide World Photos; p.76 © Churchill Downs, Inc./Kinetic Corp.; p. 77 © Churchill Downs, Inc./Kinetic Corp.; p.78 Jose Lopez/New York Times Co./Archive Photos; p.79 © Corbis/Bettman-UPI; p.81 (top and bottom) © Corbis/Bettman-UPI; p.82 © Corbis/Bettman-UPI; p. 83 © Corbis/Bettman-UPI; p.84 © Camera Press Ltd./Archive Photos; p. 85 © Corbis/Bettman-UPI; p.86 © Houston Chronicle; p. 87 © Corbis/Bettman-UPI; p. 88 © Houston Chronicle; p. 89 © Houston Chronicle; p.90 © AP/Wide World Photos; p.92 © Reuters/Tom Russo/Archive Photos; p.93 © AFP/Corbis-Bettman; p.94 © AP/Wide World Photos; p.95 © AP/Wide World Photos; p.96 © AP/Wide World Photos; p.97 © Corbis/Bettman-UPI; p.98 © Richard Mackson/Sports Illustrated, Time Inc.; p.99 © AP/Wide World Photos; p.100 © Corbis/Bettman-UPI; p.101 courtesy of Francis Oiumet Scholarship Fund; p.102 © Corbis/Bettman-UPI; p.103 © Rich Clarkson/Sports Illustrated, Time Inc.; p.104 © AP/Wide World Photos; p.105 © Archive Photos/Paris Match; p.106 © Corbis/Bettman-UPI; p.107 © Corbis/Bettman-UPI; p.108 © AP/Wide World Photos; p.109 © AP/Wide World Photos; p.110 © Corbis/Bettman-UPI; p.111 © David Cannon/Allsport; p.112 © The Ring magazine; p.114 © Transcendental Graphics; p.115 © Corbis/Bettman-UPI; p.116 © Transcendental Graphics; p.117 © Photofile; p.118 © Corbis/Bettman UPI; p.119 © Corbis/Bettman-UPI; p.120 courtesy of the Hambletonian; p121 courtesy of the Hambletonian; p.122 © Corbis/Bettman-UPI; p.123 © Corbis/Bettman-UPI; p.124 © Ken Levine/Allsport; p.125 © Reuters/Tony Blei/Archive Photos; p.126 © Corbis/Bettman-UPI; p.127 © Corbis/Bettman-UPI; p.128 © Corbis/Bettman-UPI; p.129 © Corbis/Bettman-UPI; p.130 © AP/Wide World Photos; p.131 © Churchill Downs, Inc./Kinetic Corp.; p.132 © AP/Wide World Photos; p. 134 © Simon Bruty/Allsport; p.135 © AP/World Wide Photos; p.136 © Express Newspapers/Archive Photos; p.137 © Corbis/Bettman-UPI; p.138 © Transcendental Graphics; p.139 courtesy Kansas Jayhawks; p.140 © Popperfoto/Archive Photos; p.141 © Popperfoto/Archive; p.142 © Dick Raphael; p.143 © Dick Raphael; p.144 © Corbis/Bettman-UPI; p.145 Reuters/Ulli Michel/Archive Photos; p.146 © AP/Wide World Photos; p.147 © AP/Wide World Photos; p.148 © Richard C.Lewis; p.149 © Richard C. Lewis; p.150 © Corbis/Bettman-UPI; p.151 © Stephen Green/Armytage/Sports Illustrated, Time Inc.; p.152 © John W. McDonough/Sports Illustrated, Time Inc.; p.154 © Reuters/Calvin Hom/Archive Photos; p.155 © Allsport; p.156 © Corbis/Bettman-UPI; p.157 © Corbis/Bettman-UPI; p.158 © The Ring magazine; p.159 © Corbis/Bettman-UPI; p.161 (top) © Transcendental Graphics; p.161 (Bottom) © Photofile; p.162 © Corbis/Bettman-UPI; p.163 © Corbis/Bettman-UPI; p.164 © Bruce Bennett Studios; p.165 © Bruce Bennett Studios; p.166 © Corbis/Bettman-UPI; p.167 © Corbis/Bettman-UPI; p. 169 (top, middle, bottom) © AP/Wide World Photos; p.171 © San Francisco Chronicle; p.172 © Gerard Vandystadt/Allsport; p.174 © Corbis/Reuters; p.175 © Rich Clarkson/Allsport; p.176 © Tony Duffy/Allsport; p.177 © Simon Bruty/Allsport; p.179 (top) courtesy Notre Dame; p.179 (bottom) courtesy Notre Dame; p.180 © AP/Wide World Photos; p.181 © Corbis/Bettman-UPI; p.182 © Corbis/Bettman-UPI; p.183 © Corbis/Bettman-UPI; p.184 © Archive France/Archive Photos; p.185 © Corbis/Reuters; p.186 © John Biever/Sports Illustrated, Time Inc.; p.187 © Reuters/Gary Hershorn/Archive Photo; p.188 © Transcendental Graphics; p.189 © Roger St. Jean/La Presse; p.190 © Corbis/Bettman-UPI; p.191 © Archive Photos; p.192 © Corbis/Bettman-UPI; p.193 © AP/Wide World Photos; p.194 © Corbis/Bettman-UPI; p.196 © Reuters/Eddie Motes/Archive Photos; p.197 © Mark B. Sluder; p.198 © AP/Wide World Photos; p.199 © Corbis/Bettman-UPI; p.200 © Popperfoto/Archive Photos; p201 © Allsport/Hulton Deutsch; p.202 © AP/Wide World Photos; p.203 © AP/Wide World Photos; p.204 © Churchill Downs, Inc./Kinetic Corp.; p.205 © AP/Wide World Photos; p.206 © Ronald C. Modra/Sports Illustrated, Time Inc.; p.207 © Richard C. Lewis; p.208 © Dick Raphael; p.209 © AP/Wide World Photos; p.210 © Corbis/Bettman-UPI; p.211 © Corbis/Bettman-UPI; p.212 © Corbis/Bettman-UPI; p.213 © Transcendental Graphics; p.214 © Corbis/Bettman-UPI; p.215 © Corbis/Bettman-UPI; p.216 © Corbis/Bettman-UPI; p.217 © Corbis/Bettman-UPI

INDEX